MINDFUL THERAPY

"This is the voice of a wise and sincere practitioner of both emotional healing-mindfulness and psychotherapy. Tom Bien reminds helping professionals to fully embody mindfulness in their lives—to be present—if they wish to share it with others. He explains the core ideas of Buddhist psychology in language that is likely to make sense to beginners and seasoned practitioners alike, and he provides a wealth of insights and techniques to make the teachings more accessible to clients. This book is a rich and timely contribution to our understanding of how to integrate the ancient practice of mindfulness into modern-day psychotherapy."—Christopher K. Germer, PhD, Harvard Medical School, and co-editor, *Mindfulness and Psychotherapy*

"Using theoretical groundwork, personal experience, case studies and practice exercises, *Mindful Therapy* offers ways to bring the teachings of Buddhism into a psychotherapeutic practice, and provides a thorough explanation of the benefits of doing so."—*Albuquerque Tribune*

Dr. Bien skillfully weaves through his book the essentials of Buddhism, of which he has an excellent understanding. [...] Replete with exercises for the therapist outside of the consulting room, as well as practical suggestions for the therapeutic interaction itself, the book covers a wide territory. [...] *Mindful Therapy* has a kinship with Carl Rogers and *On Becoming a Person*. The general reader will easily appreciate from this book the salutary effects of the practice of mindfulness, and the interconnection of mindfulness and emotional well-being."
—*Wildmind Newsletter*

MINDFUL THERAPY

A Guide for Therapists and Helping Professionals

Thomas Bien, Ph.D.

WISDOM PUBLICATIONS • BOSTON

Wisdom Publications, Inc.
199 Elm Street
Somerville MA 02144 USA
www.wisdompubs.org

Library of Congress Cataloging-in-Publication Data
Bien, Thomas.
Mindful therapy : a guide for therapists and helping professionals /
Thomas Bien.— 1st ed.
p. cm.
Includes bibliographical references and index.
ISBN 0-86171-292-7 (pbk. : alk. paper)
1. Psychotherapy—Religious aspects—Buddhism. 2. Healing
—Religious aspects—Buddhism. 3. Buddhism—Psychology. I. Title.
BQ4570.P76B54 2006
294.3'36616891—dc22
2005036443

ISBN 0-86171-292-7
First edition
10 09 08 07
5 4 3 2

Cover design by Katya Popovich.
Interior by Dede Cummings.
Cover photo by Gregory Palmer/kinworks.net

Buddha was not a philosopher trying to explain the universe.
He was a spiritual guide who wanted to help us put
an end to our suffering.

THICH NHAT HANH

———◆———

To Beverly

CONTENTS

———•——

PREFACE

———— ·✦· ————

WHILE THIS BOOK seeks to outline an overall approach to therapy, it cannot of course be a complete text in this regard. It cannot tell you everything you need to know about therapy. And if I cannot claim this is a complete manual for doing psychotherapy, I also cannot claim the ideas herein are in any sense definitive, or that they amount to more than one therapist's view of how Buddhist ideas can be worked with in clinical practice. And while both new therapists and experienced therapists might read this book profitably, its purpose is as much inspirational as technical.

Although *Mindful Therapy* focuses on psychotherapy, other professionals who want to learn to listen more deeply to the people they work with will also find content of interest here, including physicians, attorneys, teachers, and so on.

A word about words:

Therapy and psychotherapy. I use these terms in the broadest sense, not differentiating these from counseling, pastoral counseling, analysis, and so on.

Patient or client. Both of these terms present problems. Both have their limitations. On the one hand, *client* always sounded to me like someone that we are trying to sell to. A client is someone the insurance agent, the stockbroker, or the banker deals with. It doesn't strike quite the right note. On the other hand, *patient* seems to emphasize the dominance and superiority of the therapist too much. Patient implies a far too passive role for what the person in therapy or counseling must do. In everyday life, I use these terms interchangeably. But for consistency's sake, I have used patient throughout the book for several reasons.

First, using the word *patient* is to my mind in keeping with the Buddhist principle of acknowledging the truth. In this era of political correctness, there is a tendency to use terms for things which disguise what they actually are. The word *patient* seems in some ways more honest, since it denotes an important part of the reality of the therapeutic relationship: patients come to us because they are suffering, and because they hope we can help.

When we use the word *client,* we may do so with the admirable goal of reminding ourselves that all beings are equal, that none should hide behind an assumed professional superiority. In practice, however, I think this term does little to help with this. The end result of avoiding the use of the word *patient* may actually be to devalue the role of the therapist rather than to elevate the person on the other side. And these days, I think therapists could use some help in remembering to value what they do, and in teaching the world to do so.

Whichever term is used, however, the practitioner of mindful therapy is hardly someone that will dominate, manipulate, or control the people she works with. Calling someone a patient will not present any difficulty in the atmosphere of mindful therapy, which by its nature communicates a deep respect. Like the bodhisattva named Never Disparaging, we should remember that everyone is a future buddha.

He and she. I have alternated use of masculine and feminine forms of the third person singular pronouns in an approximately equal fashion to indicate a person in general. As with the use of *patient* and *client,* there are other options worth considering. But overall, I find this the least awkward way to avoid gender-biased language.

Finally, I wish to address the issue of the identities of patients discussed herein. Case histories in this book are generally based on composites of multiple individuals to crystallize important points that might take much longer to explicate through presentation of single cases. They are all based on reality, however, and are not purely fictional.

Even when a case history is based primarily on a single person, identifying information is altered to disguise the identity of patients. In other words, if it sounds just like you, it isn't.

So many beings go into the making of a book that an acknowledgment can easily sound like one of those endless Oscar acceptance speeches. But let me thank all whose love, support, and friendship provide the needed encouragement to write a book. Especially important in this regard are my wife Beverly, my son Joshua, and my dear friends Joe Boroughs and Steve Barrilleaux. I would like to thank my many spiritual teachers and psychological teachers, among the former, Thich Nhat Hanh, Rollo Michael, and Jim Harris, not to mention Siddhartha Gautama and Jesus of Nazareth; among the latter, Bill Miller and Chuck Elliott. Bob Weber has provided helpful guidance and feedback along the way. Scott Love, as always, deserves many thanks for keeping my computer running. I often wonder what I would do without him.

At Wisdom Publications, I would like to thank my editor Josh Bartok for seeing the value of this project and helping to bring it into being. His insight has helped this be the best book it could be. I am also grateful to production editor Tony Lulek and promotions and marketing coordinator Rod Meade Sperry.

Last but by no means least I want to thank the many patients I have worked with over the years. Some of these have been difficult teachers—the kind of Zen master who beats you with a stick when you get it wrong, or even, in some cases, when you get it right! Many more have appreciated my efforts to offer presence, support, and guidance. Every single one of them has been my teacher.

Thomas Bien, Ph.D.

April 2, 2005

Albuquerque, New Mexico

INTRODUCTION

—◆◆◆—

A S PSYCHOTHERAPISTS, we know that how much our patients suffer often has more to do with the conceptual lenses through which they view their experience than with what they actually experience. Buddhist understanding takes this insight further, teaching us that when we free ourselves entirely from our concepts, we can experience reality in a new and wondrous way. That way is called nirvana, the direct perception of wondrous becoming.

Consider some simple, everyday examples. We tend to classify tasks as either things that we have to do or things that we want to do. Going to work, doing chores and running errands, cooking and cleaning, taking out the trash, mowing the lawn—these often fall into the category of things we have to do, while enjoying a meal, going to the movies, watching television or doing pleasure reading, drinking our coffee or tea—these are often seen as things we want to do. Frequently the list of things we have to do dominates us. It dominates us so much, that we may not notice that many of the things we have to do contain enjoyable elements. It dominates us in the sense that we often do not even question whether these tasks are really necessary. And it dominates us so much that we may rush through even the things we want to do without really experiencing them.

We may also classify all the moments in our lives as either time for ourselves or time for others. As psychotherapists, the time for our patients is their time, not ours. But that does not mean we feel the rest of our time is ours. The time spent with a spouse, a child, a family member, or a friend, when involving activities that are more their choice than our own, may also be seen as their time. Maybe at the end of the day we finally get to the time that is "our" time, but by then we may be too exhausted to do much.

One solution to this problem is mindfulness. Described by the Buddha over 2,500 years ago, mindfulness is a way of learning to see life as a unified whole. When we live mindfully, life is no longer divided between what we have to do and what we want to do. Life is no longer divided between "our" time and time for others. All of life becomes our time. All of life becomes an opportunity to be alive and aware. When we live mindfully, we learn to be happy and content, whether interacting with our patients, filling in an appointment time in our calendar, enjoying time with someone we love, or relaxing with a cup of coffee.

Mindfulness is a way of facing the truth. And one of the truths we must face as psychotherapists is this: *psychotherapy is difficult work*. It may not seem that way to our patients or lay peers. From the outside, it may seem as though we just sit and listen, and occasionally offer reflections, suggestions, interpretations, or advice. And yet to sit and listen that way is one of the most difficult things one can do.

Like many of our patients, we therapists may also be searching. Perhaps we are searching for a way to envision our work as a work of healing, beyond the technical proficiencies, beyond the theories we have learned. We may search for a way to be more fully *present* with our patients, one that can help us in helping them. Or perhaps we search for a way to defragment our work life and reunify it with the rest of our time. Others of us are looking for a way to approach therapy as a spiritual task while still following professional standards and without triggering fear in our patients that we are trying to convert them to our form of spirituality.

Mindful Therapy is designed to help with these concerns. Mindful therapy emphasizes that whatever else we have to offer, the most important thing we offer is our true presence and our deep listening. Yet since we are not ourselves enlightened, since we are torn and fragmented by the same suffering and by the same powerful cultural forces and conditioning that bedevil our patients, doing this is not so easy. To offer true presence and deep listening, we need ways to approach our work and our life that are free of clutter and distraction. We need ways to become more clear and centered. If we are not clear and centered, how will we offer these qualities to those who seek our help? For this reason, this book is as much about how therapists and counselors can take better care of themselves through mindful living as it is about how we can use mindfulness clinically.

Mindfulness offers us an approach to living and an approach to therapy that can help us deepen our presence and our listening. While rooted in Buddhism, mindfulness does not require us to "be a Buddhist," or to share specifically Buddhist insights with our patients. Depending on our patients' needs and our own style, we can do more or less of that. Since Buddhism teaches us to hold our opinions lightly—even our Buddhist ones—we can offer mindfulness simply and directly. We can offer mindfulness without religious or metaphysical assumptions, allowing us to talk comfortably with people of different religions or of no religion at all.

Mindfulness is also something we can offer ourselves. Since mindfulness is ultimately the art of living deeply and happily, this is not a burdensome task. One of the assertions of this book is that to practice therapy mindfully, we need to do our best to live mindfully in the rest of our lives. Mindfulness helps us integrate our professional and personal life, our time "for others" and "our own" time. By using mindfulness practice to care for ourselves in our non-work life, we can offer greater mindfulness in our work— and this in turn will help us to live with greater joy and with ease of well-being. Mindfulness helps us in both the private and professional areas of our lives by eliminating any rigid distinction between the two, helping us to be more at home wherever we are. It helps us both to find healing for ourselves, and to offer healing to our patients.

WHAT THIS BOOK OFFERS

Mindful Therapy consists of three parts. Part one, "Revisioning the Role of the Psychotherapist," puts the task of the therapist in the context of its ancient lineage of healing. The first chapter offers the perspective that, in a world of increasing alienation, fragmentation, and disconnection, we need therapists who are true healers rather than mere technicians. To become true healers, we therapists might consider trying to see ourselves in the context of the ancient roles of shaman, guru, and healer. While we may not be able to adopt these models wholesale into our twenty-first-century role, we can nonetheless find inspiration in them that goes beyond our technical training. This inspiration also helps to inoculate the therapist against the difficulties of the work.

The second chapter introduces the importance of the therapist's self-care, or care of the self. Without care of self, care of others becomes ultimately impossible. A *gatha* (a kind of brief versified Buddhist teaching) from Zen master Thich Nhat Hanh is used to structure an approach to greater solidity, stability, and freedom.

Part two, "Buddha as Therapist," shows how the teachings of the Buddha in general, and of mindfulness in particular, provide the therapist with a framework for understanding the therapeutic task. Chapter three discusses the practice of mindfulness in various terms: as radical acceptance, daily life meditation, surrender, reverence, acknowledging the truth of experience, and dwelling happily in the present moment. It shows how these qualities are important to the therapist. What is more, it also addresses how to share these qualities with patients and how to assess when and how it is appropriate to do so. Chapter four uses the basic Buddhist teaching of the "four noble truths" to open a perspective on suffering and its alleviation in the context of therapy. From the four noble truths we can derive a kind of practical, four-step, self-help exercise that can be surprisingly powerful. Chapter five examines the teaching of the "three poisons" of greed, hatred, and delusion, and their antidotes (love, compassion, and wisdom), and how these shed light on human suffering and the release from suffering in a clinical context. Chapter six considers the "three seals" that all things share—I will present these three as impermanence, no separate self, and nirvana*—in the context of the general alleviation of human suffering and in clinical work. When the nature of reality as seen under these seals is accepted in a deep way and harmonized with rather than resisted, suffering ends.

Chapter seven turns from the nature of suffering and its causes to consider the antonym of suffering, well-being. Every therapist has at least an implicit, if unarticulated, view of what well-being is. This chapter offers the Buddha's description of well-being as embodied in the teaching of the "noble eightfold path." It suggests that the eightfold path can even be used diagnostically to help understand the causes of suffering in our own

---

*In some schools of Buddhism, dukkha (suffering) is used in place of nirvana. But these are ultimately flip sides of the same coin, since nirvana can ultimately only be found in samsara, in the realm of suffering.

and our patients' lives. Chapter eight offers a basic model for understanding and working with emotions based on Buddhist teaching. Several traditional practices are offered in the light of working with emotions.

To the reader who may be wondering, "Okay. But what do I *do* in my life and work as a mindful therapist?", part three aims at offering specfic suggestions. Chapter nine offers specifics about what the work of the mindful therapist might look like in terms of therapeutic technique. Techniques are offered in passing throughout the book, but are intentionally confined largely to this one chapter so the reader does not confuse a mindfulness approach to therapy with technique-driven approaches. This is an essential point. Since the mindful therapist works by producing her true presence and offering deep listening, she allows technique to grow organically out of the work. Technique is never imposed artificially or arbitrarily. By contrast, many books about psychotherapy offer a disclaimer that technique is secondary. Yet even in such cases, the disclaimer is often contradicted by the content—a fate I hope to avoid here. My intention is not to present a definitive or complete set of techniques, but simply to discuss how one therapist (the author) does it. Finally, in chapter ten, I offer reflections on the unification of work and life for the mindful therapist.

PART I

------ •◆• ------

Revisioning the Role
of the Psychotherapist

CHAPTER ONE
Envision Psychotherapy as a Spiritual Path

*A therapist has to practice being fully present and has to cultivate
the energy of compassion in order to be helpful.*[1]
—THICH NHAT HANH

THERAPY IS NOT easy work. If you are a psychotherapist, a
counselor, or anyone who routinely seeks to relieve suffering
in others through any of the arts involving deep listening and true
presence, you are a special person. You are part of a long line of
healers and shamans, of gurus and bodhisattvas stretching back to
the beginning of human history and even earlier still.

Yet no time in the brief history of psychotherapy has been
more challenging than this one. We continue to live in a world
of increasing alienation, disconnection, and fragmentation. Our
patients are not immune to this, and neither are we. Those of us
who try to help in such circumstances as these will at times feel
underappreciated and overwhelmed. Every year our paperwork
increases, while our fees remain the same or are even reduced.
Sometimes we have to fight to just get a few more sessions for a
severely depressed patient. We may become the target of the

negative transference of our patients who see us as the depriving mother or the severe father, and the economic conditions and bureaucratic struggles surrounding our work make it increasingly difficult to tolerate. In decades past, people had high expectations for therapy, perhaps too high. But today we more often encounter unwarranted skepticism. Perhaps in part this skepticism has resulted because, while a wider range of people may now experience a service they've been told is psychotherapy, they have in reality received no such thing. Instead of a deep, healing human encounter, they may in at least some instances have received only a few sessions of well-intentioned advice-giving or a brief interview for the purposes of pharmacological treatment, particularly in areas where managed care dominates. And if *that* is therapy, and the world does not value it very much, can we blame them for being skeptical about it? Beyond this, in the United States there is a deeply entrenched feeling that we should rely on ourselves and that therapy is a kind of dependency, rather than the process of self-discovery it actually is. What is more, we live in a culture that is largely outside without inside, biased toward the extroverted and doing-oriented side of life. In such a context, psychotherapy and other techniques involving increased awareness are all too easily lampooned as frivolous navel-gazing.

There are no readily identifiable villains in our complex and often inadequate system of health care. We are all caught together in it, doing the best we can. It may have seemed like a good idea, some years ago, to "medicalize" psychotherapy in order to qualify for insurance reimbursement, but when the pressure of spiraling medical costs became too great, we who jumped aboard the medical bandwagon last were of course the first to pay the price, the first to have our services reduced and controlled. Unwisely so, I believe. But not surprisingly.

I want to suggest, to all my colleagues in the art of deep listening, that in order to withstand the difficulties of our work and the ups and downs of its valuation in the marketplace, we require a powerful inoculation. And in my experience the best inoculation is the capacity to envision our work as a that of a healer, a part of a long and honorable lineage—to view it as a path of service, a calling as well as a business—and to sincerely offer up this work to the good of all beings.

SCIENCE IS NOT ENOUGH

I am a psychologist. My training is scientific. I am versed in experimental design and statistical analysis. In my education I received the great mantras: "What does the research say?" and "Where are your data?" And I value that training. Whatever we can learn from science about our work is grounding and helpful.

At the same time, it is not enough.

You knew this, if you were honest, the first time you had the experience of sitting down as a therapist with a person you were supposed to help. If you were open to acknowledging it, you knew right away that you needed more than what your training had provided you.

Zen scholar D.T. Suzuki expressed the trouble with science, and scientific objectivity, this way:

Scientists . . . like to be objective and avoid being subjective, whatever this may mean. For they firmly adhere to the view that a statement is true only when it is objectively evaluated or validated and not merely subjectively or personally experienced. They forget the fact that a person invariably *lives* a personal life and not a conceptually or scientifically defined one. However exactly or objectively . . . the definition might have been given, it is not the definition the person lives, but the life itself, and it is this life which is the subject of human study.[2]

When I emerged from graduate training, my ideas about the nature of therapy were not too different from what they are now. But if you and I could watch a video of me doing therapy at that time, I shudder to imagine what we would see. We would probably have had a hard time knowing that my view of therapy was anything much like what I describe in this book. In keeping with the great mantras I had learned, I fear you would have seen someone ready to pounce on anything a patient said and trot out some prized bit of information: "Actually, research shows that . . ." Contrary to what I would have said about my work even at that time, in practice I seem to have viewed my role as providing people with the information I had accumulated in graduate school. I was like the learned scholar in the familiar story, puffed up with knowledge, who called upon the Zen master to discuss Buddhism. Sitting at tea with the professor, the master kept pouring into the scholar's cup, filling it to overflowing. The scholar said, "It is already full! No more can go in!" "You are like this," the master explained. "How can I show you Zen unless you first empty your cup?" This may be a somewhat unkind caricature of myself as a therapist at that time, but I'm afraid I resembled it rather too much for comfort, and even today, with some regularity, leave a session with the feeling that once again I talked too much.

Looking back at myself at that time, I can see that I was attempting to *lead* with my knowledge base, rather than allowing it to inform me in the background. As Zen master Thich Nhat Hanh writes, "On the path of practice, knowledge is an obstacle that must be overcome. We must be ready to abandon our knowledge at any moment in order to get to a higher level of understanding."[3]

In this perspective, we may consider the metaphor of water and ice. A living encounter is water, continually flowing, always ready to take new shape; knowledge is ice, hardened, fixed. Being mindful means allowing the ice of our knowledge to melt into the living water of a personal encounter with another human being.

It is only in such an encounter that true healing, true therapy takes place.

I believed then, and believe now, that the task of the therapist is to practice deep listening, to produce one's true presence, to be deeply available and thereby create the living water of a true encounter. This is what I call *mindful therapy*. Mindful therapists know it is the relationship that brings the healing. It is the capacity to use our own personhood in the authentic meeting with another person that is most important. "The great healing factor in psychotherapy," writes Carl Jung, "is the doctor's personality." In our context, we might talk about presence or mindfulness rather than personality, but we can readily understand Jung's meaning.

Our training may be scientific, but our true lineage is not only scientific. We are the descendants not only of scientists, but also of shamans, gurus, healers, and bodhisattvas—spiritual teachers, philosophers, and wise people of all kinds from all times and places. We might attempt to deny being the offspring of disliked parents, but we cannot deny the truth that remains in our bodies, in our genes. In this same sense, we are the descendants of these healers. Like them, we inevitably bring a worldview to our work, a philosophy, stated or not, about what the good life is and how to live it, and about how we get sick when we stray too far from that life. It is an essential and unavoidable part of our calling to be practical philosophers and spiritual teachers.

And yet, while it is necessary that we claim our role as spiritual teachers and healers, we also need a way to fulfill that role, a way that feels possible, practical, and human-sized. We need a way to do this, in today's pluralistic world, that does not include a lot of specific religious dogma that may conflict with the beliefs of our patients. To be a healer, to be a practical philosopher and spiritual teacher without ourselves succumbing to the risks of ego inflation, we need a grounded, realistic, and humanistic framework for such work.

If we are to acknowledge this as our true task, then we need a way to produce our true presence, to deepen our spiritual understanding, and to enhance our capacity to listen calmly. We require a vision for our psychotherapy practice that is at the same time lofty and practical, head in the clouds, perhaps, but feet firmly on the ground.

One approach highly suited to meet this need is the Buddhist practice of mindfulness. Mindfulness, the practice of deep awareness, of calm presence, involves a minimum of metaphysical or dogmatic belief, making it a spiritual path accessible to the agnostic as much as to the practicing Jew, Protestant, or Catholic. It is an approach to living that we can share with patients of diverse backgrounds and belief systems. Immensely practical, it is also simply a wonderful way to live. We will explore mindfulness and a mindful life more deeply in later chapters.

If you are a practicing psychotherapist, you may imagine you know enough about the science, theories, and the techniques of therapy—but at any rate, these things are not the focus of this book. In my opinion and my experience, if we are to avoid the fate of our science becoming an obstacle and of our techniques becoming gimmicks, we need to learn how to bear the mantle of the shaman, the guru, the healer, the bodhisattva. Let's take a closer look at what this means.

THE SHAMAN AND THE PSYCHOTHERAPIST

The word *shaman* originates with the Tungu tribe in Siberia, where it refers to people who heal through their capacity to deal with the spiritual realm. I use the word here to refer to aboriginal healers in general. We find shamans in the tribes of New Guinea and Australia, and we find them in Native American tribes and the cultures in the Artic circle. Human beings seem to have recognized very early on that there are people especially suited to this role.

Whether we explain this regularity by a model of cultural diffusion, or are inclined to believe that such a role is archetypal, rooted deeply in the Jungian collective unconscious, such a role is fundamentally and uniquely human. Archetypally, the career of such individuals begins with an initiatory experience, often an illness of some sort. If they survive this ordeal, the shaman emerges as a *wounded* healer, one with a capacity to interact with the realm of spirits and help others.

If not always so dramatically, this applies to many of us who practice psychotherapy as well. Many of us are attracted to the archetype of the wounded healer, and choosing to be a therapist is an expression of that attraction. The choice to become a therapist reflects an inclination to become a wise person, not only to help other people, but also to bring light and healing to our own wounds. Without such a motivation, it is difficult to understand why someone would take on this difficult work.

When I look around at a meeting of therapists, I see no psychological supermen and superwomen. If you have that kind of expectation, you will be quite disappointed in your colleagues. In many I see wounded healers—people who have come through some difficulty of their own, and have learned something along the way about how to help others. This knowledge is clearly not just what we learned in our training. Our human suffering—both specific and universal—is the very door through which we have become healers, and not our training and education alone.

THE GURU AND THE PSYCHOTHERAPIST

The Sanskrit word *guru* means "heavy." To be a guru is to be a person of weight and substance, a teacher. The exact role of the guru varies from tradition to tradition, but in its most exalted form, devotion to the guru is paramount. From a Western point of view, it often looks like such devotion is a very questionable matter at best, and indeed it has been subject to abuse. The guru relationship is particularly subject to abuse when Eastern gurus come to the West, unaccustomed to the sort of projections—sexual and otherwise—that Westerners place on them. While we in the West may view such devotion with distaste, what we may miss is the way the guru, in taking on a student, takes on an extraordinary commitment to that individual—a commitment for nothing less than that person's total salvation in this and perhaps even future lives.

In re-visioning the therapist as a kind of guru in our own contemporary cultural context, we must know that there are limits to our understanding, to the "devotion" we deserve and can expect, and to the commitment we can honestly give to the other person. Yet contrary to many media images, I find most therapists to be devoted to their patients. I know of more than one therapist who has retired, but nonetheless continues to consult with patients by telephone, feeling a continuing responsibility to them, sometimes despite serious personal health and other issues.

Some may have ethical questions about such practices. It might be better to make a good referral once we retire than to try to provide ongoing care. But such examples demonstrate the deep responsibility we often feel toward our patients. For therapy is and must be, first and foremost, a decent human relationship. And if it is a decent human relationship, it is difficult to completely confine it to fifty minutes per week. Even if we have no other contact, with the possible exception of a rare phone call, we think of our patients between sessions—and indeed I believe we *should* think about them. If it is a deep relationship, they penetrate our psyches as we do theirs. They dream about us, and we may sometimes dream about them. This surely reflects a deep commitment.

And thus, while of course we should not expect unquestioning devotion from our patients, *we are nonetheless worthy of respect* for what we offer. We are people of weight, of substance. The fee for our service is only one expression of this. In fact, if our patients do not have some minimal level of respect for us, we will not be able to help them at all. If a patient is simply too skeptical, too mistrustful of us and our intentions, or if they see us as only interested in the money—if they believe that it is not possible for us to care about them and earn our living from them at the same time, if they think we are too young or too old or in some other way too different to understand them, our capacity to help will be limited.

In some traditions, the guru is viewed with almost deifying reverence. Psychologically, this means that to be healers, we must be people who can temporarily bear for the patient what Jung called the archetype of the Self, the Jungian equivalent of the Totality or the Divine. We function like gurus in the limited sense that, in a successful therapeutic process, patients project this archetype onto us. This is a heavy burden to bear, and would in fact be unbearable were it not that we only hold it in trust for the patient until such time as the patient becomes capable of holding it for himself.

In this way, by bearing the archetype of the Self, the therapist functions as a transitional object, like a child's security blanket that stands in for the presence of the mother until the child incorporates her presence into his own psyche. An apt analogy from popular culture is that the therapist or the therapy process is a little like Dumbo's magic feather. Holding the magic feather, Dumbo believes that he can fly. Dumbo clings tightly to the feather until he learns that the capacity for flight resides in himself and not in the feather.

Fortunately we do not have to have to be god to our patients. We do not require any god-like, all-knowing, superhuman wisdom or power. In fact, patients coming to know our limitation and humanness is part of how they claim the power they attribute to us as their own. We are not gurus in the sense of being in any way superhuman, yet at the same time, we have power to heal and help. Gurus who do not know their power are dangerous.

To be healers we must be convincing and worthy of trust. We must have enough connection with the archetype of the Divine—with wholeness and full humanity—that we can receive and hold the projection of the archetype of the Self, of wholeness. In other words, patients project wholeness onto us, and then claim it back as their own. For this to work, we must be at least somewhat suitable targets for the projection. We must be people who attend to our own growth, who find our own spiritual practice. That's part of the job description of a mindful therapist.

Given the burden of the therapist to bear the archetype of the Self, the image of wholeness, it is no wonder that so many of us—especially in starting out as therapists—are comforted by formulaic approaches that seem to provide all the answers, and tell us just what to do, session by session. Otherwise, it would be difficult to know just how to begin this awesome process, to carry the weight of the therapist's role. But however useful such strategies may be for research or for learning, ultimately no formula can suffice. Only the involvement of our whole selves will do. As gurus, we need to be weighty persons, authoritative while not authoritarian, people who are authentically interested in human spirituality and well-being, and who do our human best to live in accord with these aspirations ourselves.

Psychotherapists of any school who have made their mark, from the psychoanalytic to the behavioral, from the humanistic to the transpersonal, often have one thing in common: they are *convincing*. There may be many reasons why this is so, including the clarity and originality of their thought and the lucidity of their writing. But I would like to suggest that another reason is that they all have a special presence and confidence. From Freud and Jung to Ellis and Maslow, all of them exude this quality, even if in profoundly personal and differing ways. As we learn to deepen our mindfulness, we too come to share this quality of presence. In some fashion and to some extent we become weighty persons capable of bearing the archetype of wholeness and healing.

THE HEALER

Many of the people who go to visit a physician today do not have a problem amenable to medical treatment. But they go anyway. Even if they have a cold, and know that the doctor will simply say to rest and drink fluids, they go. Why is this?

One reason may be that they are seeking something beyond the modern, scientific medical arsenal. They are seeking the presence of a person who bears the mantle of healing.

Ancient healers knew what many today have forgotten: *Every disease is at least in part a spiritual problem.* This is not to say that healing should be confined only to spiritual tecnhiques, or that being spiritual means perfect health. On the contrary, even great spiritual masters get sick, and modern medicine is an obvious blessing. But denying the spiritual component is short-sighted.

Ancient healers had to be learned in many fields. They studied human anatomy and physiology and the effects of nutrition, as we might expect. But they also were often experts on the effects of music, on the stars and planets, and much else besides. Spirituality has to do with life in its wholeness, in its unfragmented entirety. And therefore, to say every disease is spiritual means that no disease can really be understood apart from its context. Healing is therefore not only a matter of treating the symptomology, but of also aligning ourselves with the universe, of restoring harmony and balance. Any healing which stops short of that will not have reached the root of the problem. Otherwise our efforts are like treating a patient for lung cancer who continues to smoke.

Noted author and physician Larry Dossey makes this point regarding heart disease as an example:

> Heart disease cannot be understood by confining our scrutiny to single persons or to body parts . . . Transpersonal events such as misperceptions of meanings, job dissatisfaction, lack of communication between individuals, and lack of love and trust are capable of setting this disease in motion. Not only are these factors causative of illness, they can ameliorate it too, as is demonstrated by the reduction in angina in men with heart disease who have loving wives . . . [4]

The Gospels portray Jesus as a wandering healer and exorcist. In those days of course, the one belonged naturally to the other. In Judeo-Christian thinking, where there is disease there is *sin*— superficially considered as breaking the rules, profoundly considered as alienation from the Divine Ground. Where there is disease, there are negative spiritual forces (demons) at work, and these must be driven out.

This point of view, pushed to extreme, creates the problem of blaming the victim. If disease is caused by sin, in the superficial sense of rule breaking, as such tortured logic would have it, they are sick through their own fault. We then have grounds to blame and ostracize the sick for being ill in the first place. Nor is this, unfortunately, simply a benighted ancient attitude. It is one that occurs frequently in our own time as well, sometimes behind but the thinnest of veils. This error, which Christ specifically repudiated, (Matthew 5:45), pointing out that God makes the sun to shine and the rain to fall on the just and unjust alike, is not confined to spiritually-oriented people. Many interactions of healing professionals with their patients are contaminated with the same attitude. Our diagnostic categories, while designed to be descriptive, first of all, and prescriptive second of all, are used in a way that often contains a barely hidden moral judgment. This is particularly evident in the case of personality disorders, where to diagnose someone as having a narcissistic or borderline personality disorder is roughly the same as saying someone is a bad person, and that, since their problems are their own fault, they do not deserve kindness or compassion. This can be a seductively comforting point of view. Further, if we can believe that others suffer through their own fault, we can imagine that we might avoid such misfortune, since we, of course, would not do the things that would cause such ills.

Consider, for example, the attitude of therapists toward addicted individuals. Most therapists believe that people generally respond to empathic understanding. But in counseling and psychology, we used to teach, and some still believe, that empathy will not work with the addicted person, that you have to smash though their denial. It is very interesting, and very questionable, that we should reserve the harshest approach for those with diagnoses carrying the greatest stigma, especially addiction and sexual misconduct. Traditional alcohol counselors would not agree to even see a patient until he had already stopped drinking—thus requiring a positive outcome before even engaging in the treatment! Just imagine if your physician were willing to treat your strep throat only if it was already better, or if we as therapists said to a new patient who is depressed, "Okay, you can come in. But no acting sad around here, for crying out loud!"

As modern medicine has learned more about disease, we have come to see it as an isolated thing. Some doctors see only a diseased liver, not a person with a certain job, a happy or an unhappy marriage, who has found a way to feel in harmony with the world or who feels isolated and alienated, and so on. As therapists, as healers, we are the ones whose task it is to see the whole person in their life context.

If you are a true psychotherapist, you are a healer. You are someone who sees the whole person. You help the patient on the level of mind, of emotion, and of spirit, as well as of body. Your role in doing this is *crucial*. You may be the only person some ever meet who embody the lineage of human healing in this way.

THE BODHISATTVA

A bodhisattva is a person who has put off fulfillment of her own ultimate peace in order to help others. The bodhisattva vow in the Zen tradition is an awesome undertaking:

Innumerable are sentient beings; I vow to save them all.
Inexhaustible are deluded passions; I vow to transform them all.
Immeasurable are the Dharma teachings; I vow to master them all.
Infinite is the Buddha's way; I vow to fulfill it completely.

To the Western mind, this may sound overwhelming and bur-densome—to say nothing of impossible! But to see these vows like that misses the point. It may be less overwhelming if we take the point of these vows to be generating *aspiration,* to cultivate a certain attitude and intention.

There is evidence that people who view their work as a calling obtain more satisfaction from it then those who work primarily for money or for advancement.[5] The practice of vow is similar. When you do your work with a sense of satisfaction in being helpful to others, in making a difference, paradoxically, you will be the first one to benefit.

If, in facing your work day, even with cases in which you doubt your progress, your intention can provide some encouragement. With this intention, you remember that you can make a difference and at least to some extent reduce suffering in the lives of your patients, and in all the lives touched by their lives; for you have bodhisattva energy at your disposal. Even Monday morning becomes easier to tolerate.

WE'RE IN THIS TOGETHER

At one point in graduate school, I worked extensively with the cognitive-behavioral approach. I found that the techniques I was learning as interventions were also helpful in my own life. I was practicing the things I was teaching. So by the time I had recommended an exercise to identify and rebut irrational thoughts, for example, I already had intimate experience of it. I knew something about my own irrational thought patterns, had some sense of what it was like to do such exercises, how they were helpful, and what their limitations were.

In a meeting with my supervisor one day I asked whether he had worked with these ideas himself. Surprised by my question, he admitted he hadn't. That supervisor may have been caught to some extent in his categories. He was the DOCTOR and the people he worked with were PATIENTS (even if he called them clients). As he saw it, he didn't need to undertake these exercises any more than, say, a healthy oncologist needs to undergo chemotherapy. His was a treatment for the sick, and he was not one of the sick.

This is crucial: True healers do not stand outside of the struggle of those they help. Healers know themselves as wounded, know their own suffering as a part of the human condition. Buddhism is very frank and explicit on this point. Until and unless we traverse the enlightenment path, suffering is the human lot and is not something incidental or added on. A healer may be relatively free of anxiety, for example, but she may still experience it. We are all in this human dilemma, facing the same human difficulties.

I hope that you will use the exercises and practice suggestions in this book with this in mind. I hope you will use them with your patients, but I also hope you will find ways to use them yourself.

Life difficulties may trigger more severe reactions in vulnerable patients than in ourselves, but we too must know ourselves as quite capable of reacting at times in less than helpful or even destructive ways. There may be a difference of degree between the reaction patterns of our patients and our own, but there is more we have in common with our patients than there is that holds us apart.

What we can learn from ancient models of healing—shamans and gurus, healers and bodhisattvas—is that a good relationship to our patients is one of trust, responsibility, and healing in the broadest sense. We limit the scope of our responsibility primarily to the therapy appointment, as we must. This in part acknowledges that we are not literal gurus, an important distinction for us not to lose track of. But if our responsibility must have limits and boundaries, *within* these it can still have great depth. We cannot always be available, but when we are, it is our capacity for true presence that does the healing.

HOLD CONCEPTS LOOSELY

According to modern medicine, a disease is a discrete entity. It has a beginning, requires a prescribed course of treatment, and predictably comes to an end. Yet this may not always describe the truth. Dr. Dossey writes:

> . . . [O]ur picture of human illness and health will be considerably enriched and more accurate if we can relax our insistence on strict beginnings of illnesses, for they do not exist. They can be defended only out of a kind of clinical or therapeutic convenience. In effect, we detract from our role as participants in the universe when we install the "strep" bacterium as the sole progenitor of disease in this case. This is a bad habit not only in this illness, but in all illnesses. It denies the richness of the world . . . and it installs simplicities where a greater complexity always reigns.[6]

In psychotherapy illness is even less clear. Often the "disease" we are treating is part of the human condition itself, a condition in which we sometimes lose what we love most, fail to attain what we want, and are faced ultimately with the prospect of our own death. Our task is to be helpful. And if we are prepared to do depth psychotherapy but a patient turns out to only need a little practical advice and enouragement, so be it. This fits nicely with Buddhist teaching, which encourages us to go beyond our cherished concepts and deal with what is real and practical. In Buddhist practice one strives for the extinction of notions and concepts that we interpose between our awareness and reality. Zen Buddhism especially teaches that we must hold our concepts lightly—even our Buddhist ones.

In light of this attitude, we must recognize that our diagnoses, for example, are not ultimately real things, and we do not reify them. For example, if you think depression is a real entity, try to take it out and show it to someone! When we talk about a diagnosis, it is important to remember we are talking about a convenient description rather than reality itself. A diagnosis is simply a collection of signs that more or less cohere, and which give us an idea about what kind of treatment may be helpful—especially with regard to medications. While great strides have been made in making our diagnoses more consistent and valid, they remain, inevitably, imprecise. Or if you regard diagnoses as something real, you will miss the obvious absurdity of our diagnostic criteria, by which a person with seven symptoms qualifies for a diagnosis, while a person with only six does not and, by implication, is therefore just fine.

Placing therapy within the tradition of healing, however, does not require discarding diagnostic terms. Discarding diagnosis may be a worse error than giving diagnosis ultimate credence. So long as we hold our diagnostic concepts loosely, they can be a help rather than a hindrance.

In mindful therapy, diagnosis is considered broadly. The most useful sort of diagnosis is to see the person as a whole and his life context as a whole. The label is only the palest reflection of this broad, holistic, contextual process. It is the difference between the letters *p-e-b-b-l-e* and the feel of a small stone in your hand.

Looking at therapy this way, as a deep, healing relationship not always capable of being contained by labels and not always subject to discrete, specific endings, helps us avoid being caught in our concepts. Ours would be a healthier society by far if we all had someone to provide us with an hour of deep listening once a week—whether we qualified for a clinical diagnosis or not.

The specter raised by the prospect of interminable therapy is unhealthy dependence. Yet I find this to be largely chimeric. Contrary to expectation, my experience in practicing mindful therapy has been that an unhealthily dependent relationship is rare, and when it does happen, can develop as easily in a shorter-term therapy relationship as in a long one. Few people in our society schedule a weekly appointment and pay even a modest copay unless they feel that they benefit. The reason I think that dependence occurs so rarely has to do with the nature of mindful psychotherapy—therapy as a practice of deep listening and true presence. Unhealthy dependency is more likely to develop in cases in which the therapist attempts to offer advice for every problem or dilemma the patient encounters in living than when the basic therapeutic stance is one of offering deep listening, understanding, and acceptance.

In mindful therapy, dependence is unlikely because its very nature is to help people connect with their own wisdom, their own Buddha nature. Sometimes a patient who has never been in therapy comes for a first session, and immediately declares his ambivalence about therapy, contending that one should solve one's own problems. I always agree heartily. I tell the patient that I also believe that we have to solve our own problems. And I add that therapy is not about someone else solving our problems for us, but about creating a space in which we can connect with our own capacity to find what we need. But this concept, too, must be held lightly, and there will always be those people who benefit from a bit of concrete advice.

UNIFYING WORK AND LIFE

In former times, and still in traditional societies today, "work" and "life" were more of a piece. Work was not a separate fragment of life existing apart from the rest. It did not need to be isolated, removed from personal and family life. The farm was a family endeavor: everyone contributed. The work of the farm was not a job outside of the rest of one's life, but very much part of it. The shopkeeper often lived over his store, so that when he was in the shop, he was never far away from other family members.

Our work, too, can feel quite different when it is integrated with the rest of life, when it flows naturally out of our mindfulness, our sense of what needs doing rather than being something artificial, added on from the outside to meet financial need.

Of course, as therapists, we cannot completely eliminate boundaries between our work and life; we require some protection from patients who might abuse their access to us, perhaps calling us continually at all hours or otherwise failing to respect emotional boundaries. Yet once again, in my experience, those who actually abuse access are few. Most people are respectful of my time, unwilling to intrude too much into my life beyond our appointed meetings. In fact, I am more often in the position of having to *encourage* people to call me when doing so is actually appropriate, such as when feeling a suicidal despair or other major crisis, than of having to set limits with people who take advantage of my willingness to be available.

Unifying our work and personal time means first and foremost having a *unified vision* of our life. If you connect with the shaman, the guru, and the healer in yourself, you know that your healing work grows organically from the ground of who you are. Knowing that we ourselves are not always wise, we see the importance of being devoted to our own growth as well as to that of our patients. We know we are in the same predicament as our patients, trying our best to deal with the dilemma of human life, practicing with them, meditating by ourselves before work and then teaching what we have found helpful.

Therapy thus is a calling, a way of life. If mindful therapy is not part of our way of life we run the risk of becoming only technicians, not healers.

CAN I LIVE UP TO THIS VISION?

The vision that our work fits into the lineage of shamans, gurus, healers, and bodhisattvas has an edge to it. If we can hold this vision of our work, we may be able to tolerate the skepticism, the negative transference, and the other difficulties of being a therapist more easily. If we see ourselves as healers, we can accept these realities, and need not be crushed by them—because we then have a wider vision in which to hold these experiences. Without such a vision, we are more vulnerable. The mindful therapist knows that her compassion, growing out of a clear vision of her task, is her greatest help and protection. Yet it is challenging to think of ourselves this way—to think of ourselves as healers or shamans or gurus. Who are we to adopt this role? Is this not a little grandiose?

Let us first clarify that in taking on such a vision of our work, we do not mean feigning some in- or superhuman perfection. Nor does such a vision require us to squash our sense of humor, our playfulness, our sensuality, or any other aspect of ourselves that gives our humanity its authenticity. It is enough to be dedicated to our own inner growth and well-being, working on our spiritual life, progressively shedding ourselves of limitations and blind spots—in full knowledge that we are always beginners, and there is always more to be done. If this is the case, our life and our work will teach us what we need to know.

There is a Jewish tradition of the *zaddik*—the holy person. The zaddik differs, it is said, from ordinary people, in that the zaddik is *more fully human*. In the Christian tradition, Saint Irenaeus says something similar. He says that the glory of God is a human being fully alive. Buddha too was nothing more than fully human. Buddhist teaching stresses that the Buddha is a human being in order to emphasize that we can accomplish what he accomplished. When asked if he were a god or a saint, he always denied both, saying simply, "I am awake."

To be fully and completely alive, fully and completely human, is goal enough. There is no other sort of completeness or perfection to attain. The plum tree in my back yard can only express its plum tree–ness. No other kind of perfection is available or needed. A flower is only itself. It does not have to strain and struggle to be a flower, but lets its flowerness unfold of itself.

You may ask, "Who am I to do this work?" and I might respond, "Who are you *not* to do this?" "You are the light of the world," said Christ. And that light must be allowed to shine. You already express Buddha nature. To become a full and whole human being is your main task in life—not some secondary one to be taken care of after you somehow find a way to earn a living.

AVOIDING A GREAT MISUNDERSTANDING

We mustn't confuse spiritual aspiration with a striving for some kind of insipid, limp *goodness*. The therapist who goes into the consulting room hoping to be liked is sunk from the start. For while some of our patients will appreciate us more than we deserve, many will not understand that what we do is difficult. And in fact, the better you are at it, the easier it seems from the outside.

In a seldom-discussed passage of the Bible, Christ himself rejects being called good (Mark 10:17). In this account, a man approaches him respectfully with a question, calling him "Good Teacher." Christ responded, "Why do you call me good? No one is good but God alone."

A healer must be on the way to to full humanity. But "trying to be good" in the sense of achieving a superhuman perfection inevitably activates the opposite. Striving in this sense creates a sense of lack of acceptance, not only toward ourselves, but toward our patients as well. The work we do requires faith in our humanity.

THE NEED FOR PRACTICE

Most of the time we live in forgetfulness. We are distracted. We are not really present to what we are doing or saying, but are already planning what we will do or say next, and perhaps a few things after that. That is why it can be such a relief to do a simple thing like mindful breathing. If you can be fully aware of the sensation of breathing in and out for the space of one breath, then you have brought body and mind together for that length of time. The essence of becoming a fully awake, mindful human being is to know that you are already Buddha. And remember, if this feels overwhelming, it is really very simple—as close and available as your next mindful breath. In the context of mindful therapy it is essential to listen deeply. Yet we cannot become capable of deep listening in the therapy room if we do not practice mindfulness elsewhere.

In order to be deeply present, in order to truly listen, we need a way to calm the mind. This is in fact what mindfulness is about, and part of what meditation is about. Meditation is simply a process by which we calm the mind, or more precisely, allow the mind to calm itself, without our forcing it. This takes a little time and a little practice. Our minds are extraordinarily busy places, as we learn the first time we try to meditate. If we cannot develop a calm, clear mind while we are sitting in meditation, how can we expect to have one in daily life? How can we expect to suddenly have this when we listen to patients? But if we can establish a base of mindfulness in meditation, we can then begin to learn how to bring the same calm, clear awareness out into our life and into our work.

EXERCISES

Mindful breathing is the basis of many exercises in this book, so let us explore it here. Please take a few moments to try it after you have read this.

To breathe mindfully is in essence simply to be fully aware of your breathing. First sit in an upright, comfortable position. You might like to take a few deep breaths to start, just to get in touch with the sensation of breathing. Then imagine your awareness sinking down into the abdomen. From there, become aware of the gentle rising and falling of your diaphragm with each breath, letting the body breathe just as it wants and needs to, letting your awareness just rest on the breath without struggling or forcing. When your mind wanders (as it will!), just treat this as the most natural thing in the world (as it is!), and gently bring your attention back to the breath. Remind yourself that you are not trying to do or accomplish anything special. You are just allowing your mind to rest on the breath. Please take care of yourself every day by allowing some time to breathe mindfully.

Become the Guru

In talking about re-visioning the role of psychotherapist, I am not talking solely, or even primarily, of an intellectual vision. Intellectual vision is important. It is the beginning of the process, but it is only the beginning.

For this exercise, spend a little while deciding first upon an image of a person who for you personifies numinous wisdom. It might be, for example, the Buddha, Christ, a saint or bodhisattva. It might be an image from an old photograph you have of a Native American healer. It might be an image of someone very loving and wise that comes from your own imagination. (But it should not be someone from your actual life, as we are seeking an image of transcendent wisdom.)

You may know right away who it is you want to choose for this purpose, or it may take a few days to work this out and make the choice that feels right. When you have decided, you are ready to take the next step.

Now spend a few moments sitting quietly. Allow the body and mind to rest by bringing your awareness to your breathing. Experience the body breathing in and breathing out, at its own pace and rhythm. Now imagine the wise person you have chosen standing before you. You may envision this person in some detail, or just form a sense of her presence.

Spend a little while with that person before you. Imagine him smiling to you, transmitting light and love and wisdom. Take your time. Don't rush.

Finally, imagine that person becoming all light and energy, or perhaps something like smoke, rising up before you and entering your body through the top of your head, then dispersing through every part of your body. Experience the warmth and wisdom of this person permeating every cell. Notice how this feels: in your thinking, your emotions, and in your body. Then imagine yourself going through your day feeling this way: driving, talking on the phone, meeting with patients, being at home. See yourself as going through the day in peace, understanding, and joy—full of concentration and loving-kindness.

Then imagine yourself being challenged in some ways during the day, perhaps losing this peace for a little while, but then finding your way back to it.

Make it a practice to take this person into you again at the start of every work day, and again briefly between sessions.

Know yourself as guru, as shaman, as healer.

CHAPTER TWO
Cultivate the Spiritual Life:
Freshness, Stability, Stillness, and Freedom

Nirvana teaches that we already are what we want to become.
We don't have to run after anything anymore. We only need
to return to ourselves and touch our true nature. When we do,
we have real peace and joy.[7]
—THICH NHAT HANH

MUCH HAVOC IS WROUGHT in the world through the efforts of self-conscious do-gooders. With the best of intentions, they set out to reform the rest of us. But often, it backfires. In psychotherapy, for example, we know that sometimes we try too hard to help. Perhaps we dispense advice too readily. We jump in with our favorite exercise or homework. And yet somehow, we are surprised to find the patient resisting. We are trying to heal the world. But when we are in the flow of psychotherapy, just relaxed and paying attention, often wonderful things unfold, seemingly without effort. It is this effortless effort from which change and healing flow.

On a broader level, consider the example of social activists. Activists may act with the best of intentions but are often too angry, too hostile to be effective. Rather than convincing any but the already persuaded, they make enemies of those with a different opinion. Rather than helping others to see differently, those who think differently become even more entrenched in their opinion in the face of such hostility. The net result is the polarized society now so familiar to us all.

Consider the not-so-distant example of the Vietnam War. We ended the conflict in southeast Asia, but at the cost of bringing it home. What both protesters and war supporters did not know back then was how to listen deeply and make the person with a different view a friend rather than an enemy. Perhaps the protests contributed to the end of the war. But perhaps also, if they had protested with mindfulness—with understanding—the war would have ended even sooner. People would not have become so entrenched in their positions. And our country's political landscape might be more civil today. The current situation in Iraq may also have evolved quite differently. There was not a lot of dialogue going on before our invasion of Iraq—just angry people on both sides shouting. People perceived that deeply held values were threatened. Once that happens, listening becomes impossible. If we could have found a way to continue to listen deeply, and to talk without anger or rancor, we might have found another way to accomplish our ends, one without violence and the attendant risks of backlash.

Even when we do good things, if we do it full of anger and hatred, only anger and hatred result. On the other hand, if we are able to take good care of ourselves, and preserve our freshness, solidity, stillness, and freedom, we can keep the relationship open with those whose opinions differ from our own. We will not make enemies of those who disagree with us. By taking good care of ourselves, we give anger and hatred no foothold in us. In this way, we become a true source of healing in the world.

One great paradox of the spiritual life is rooted in the notion of nonself or interbeing: *If you set out to heal the world, you will lose yourself. If you set out to heal yourself, you heal the world.*

The best way to take care of yourself is to cultivate mindfulness—to cultivate a calm, spacious, accepting, open awareness of what is happening in the impermanent and ever-changing world inside and outside our skin. By taking care of yourself in this way, you are at the same time of the most help to others.

KNOWING WHAT NOT TO DO

When we illuminate each circumstance and situation with our awareness, and let it be, without resisting or struggling against what is, we begin to increase the positive elements and decrease the negative ones. When you feel happy, and are aware that you are happy, your happiness increases. When you feel sad, and allow yourself to have the feeling of sadness without resistance, suffering is reduced, seeking its own natural level in the economy of the psyche.

One of the properties of the mind articulated in Buddhism is that the mind takes on the quality of what it dwells on. Like the chameleon that becomes green on a leaf and brown on the trunk of a tree, we take on the character of what we focus on. When we struggle *against* something difficult or negative or painful, this only gives it more energy, and the negative aspect gains strength. When we acknowledge the difficult element, letting it simply *be,* it comes and goes: but it does not get stuck. It does not gain power.

One always has to add, in a Western context, that the mental state of *letting be* is not passivity. By way of illustration, consider the example of a person standing in a cold rain. The mindful person knows: *this rain is cold.* She does not have to ponder very much about taking appropriate action. She gets out of the rain. (Or, if that is not possible, she equanimously gets wet.) It is the person distracted by all her busyness that does not experience the cold rain and take care of herself.

The Buddha said that "All things can be mastered by mindfulness."[8] And Gestalt therapist Fritz Perls tells us:

> And I believe that this is the great thing to understand: *that awareness per se—by and of itself—can be curative.* Because with full awareness you become aware of the organismic self-regulation, you can let the organism take over without interfering, without interrupting; we can rely on the wisdom of the organism. (Italics original).[9]

In other words, nothing else is needed. Awareness is sufficient because doing naturally arises out of awareness when you trust your organismic responding. And what Perls calls the "wisdom of the organism" is synonymous with what others call our Buddha nature or the divine within.

The famous Thai meditation master Ajahn Chah recalls a student who, when a strong wind blew off the roof of his hut in the rainy season, did not bother to repair it, saying that he was practicing "not clinging." The master commented: "This is not clinging without wisdom. It is about the same as the equanimity of the water buffalo."[10]

The idea is not that you do not do what needs doing, but that you do it mindfully. Also, if you are mindful, you learn that many things indeed do not need doing, that every itch does not need to be scratched. And knowing what not to do is at least as much a part of wisdom as doing what needs doing, and often more so.

Unless we are open and aware, in touch with what really is, we continue to act out old conditioning, old scripts. We do not respond to the person before us, but to the punishing mother or absent father of our childhood. Only if we are calm and open and sensitive can we do what needs doing, do it in the way it needs doing, and also know what not to do. The practice of therapy does not entail simply blurting out advice that a patient may find judgmental or insultingly obvious. But because we are listening deeply, in touch with the patient and the moment, we more clearly know what is needed and what is not needed. If we act out of our own need to feel helpful, we will be less able to resist saying unhelpful things.

TOUCHING YOUR BUDDHA NATURE

The word "Buddhism" is essentially a western invention. Usually Buddhists will refer to it simply as the *dharma* (in Sanskrit) or *dhamma* (in Pali).[11] Buddhism is not best understood as a religion among other religions, such that if you are a Buddhist you must adamantly oppose all other religious or philosophical points of view. Rather, it is a teaching that leads to the end of suffering, to peace. And these teachings are compatible with a wide variety of religious and non-religious views. I have always been intrigued by the multiple meanings of the word *dharma*. In this context, as the word used in place of what we would call Buddhism, it means the "teaching"—the practice that leads to liberation from suffering. The other meaning of *dharma* is "phenomenon" or more simply, "thing." These multiple meanings of *dharma* imply that the teaching and phenomena can be seen as ultimately the same thing. A mountain teaches dharma. A stream teaches dharma. A bird teaches dharma. And yes, heavy traffic teaches dharma. Weeds teach the dharma. Suffering—perhaps especially suffering—teaches dharma.

Working with Natural Images

Zen master Thich Nhat Hanh uses this idea to offer one way to be in touch with our Buddha nature by touching our kinship with flowers, mountains, water, and space. The following exercise is a wonderful way to meditate, to heal and restore your calmness, your well-being, or to prepare to listen deeply to a patient. It is also a wonderful meditation to teach your patients.

Thich Nhat Hanh offers this meditation practice:

Breathing in, I know I am breathing in.
Breathing out, I know I am breathing out.   *(in, out)*
Breathing in, I see myself as a flower.
Breathing out, I feel fresh.   *(flower, fresh)*
Breathing in, I see myself as a mountain.
Breathing out, I feel solid.   *(mountain, solid)*
Breathing in, I see myself as still water.
Breathing out, I reflect things as they are.   *(still water, reflecting)*
Breathing in, I see myself as space.
Breathing out, I feel free.   *(space, free)*[12]

Statements like the ones in this exercise are known as *gathas.* To work with these statements, take each pair in turn. As you draw a breath, tell yourself silently, "Breathing in, I know I am breathing in" and then as you breath out, "Breathing out, I know I am breathing out," using the words to guide your attention. Since it is a little unwieldy to say the whole sentence each time, after the first breath you can just say the words in parentheses, in on the inbreath, out on the outbreath. You can repeat this process as many times as you like, and then move on to the other statements—flower/fresh and so on.

If your concentration wanders, first of all you should know that there is nothing wrong with that. In meditation, you are allowing the mind to calm down in its own time and way, not imposing calm upon it. The word *concentration* is a bit misleading insofar as it connotes strain or struggle. The process of calming or concentrating is more like a broad, flat, light stone slowly settling to the bottom of a deep cool lake. You don't have to try to push the stone to the bottom: it will settle there on its own.

When you do wander, though, you might enjoy coming back to the full statement, not just the pair of words. You may also find it helpful to say the full statement out loud a time or two when you are alone and will not disturb others (or embarrass yourself!).

In the subsections that follow I will explore each of the pairs in this gatha.

THE IN- AND OUT-BREATH

Most Buddhist meditation begins with the breath. Breathing is the most fundamental act of life. We can live without food or water for days, but only for a few minutes without breathing. As we breathe in and out, we know that we nourish every cell in the body. As we breathe in and out with the first part of this gatha, we touch how nourishing it is for our body and mind to draw and release breath.

The breath lies uniquely on the boundary between the voluntary and autonomic nervous systems. It does not require conscious cooperation to breathe, and yet when we bring mindfulness to our breath we experience more of the full benefit of breathing: its full calming, healing, nurturing potential.

When we are anxious or sad, when we entertain a disturbing thought, or even when we struggle to solve a problem in arithmetic, we may catch the breath, and breathe in a shallow and uneven way. When we breathe in this way, we are not taking such good care of body and mind. Our cells may be just slightly deprived of oxygen, and may build up toxins. Further, there is a feedback loop between breath and emotion. Feeling anxious, we breathe shallowly. Breathing shallowly, we begin to feel more anxious. Fortunately, the opposite is true also: As we begin to breathe more calmly and deeply, we start to feel calmer. We can be present with negative emotions without being overwhelmed by them, without denying them or avoiding them. Yet since we increase our calmness and our capacity for mindfulness, we also do not get stuck in these emotions.

The breath gives us a foundation from which we can take care of our emotional life.

Another aspect of breathing is that, since it lies on the boundary between voluntary and involuntary, it is a way of bringing body and mind harmoniously together. We can avoid being like the James Joyce character who lived just a few feet from his body. Our minds may be preoccupied with dreams of greatness or fears of humiliation and defeat, with the past or the future, and thus our energy, our vital force is scattered.

When you can use the breath to be calm and present, you become someone that others—including your patients—can trust to be present with them even through difficult emotions and life problems. You become more capable of holding the patient in your kind, compassionate, equanimous attention.

Working with the breath is a basic practice, but that does not mean it is not also an advanced practice. In the Anapanasatti Sutra, the Buddha shows that the breath is a vehicle one can ride all the way to enlightenment. It is not just for beginners.

It is a wonderful practice sometimes to do nothing more than meditate on the breath, on *in* and *out,* for a whole period of meditation, or to work just with this for a period of days or weeks.

Even when moving on to the other word pairs in this gatha—*flower/fresh, mountain/solid* and so forth—you still maintain contact with the breath.

FLOWER/FRESH

Since the mind takes on the qualities of whatever it attends to, what better thing to meditate on then a flower? If you have a beautiful flower available, you can help make this part of the meditation vivid by gazing at it as you practice *flower/fresh.*

The stressors of daily life wilt the flower in us. If we allow it, they can destroy our well-being. But by practicing *flower/fresh,* we give our flower cooling, vitalizing water, and quickly restore its beauty.

When you have a beautiful flower, you want to take good care of it. When you are in touch with your own flowerness, you want to take good care of yourself as well. Since you are a precious and beautiful flower, why willingly expose yourself to toxins that wilt you? You naturally want to practice mindful consumption, eating and drinking in a more healthy way, not exposing yourself to too many images of violence, to too many empty television shows, to advertising that waters feelings of deprivation and greed. You want to avoid people and situations that are too strong in their negativity for you to change, that will only wilt you.

This has a very real consequence for the mindful therapist: If patients' difficulties are too much for you, if their interactions with you are too difficult for you despite your best effort to deal with them mindfully, you must recognize and acknowledge this, and then make an appropriate referral. *No one* is served by your going down with your patient.

A flower is something very precious. Its beauty is fleeting and impermanent, as we ourselves are, as our patients and loved ones are. Since we know the flower is transient, we value it even more.

MOUNTAIN/SOLID

Every morning when I jog around the neighborhood, I see my old friends the Sandia mountains, and I remember to practice *mountain/solid*. On a cold winter morning I may shiver. On a summer afternoon I may be hot. Strong winds may make it difficult to breathe or move forward. Rain may dampen both my body and my spirit. But the Sandias do not care. They do not shiver in the cold, or wilt in the heat. The winds do not move them in the slightest. The rain rolls off them playfully, while the mountains just smile.

When you see a Zen master like Thich Nhat Hanh walk, you may be struck by the quality of stillness and solidity he embodies. He looks like a mountain moving in a smooth and stately way. We can practice moving in this way, bring mindfulness to every step we make. This is the practice of embodying the solidity of the mountain.

When we practice *mountain/solid*, we get in touch with our own solidity, our own strength. We sit in a solid way when we do this practice, to get the feel of it in our bodies. We may also focus our attention on the area just below the navel, the hara. The hara is the physical center of gravity in our body, which is a very solid part of ourselves. By focusing on the mountain, we take on its strength, its solidity. Our emotions may rage and blow on one level, but this solid aspect of ourselves remains undisturbed.

When I say we are undisturbed, I do not mean that we do not feel emotions. We *feel* them but are not *disturbed* by them, and do not have to struggle against them. They simply are allowed to come and go in their own time and rhythm.

Buddhas feel emotion. It is not the goal to become unfeeling, like a hunk of metal. For while buddhas feel emotion, they also know that they are more than these emotions. They are in touch with their emotions, but are at the same time in touch with their inner strength and solidity. Emotional storms may rage, but buddhas can bear them as a mountain bears a rainstorm, solidly and with complete freedom.

Patients come to us because they do not feel very solid. There are storms blowing constantly around them and inside them, and since they are not in touch with their solidity, this is painful for them to bear. The first gift we offer them is our own solidity. Practicing *mountain/solid*, we empathically feel their feelings along with them, but we are not lost in these feelings and we are not blown away. We do not get caught in the repetitive and hurtful dramas of our patients, even when they do their best to hypnotize us into playing the roles complementary to their own. We offer them our solidity, our strong, true presence, relating to them from the solid place in ourselves.

And when appropriate, if the time comes, we can teach them the practice of *mountain/solid*.

STILL WATER/REFLECTING

Imagine a high mountain lake on a windless, clear day, its surface smooth as glass. It reflects everything vividly: the sun, the moon, a human face. Whether it is something beautiful or ugly, soothing or troubling, the lake reflects it clearly, without judgment or prejudice. As Zen master Seng-tsan expressed it, "The perfect Tao is without difficulty, save that it avoids picking and choosing."[13]

Since the human body is itself mostly water, it is not at all far-fetched to envision yourself this way, fully at rest, reflecting what is real, what is true, without prejudice or ban, without choosing. Unless we are still, we cannot perceive clearly. When we are agitated, the garden hose on the ground may look like a snake. Our actions and responses to the world will be off too, in accord with our misperception. When you become still and clear like a calm lake, you see reality clearly, and respond appropriately. When you are calm and clear, you can also be in touch with what is positive and healing. You see the blue sky, the eyes of the child, the trees and grass. You see everything. And you realize, no matter how many difficulties there are in the world, there are always beautiful things to appreciate. Perceptions of the positive elements of our experience provide the strength needed to bear what is difficult.

You may be full of uncertainty about yourself. You may be full of judgment about your patient. You may be full of reactions, deciding whether you agree or disagree with your patient, or you may be thinking about what kind of advice to give or treatments to offer. But if we are not first still and open, receiving the person that is before us as the quiet water receives the full moon, without resistance or dissent, our vision will be murky, and our decisions dubious.

When we are still and clear, we can also have patience, and know when to act and when to wait. To listen as still water is to really hear.

SPACE/FREE

When I practice *space/free,* I like to picture myself as the wide-open blue sky. Thoughts and feelings move across the sky like clouds. Some are dark and threatening, some bright and reassuring. But in any event, I know they are clouds and I know I am the sky.

When I know I am the sky and not the clouds, I am free amid the clouds. Clouds come and go, some are beautiful and some are threatening. That is the nature of mind and that is the nature of life. We are not free so long as we insist on only *certain types* of thoughts, feelings, and experiences—the ones we like or approve of. We are free only when we learn to be present to life, whatever is happening, even when we would prefer things were otherwise. When we practice sky-like awareness, everything becomes luminous, because we have stopped picking and choosing. We are open and free.

Practicing *space/free* is a challenge. So often, before we even get out of bed in the morning, we are already running internally. Before one foot touches the ground, we are already planning our steps, anticipating the many things we will need to do that day, and deciding on the order in which we need to do them—everything from making coffee, showering, and getting dressed to important meetings and work tasks. As therapists, you may even know at times which patients are coming in that day, anticipating all this with your own mix of dread or relief, anticipation or anxiety. When we practice *space/free,* we disidentify with these thoughts. We are aware of them, but we know that thoughts and feelings are fleeting and impermanent. We can let them come and go, neither fearing them nor chasing after them. After all, to avoid or pursue a cloud is foolishness when you are the sky itself!

Practicing *space/free* awareness, you know that you are not these thoughts and feelings. Practicing *space/free* you are not clinging to or fearing your thoughts and feelings. They simply move through your awareness, arising and departing in accord with their own nature. As you allow them to come and go, you can look into them, release them, and come back to the present moment, knowing that the moment of *reaching* toward your coffee cup is already a wonderful moment, no less so than the moment of tasting the coffee.

To put the exercises in this gatha into practice, it helps a great deal to begin at the start of the day. In principle, we can become mindful at any time. But as a practical matter, if you do not find a way to generate some mindfulness at the beginning of the day it becomes even harder to find the time as the day continues and you get caught up in your inevitably busy life.

One such practice is to find a way to remind yourself to breathe and smile even before you sit up in bed and place a foot on the ground. Remind yourself that this day is a gift, that it is wonderful to be alive, even if the day before you is busy and includes people and tasks you would rather not have to deal with.

Try to find a way to touch the wonderfulness of life even before you get out of bed. Some of the clouds passing through may involve planning and worrying about the day ahead, but at least you can create, alongside such thoughts, the awareness that at its base this is all wonderful.

But be patient with yourself! Our mindfulness is not very strong at first. It is like the sun trying to shine through a thick layer of cold winter clouds. But if we can find a way to create the energy of mindfulness first thing in the morning, and do our best to return to this energy throughout the day, pausing periodically to breathe and smile, the light of our awareness becomes much stronger.

After you have showered and dressed and had your breakfast, you might like to create some time in the morning to read a little bit and meditate. Rising early enough to allow this is immensely worthwhile. Spend a little time with a book that inspires your mindfulness and sense of the spiritual. It need not be a long time. If you choose the right kind of book, a few minutes may suffice. Then spend a little time in sitting meditation, breathing and smiling, practicing *flower/fresh*, and so on. This may be just a few minutes at first, keeping it within a time frame that you can enjoy, and gradually lengthening to allow the mind to settle more fully in meditation.

Traditionally, Buddhists generate energy for their spiritual practice through vows, which create aspiration. Many of us in the West don't like vows very much. They create a tug of war in ourselves between following the vow and rebelling. A better way for us may be to practice visualization. At the end of your meditation period, when you are a little more relaxed than you were to begin with, picture yourself going through the day in a mindful way—driving mindfully, in an unhurried way, talking on the phone pleasantly, being calm when patients are difficult or come late or don't show at all, enjoying the more pleasant patients, pausing often to breathe and smile, and so on. I find this to be a very powerful practice, and I recommend it highly. Please try.

Jorge returned to therapy one day distraught. He had been sober for five years, but suddenly began drinking heavily again, feeling powerless to stop. I stayed with him in his despair. I did not rush in with advice, but listened, reflected—still water. After wallowing in these feelings for about forty minutes, suddenly there was a shift. Jorge recalled how wonderful it was to be sober for five years.

It was not until Jorge spontaneously made this shift that I offered a suggestion to help. Building on what was already happening spontaneously, I asked him to close his eyes, breathe a few mindful breaths, and conjure up specific, clear images of what his sober life was like, noting how this felt in his body and his mind, then suggesting also that he could choose to remember these feelings the next time he felt an urge to drink, and that maybe he would be able to make another choice. Jorge left my office smiling, and was able to interrupt his downward spiral.

If I had not been in a place where I could practice still water that day, the result might have been quite different. If I had rushed to offer advice because Jorge's despair created an anxiety in me that I wanted to bring to a halt by offering him something, this would not have worked so well. If I had offered this visualization before he was through processing his despair and hopelessness, I might have encountered resistance and arguing. As it was, I simply aligned myself with the emerging force of healing that was already in evidence.

DISTORTED PERCEPTION

A fundamental tenet of Buddhism is that our perception is by its nature distorted. Where there is perception, it is said, there is deception. We see through the distorting lens of a separate self, one we often imagine to be somehow permanent and unchanging. But this separate self is illusory. We will explore this further in chapter six.

What's more, we instantly layer judgment upon perception. We don't allow anything to just be in itself, but continually judge whether we like it, dislike it, or find it neutral. And then we react to our judgment. If we like it, we want to move toward it or even possess the pleasant object of perception. If we dislike it, we want to move away from it or destroy it. And if it is neutral, we may scarcely notice it at all. We judge it irrelevant and ignore it.

We view every opinion we encounter from the standpoint of whether we agree or disagree with it or simply do not care about it at all. If we agree, we have a pleasant feeling, and if we disagree, an unpleasant one. And if we feel neutral, that too can become the unpleasant sensation of boredom if we need to continue to attend.

I have taught a workshop on Mindful Living at the University of New Mexico for many years now. In that workshop we do some exercises to increase sensory awareness. One of these involves listening. The room I teach in has a rattle in the ventilator that every class notices during the listening exercise and comments on in some way. When this sound is in the background, it remains a minor irritant. When people begin to attend to it, at first it may become even more irritating than when it was simply in the background, but then, at least for some, as people begin to listen in an open, interested way, it becomes neutral. It is neither pleasant nor unpleasant. Some people have even been able to hear the sound as pleasant, realizing that it is a wonderful thing to have two good ears, that hearing is in itself wonderful once we step outside of our labels.

To use a familiar example, the sound of our phone ringing may be pleasant, unpleasant, or neutral. If you experience phone calls as an interruption, it may take on an unpleasant association. The ringing may seem very irritating. On the other hand, if you have been expecting your new love to call you, the sound of the phone ringing may be very pleasant. But whether you experience it as unpleasant, pleasant, or neutral because of such factors as these, you are not really hearing the ringing. You are hearing something like an annoying interruption, the voice of your beloved, or just a signal that it is time to answer the phone.

When you hear the phone ringing with mindfulness, you may be aware of all those kinds of meanings, but at the same time, you hear the sound in itself. And that is always pleasant. Experience is pleasant in the sense that it is life or part of being alive, part of having this wonderful, human sensory apparatus. Mindfulness means learning to hear in such a way that we know hearing is in itself a miracle. It is learning to see in such a way that we know seeing is a miracle. It is learning to see that being alive is a miracle.

When we hear our patients speaking, we can get so caught up—in whether what they are saying is affecting us in a pleasant way, whether we agree with it, whether we think it healthy or unhealthy, and what sort of diagnosis may underlie their remarks—that we do not really hear the patient. We do not really perceive the other person. At this level, it is not so much about hearing the person's voice as pure sound, though that may indeed be part of it, but of hearing the person behind the words. To understand someone deeply is a pleasant experience, even if the content is not so pleasant, is filled with sadness, suffering, or anger.

When we listen to our patient as still water, when we practice mindful therapy, we hear what is said and what is left unsaid. We sense things that may not be immediately available to verbal expression or cognition. We are available.

MINDFULNESS DURING THE WORK DAY

On a retreat with Thich Nhat Hanh in Santa Barbara, someone asked him how long one should meditate. The wise Zen master responded that one should meditate all day. Of course he did not mean that you should only sit on your meditation cushion and not do anything else, but rather that we should bring the meditative attitude into the rest of our lives, practicing calm, clear awareness, acceptance, peacefulness.

To be able to do this, it is helpful to look at your daily schedule. Consider ways in which you can try to do less rather than more, not trying to squeeze so many things in. When you have the energy of rushing in you, you do not have the energy of mindfulness. They are mutually exclusive. Allow yourself a little extra time for the drive to work. Consider limiting the number of patients you see in a day, or consider alternative scheduling ideas in so far as these are possible.

Psychiatrist and author Irvin Yalom recommends spacing appointments more than an hour apart. For example, if your first appointment is at 9:00 A.M., begin your second at 10:05, your third at 11:10, and so on. This gives you the time to complete a note, return a phone call, and practice a little mindful breathing between patients. Or you might consider limiting the number of new patients you see in one day, since these may take more time and may require more energy. When you come home, see if you can practice a little mindful breathing, letting go of the pressures of the day. Find ways to spend the evening that are quiet and restorative. Spend some time in the fresh air, enjoying the beauty of nature, even if it is just a lone tree in a small city park. Pay attention to nutrition, rest, and exercise needs. All of this is part of your calling.

I leave it to your own intelligence to find ways to take good care of yourself and live more happily and mindfully. But please do so. Please remember that nothing is more important than your own peace and equanimity. For if you are not peaceful, you will create more suffering than you heal. Make this your vow, your aspiration, your visualization. Everything depends on this.

Indeed, everything depends on everything else in our interconnected and interpenetrating universe, so if you are not happy, how can I be happy? How can your patients be happy? Your family? Your friends? If you take care of your own happiness, that is the first and greatest gift you can give to the world.

Morning Meditation

I find the following practice, which builds on those from chapter one, very helpful and healing to do in the morning to set the tone and the intention for the day. It combines mindful breathing with positive imagery.

When we visualize something, we utilize the faculty of the imagination. This aspect of our inner life has fallen upon harsh times. In our modern, scientific age, "imagination" often connotes something unreal. And yet all great advancements, technological and otherwise, depend upon this faculty for their existence. Imagination can be an important tool in becoming more whole and complete human beings.

Begin by sitting comfortably in meditation posture. It does not matter so much whether you sit on a meditation cushion cross-legged or in the lotus position, or comfortably in a chair. The main thing is that you are upright—in a relaxed, balanced, comfortable way.

Take a few moments to look around you and notice your surroundings, cultivating a sense of gratitude for having this wonderful space to meditate and the time to do so. Gently let your eyes close, aware of any sounds around you, in touch with your surroundings. Smile a Buddha-like half-smile. Smiling this way "tells" the brain that everything is okay, and the brain in turn tells the body it is okay to relax. Now say to yourself: I see myself moving through this day with peace, joy, and ease, performing each action in mindfulness. I see myself driving mindfully, speaking on the phone mindfully, eating mindfully, doing my work mindfully, sitting down mindfully with my patients, producing my true, radiant, healing presence with them. If ever I feel my mindful awareness beginning to slip, I see myself being aware of this (which is already mindfulness), and I return to my breathing and smiling. I see that whenever something comes along that is difficult for me, that triggers sorrow, anger, envy, or sadness, I can always return to my mindfulness, remembering my true nature in the midst of this human experience, experiencing these things clearly without avoiding or repressing. Continue to enjoy this for a while.

(Those familiar with the use of imagery in psychological practice may recognize that this exercise combines mastery imagery with coping imagery.)

Finally, simply return to your breathing in and out, enjoying each breath, smiling your Buddha smile.

PART II

Buddha as Therapist

CHAPTER THREE
Mindfulness Is the Key

*We only need to practice acceptance and there will be progress
without struggle.*[14]
—THICH NHAT HANH

OUR MARVELOUS INTELLIGENCE may be said to have
two basic functions. First, it divides things up and differentiates them. This is the analytic function. With regard to ourselves and others, this intelligence emphasizes how we are each
separate and distinct from the rest of the world. It predominates
in Western culture, often to the point that it is equated with intelligence per se.

Yet the second function of intelligence is at least as important.
Its role is to connect, to see similarities. This is synthetic intelligence. With synthetic intelligence, we see how things are alike,
how they are related. Spiritually, this aspect recognizes how we are
connected with the world, how everything interpenetrates everything else. This kind of intelligence is seen more often in traditional Eastern culture.

Both kinds of intelligence have their place, though indeed
they cannot truly be separated. But since our culture values the

analytic over the synthetic, the latter is important for seeing inter-connection, both among various teachings and among all phe-nomena. Understanding the Dharma is like entering a seamless garment: it may be difficult to get into it, but once on, it fits very nicely. It is important to come to see that the four noble truths, for example, are related to the practice of mindfulness, or that the ele-ments of the eightfold path are actually connected and interre-lated. To understand one element of Buddhist teaching deeply is to understand all the other elements, and as you learn more about the other elements, they shed additional light on the first.

In this spirit, I would like to offer you some other terms and practices that I think may shed light on how we understand and practice mindfulness. Each of these is not necessarily an adequate technical definition of mindfulness itself, but all point to impor-tant aspects of connecting with our experience in the present and are therefore closely enough related to be valuable to us.

CALM, CLEAR AWARENESS

What happens, for example, if you are intending to practice calm, clear awareness, but what you become aware of is that you are nervous, or sad, or angry—or anything other than calm? The temptation at that point is to try to *repress* your awareness of these feelings. If you do so, you are worse off than if you knew nothing about mindfulness; for now you are divided into two hostile camps, the part of you that is trying to be calm, and the part of you that is nervous or angry or sad.

When you are sad, mindfulness means that you know you are sad. When you are afraid, mindfulness means that you know you are afraid. When you are angry, you know that you are angry. Once in a therapy group I encountered a man who stood up, shook his fist, and *yelled* at the rest of the group that he was not angry! When you are mindful, you know it when anger arises in you, and you bring acceptance to such states of mind, even though you might prefer not to have them. You open to the experience, rather than closing down against it. Author and physician Donald M. Pachuta describes this attitude well:

> It takes no effort and no energy to feel sad when we feel sad or to feel angry when we feel angry. Yet we spend a great deal of energy trying to be unlike ourselves. For example, if we begin to "feel" a little depressed, we waste all our energy trying not to be depressed or blaming ourselves for being depressed, since we believe that we should not be depressed. It is more natural to feel and experience the sadness, and then it quickly goes away. At the very least, it does not interfere with our functioning. To live fully and be the master of your own emotions is to feel angry when you feel angry, sad when you feel sad, afraid when you feel afraid, and so on. Mastery is being how you are.[15]

When we practice in this way, positive experiences become more positive, and negative experiences, by not being resisted, find their own level. But when we resist the negative experience, it only grows stronger. And don't forget: if you realize that you are not mindful, that, too, is already the beginning of mindfulness!

What Is Happening Now?

Pause to ask yourself many times during the day, "What am I experiencing now? What's the truth of what is happening in my body, mind, and feelings?" If something unpleasant is there, try to open to it rather than push it away. If something pleasant is there, notice how your mindfulness increases the pleasantness of this experience. The energy we get from the experience of the pleasant can help us deal with what is not pleasant without denying or repressing.

MEDITATION

On one level, mindfulness refers to awareness in daily life, and on another to meditation, to the time when we sit in a formal way to practice meditation. Mindfulness and meditation are aspects of the same thing. A simplistic understanding of meditation is that it is something you do to rest and relax and restore yourself, a kind of stress-management practice. And as far as this idea goes, it is correct. But the essence of mindfulness meditation is to rest in clear awareness.

We do not meditate, however, just to have clear awareness while sitting, but in order to have clear awareness, as Thich Nhat Hanh suggests, all day long.

Meditation is something to do throughout the day. We sit in order to generate the energy of mindfulness, but then the practice is to carry this energy with us into the rest of the day. If you sit in meditation for a short time, perhaps you will be able to enjoy some moments of calm and peace. And that is already good. But true meditation is much more. True meditation is the capacity to have that same attitude in any activity. We sit in formal meditation so we have a chance to create the same kind of awareness throughout the day. And in fact this works both ways. If on the one hand we sit to meditate so we can be mindful all day long, on the other hand we also practice mindfulness during the day in order to support our sitting meditation.

The expectation that meditation as an isolated practice will solve all your problems just by doing it mechanically is a kind of magical notion, not grounded in reality. But if you seek to bring the same sort of awareness to daily life that you have in meditation, then your daily life supports your meditation, and your meditation supports your daily life. And while it may take a while before you can cultivate much mindfulness in the midst of daily activity, if you understand this interconnection, and keep returning to your mindfulness as best you can, then you indeed have a powerful practice that will bring about a deep transformation.

As psychotherapists, we can fall into the habit of talking about mindfulness and meditation for the benefits these bring. This is an expedient way of talking, but is not correct in the deepest sense. At its most profound level spiritual practice is always for its own sake rather than for attaining even the best of goals. In this spirit, the Buddha declared that he did not gain the least thing from unexcelled, complete enlightenment.[16]

While the practice of mindfulness and meditation have many benefits, you actually reap those benefits to the fullest extent by not approaching it as another task that you are doing in order to get something out of it. If you approach meditation in that way, it becomes just another chore. Your meditation gets co-opted into the rest of your life, into doing and accomplishing, rather than it being a process for deep transformation. This is why the Buddha said, "My practice is non-action, non-practice, and non-realization."[17]

Moments of Meditation

Begin each day with a period of sitting meditation. Start with a comfortable period, perhaps only ten or even five minutes to start, and very gently, very gradually, extend it as you feel comfortable. Return to this periodically during the day by pausing frequently to take a few mindful breaths.

RADICAL ACCEPTANCE

As we have seen, Thich Nhat Hanh teaches that acceptance leads to progress without struggle.

When you accept deeply the reality in which you find yourself, you know what to do and, just as importantly, what not to do. Your doing arises naturally from this knowing. You allow the doing to flow just as you allow your emotions to flow, without trying to impede or resist them, just bringing awareness to what is going on. And in far more situations than we tend to realize in our *doing*-oriented West, the best thing to do is non-doing.

Imagine two people sitting by the river. One is watching the river flow by, wishing that it would stop flowing. The other just notices the flow and opens to the experience of the river as it is. Which one will be distressed? How often do we find ourself acting like the first person?

The river of life flows whether we wish it to or not. Our task, if we can speak of it as a task, is to harmonize with what is. Our internal resistance does not change anything.

Letting Go, Letting Be

All day long, remind yourself to be with what is. You can help cultivate this kind of attitude with this gatha: "Breathing in, I let it all go; Breathing out, I let it all be."

SURRENDER

Psychiatrist Murray Bowen was known for his work with people with schizophrenia and their families. In the course of his research, he and his colleagues tried many interventions—with little success. Then they decided to stop trying to intervene and just try to understand. They began to carefully observe and study these patients and their families, asking them questions, all with a goal of understanding. They surrendered their desire to change and control their patients, or even to help them. Much to Bowen and his colleagues' surprise, however, when they adopted this attitude, these families began to improve and appeared less dysfunctional.[18]

There is power in surrender. You can surrender to God, the Universe, the Buddha within, or just to reality itself. Hindu saint

Ramana Maharshi said, "God . . . never forsakes the devotee who has surrendered himself."[19] Often, however, we are afraid to do just that. Thich Nhat Hanh said, "Usually we think that if we let go, we will lose the things that make us happy. But the more we let go, the happier we become."[20]

REVERENCE

Christian theologian and missionary doctor Albert Schweizer summarized his approach to the spiritual life with the phrase, "reverence for life." This implies a sense that everything is holy, or, as a Buddhist might say, everything calls for non-discriminating acceptance and a sense of wonderful becoming.

Years ago I had the opportunity to see the surprisingly tiny Leonardo da Vinci portrait known as the *Mona Lisa* in the Louvre. I had made a point, as many Louvre visitors do, to find this famous work of art. I had never understood before what was so special about it. But standing there, I knew that reproductions simply do not do it justice. I was swept up in the painting as I stood before it, caught in a moment of awe and reverence. In such moments, we are simply present. We are neither critiquing or judging. Imagine standing before a painting by one of the great masters—a work by Cézanne or Monet, by Leonardo or Rembrandt—and instead of taking in the beauty of the painting before you, thinking to yourself that the painter should not have done it this way, should have used a different color, a different brush stroke, should have composed his subject differently, and so on. What a loss that would be!

When we experience something deeply, reverently, we open up to it. When we criticize and second guess, we close down. When you can start to see your back yard, your whole life, every struggle, every patient with the same eyes with which you see the *Mona Lisa*, then you are really seeing. Then you know what reverence is.

Mindfulness is not seeing "objectively," but warmly, openly, and poetically. When we see mindfully, we experience that subject and object cannot exist independently, but represent a unified field. There is no seeing without both seer and seen, no hearing without both hearer and heard. One implies the other, inseparably and inescapably.

ACKNOWLEDGING THE TRUTH OF OUR EXPERIENCE

Normally we are so busy evaluating and judging, planning the future or reworking the past, that we do not experience what is here. We confuse what is here with what we wish were here, or what we fear. Every experience is colored by the basic decision of whether we like having this experience, or don't like having it. If we don't like it, we may well try to distort our perception in order to avoid the pain of having this undesirable experience. We try not to notice; we tell ourselves it is something good; we distort and evade. This is a kind of lying to ourselves. If we like it, we get caught by wanting more of it or fearing it will not last.

When we are calm and mindful, we come to see what is really there. Of course, not everything goes as smoothly or easily as we wish. But ultimately what is there is wonderful, because to be alive itself is wonderful. And when we stop resisting, things often seem to flow more harmoniously.

DWELLING HAPPILY IN THE PRESENT MOMENT

We seldom live in the present moment. Very often, we are busy rushing into the future. We do this in ways large and small. We may, for example, be taking a class, but if we are only interested in taking it to meet a degree requirement, we do not really have the experience of the class itself. We can get so busy asking what will be on the test (as anyone who has taught knows too well) that we preclude an experience of learning. We do not learn; we meet requirements. Or you may be out on a date with a wonderful person, but find yourself so busy wondering whether she likes you, or whether he is the one that you can build a future with, that you are not really there. You do not really see the person. You may have a good job, but miss it while you concentrate on the arc of your career, impatient to move on to something bigger and better. In the shower, instead of showering, you may be thinking about the day ahead, planning and daydreaming, missing the experience of showering.

To be mindful means to come around to the present moment. Life can only occur in the present tense. The future is uncertain, and has not yet come. The past is gone. It is only in the present moment that we can encounter life. Can you enjoy a future meal? Can you drink a glass of water from the past? You can only do these things now. So why not be where you are? To do that is to be mindful.

UNDERSTANDING, LOVING-KINDNESS, COMPASSION

One aspect of mindfulness concerns awareness of other people. Just as we concentrate on being in our experience rather than judging it, the same applies in the interpersonal sphere. To be mindful of other people is to *understand*. And where there is understanding there is love, kindness, and compassion.

Patients whose perceptions are not radically distorted by their past experience will tend to perceive our attention and understanding as loving, and they are not mistaken in doing so. And even those who do not at first may come to this perception. Love is made of understanding. Love *is* understanding. If we say we love but do not understand, I would question whether we really love. That kind of love, love without understanding, is only a kind of dependence on that person, a bond of familiarity, or a type of enmeshment.

If someone says something to us that is unkind or treats us in an unkind manner, the crucial thing is to understand. If we know that the person said that because she has the flu and is not at her best, for example, then we will naturally be more understanding, and therefore we can have love and compassion. We do not have to retaliate. If we know that he said an unkind thing because he has not received much understanding in his life—because of the suffering he has experienced, we can understand. At the same time, we give ourselves a lot of understanding. We do not deny that what the other person said or did hurt us. In kindness to ourselves, we may need to tell the other that we are hurt and ask them to stop doing what they did. But no retaliation is necessary. The behavior of human beings has causes, just as much as hurricanes or earthquakes. We would do well to adopt the same attitude toward human behavior as we do toward "natural" events.

Again, we may fear that by doing this, we are losing something, giving up or giving in to the other. But in fact, we always benefit by living in a kind and understanding way. From one perspective, this may seem a certain kind of self-centered point of view, but it makes sense in the light of interbeing, in which we are not taught to love all sentient beings except ourselves, but ourselves also.[21] I recall a study that was done with college students who were shown a film about Mother Teresa caring for the sick. Students who saw this film showed a rise in immune function in their saliva compared with those who saw a control film. And this happened whether they agreed with what Mother Teresa was doing or not. Compassion is good for us. It is not a matter of belief. It is something you can experience.

When we are mindful, we approach ourselves and others with an open attitude, an attitude of understanding, which is the same thing as love.

GRATITUDE

We may take so simple a thing as breathing for granted, but someone with asthma or emphysema knows that breathing is wonderful. We may take walking for granted, but someone in a wheelchair knows that to be able to walk is a miracle. We may take our small motor movements for granted, but someone with crippling arthritis knows that to be able to move without pain is a pleasure.

The point of reflecting on these things is not to induce guilt, as our parents may have done in telling us to eat our food because of the hungry children in faraway places. The point is, rather, to prevent us from taking our experience for granted. When you are mindful, you know that to be alive is itself a sacred, awe-inspiring thing. We knew this as children. Anything that can help us reawaken that awareness will help us live more fully.

Erich Fromm provides a clear sense of the way in which children already know this:

> When the child plays with a ball, it [sic] really sees the ball moving, it is fully in this experience, and that is why it is an experience which can be repeated without end, and with a never ceasing joy. The adult also believes that he sees the ball rolling and that is of course true, inasmuch as he sees that the object-ball is rolling on the object-floor. But he does not really *see* the rolling. He *thinks* the rolling ball on the surface. When he says "the ball rolls," he actually confirms only (a) his knowledge that the round object over there is called a ball and (b) his knowledge that round objects roll on a smooth surface when given a push. His eyes operate with the end of proving his knowledge, and thus making him secure in the world. (Italics original.)[22]

Children see things with fresh, clear eyes, and Jesus taught that we need to become like little children to enter the kingdom of heaven. To become like a child is a metaphor, of course, and one is certainly not to become childish in the sense of self-centered or unable to take any perspective beyond the immediate situation. Where a child's knowing is unconscious, our knowing must be conscious. Our knowing must be done with depth and awareness or risk being superficial and ineffective. To see mindfully is to see with fresh eyes, to know that you see that way, and yet not by that act of knowing to interfere.

Imagining Nothing

Close your eyes and imagine nothing. Go on, do it. Spend at least couple of minutes imagining *nothing* as vividly as you can. Do not read any further until you do.

Okay. What was that like? Chances are, that in trying to imagine nothing, you imagined something like black, empty space. But space is something. Blackness is something. Close your eyes and try again before moving on.

Most likely you were not literally able to imagine nothing (this is essentially impossible). That's okay. But after having made the effort, look about you now. Has the way you experience the *something-ness* of the world been altered, even slightly? Can you appreciate the miraculous fact that there is something? There did not need to be *something*. But there is. How wonderful!

Keep bringing yourself back to this awareness throughout the day.

THE KINGDOM OF GOD / THE PURE LAND

In some sects of Buddhist teaching, there is a place called the Pure Land where the Buddha Amitabha dwells, the Buddha of Light. This is a perfect place, a place of peace, happiness, and joy, a place where once one has been reborn there one can rapidly attain complete enlightenment. In some ways, it resembles the Kingdom of God in Christianity.

But the idea of going to the Pure Land after we die is a

superficial view. The Pure Land is here and now, or it is nowhere and nowhen. Whether you are living in the Kingdom of God or the realm of suffering depends upon your way of perceiving. When we stop seeing things from the perspective of ego, from the perspective of "I like this" and "I don't like that," we develop Pure Land eyes. We see that we are surrounded by wonders, and that we ourselves are a wonder—that to be here, alive, seeing and hearing, walking and touching, is already a miracle.

To live mindfully is to live already in the Pure Land. To live mindfully is to inhabit the Kingdom of God. We do not have to wait for the future. In fact, it is only available in the present moment.

MINDFULNESS AND PSYCHOTHERAPY

Seen from the perspectives offered above, mindfulness is clearly not *detached*. It is not the removed, distanced, objective awareness of the scientist. It is a warm, human awareness, a caring and understanding kind of awareness.

In the Sutra on the Four Establishments of Mindfulness (*Satipatthana*), the Buddha describes mindfulness as mindfulness of the feelings *in* the feelings, and mindfulness of the body *in* the body.[23] Practicing in this way is an antidote to the mistaken effort to disown your emotions and other aspects of your experience. More accurately, mindfulness is entering fully into each experience, knowing that this experience is precisely what it is and neither more nor less, knowing that it is impermanent, and knowing that you are more and larger than the experience.

To clarify this further, one could say that there is a delicate balance to be found in perception, especially, in mindful therapy, regarding feelings or emotions. The balance is between total identification with the feeling, which threatens to drown and overwhelm the individual, on the one hand, and disowning or repressing on the other. Sometimes I describe this metaphorically as touching the feeling, holding it, and moving right up to it without getting lost in it.

This is also important when it comes to the kind of presence we produce in the therapy room. Psychotherapy patients want to be listened to and understood. They don't want a therapist who is too detached, but someone who sees them as human beings, who attempts to understand what they feel from the inside. They do not want their therapist to be so caught up in analyzing and diagnosing that she forgets they are struggling and in pain. At the same time, they also don't want a therapist who becomes overwhelmed by their patients' emotions. That also is not helpful.

Intriguingly, patients sometimes treat *themselves* as entities to be diagnosed rather than human beings. You can hear them sometimes slip into a detached, clinical sort of language about themselves. Perhaps they are trying to be "objective." Perhaps they are trying to show you that they are intelligent or sophisticated. But perhaps also, they are trying to identify with you or tell you, in effect, "Look, I'm not just a patient. I am an intelligent person. I am like you." When a patient does this, sometimes I will make a process comment about it. I may say something like: "You are talking about yourself as though you weren't in the picture. How does that feel to do that? What purpose do you think that might serve?"

My patients may acknowledge this point, or they may respond more defensively, but in either case they usually stop doing this. And of course, this must be done in a very gentle way, as an invitation to greater acceptance rather than a cause for embarrassment or shame.

If you have been fortunate enough to have been in therapy or counseling yourself, whether as a training experience or, even better, out of your own personal pain, then you will know how your patients want to be listened to. They want to know that you see them as a human being, that you care about them, and do not see them as just a diagnostic entity or another clinical hour filled. If you have had this experience, remember it every day you work as a therapist yourself. You will know how very much your patients want to be valued and prized.

Being the Other

Before the start of your work day, review the patients you will see that day. Imagine life from their perspective, what it feels like to be them. Imagine what it is like for them to be in therapy with you, and what they want from you. Spend a little time meditating on each patient this way, entering deeply into his or her experience, breathing and maintaining your mindfulness throughout.

DO YOU REALLY CARE ABOUT ME?

The issue of feeling valued can come up in the form of discussions about a therapist's fee. Of course money is a practical reality in psychotherapy, and some people find it difficult to pay for therapy even if they have insurance that covers a good portion of it. I had a client who brought up money in nearly every session. He was a wealthy person, always involved in quarrels and lawsuits, and often conveying the impression that his attorneys seemed to just be out to take his money rather than wanting to be of help. I sensed that he was talking just as much about me and our relationship as he was about the attorneys. Of course, I am sure his attorneys in fact do want to earn money, as every working person does. But it was difficult for this person to imagine that anyone could earn money from working with him and care about him at the same time. Part of this was his own preoccupation with money, a projection of his own shadow onto the attorneys and no doubt also to some extent onto me. But I could also hear the unspoken question behind this obsession: "Do you really care about me?"

If we are calm and aware, if we cultivate understanding, caring will flow naturally from us to the people we work with, even with the patients we may find difficult to work with. We will be able to remember that to understand is already a great gift, maybe in fact the only gift of any importance in therapy. Being less anxious, or at least dealing mindfully with our anxiety and our need to be helpful, we can offer our true presence. We will not rush headlong into some technique or interpretation, but will wait for the right time to offer these if we even offer them at all.

In their fine book, *Mindfulness-Based Cognitive Therapy for Depression,* Zindel Segal, Mark Williams, and John Teasdale report that they initially thought they could teach mindfulness to clients without practicing it themselves. But as they consulted with mindfulness trainers and observed how they taught, they realized that their calm, mindful manner was as much a part of the teaching as the content. They realized that to teach mindfulness effectively, they had to *embody* it.

It is challenging not to be swept away by the difficult emotional situations that arise in therapy. And every course of therapy will present us with some of these. If you are not blessed with an extremely resilient personality, you will experience difficult moments even in the best therapeutic interactions, as we do in any human relationship. Some of what passes for such "resilience," though, is in reality a kind of distancing and objectifying. But if you practice mindfulness as a way of life, and not just a therapeutic technique, you will not be swept away so much. Of course difficult situations will arise. But just as you are teaching your patients how to relate differently to their emotions and other experiences, so you will change how you relate to these difficulties. You will expand your capacity to be present even with what is uncomfortable. You will also know that this is not always an easy thing to do.

THE CORNERSTONE OF THERAPY

In a marvelous but seldom discussed teaching, Jesus quotes the Psalms, saying that the stone the builders rejected has become the head of the corner—the cornerstone (Mark 12:10). In a Christian context, this is usually taken as signifying the rejection of Jesus as the Messiah. Yet there is a truth in this teaching that is both more general and more profound. Psychologically, human beings tend to ignore the very things that are of greatest importance. When we run after money, fame, or success, we fail to attend deeply to things like friendship and love, let alone the quest for meaning and spiritual attainment. In psychotherapy, clients want to run away from their painful or difficult feelings. And indeed, some types of psychotherapy seem designed to help them do this, and seem to try to "fix" these feelings before they are even experienced. Yet these very things contain within them the seeds of new growth and possibility.

In mindful therapy, the therapist knows that what is pushed away is often what is most important. It is important to help the patient stay close to the depressed mood, the anxiety, the suicidal feelings, the relationship conflict, the apparently irresolvable life issue, yet to help patients be able to experience these things with greater clarity and calm, shining the light of mindfulness on them.

Some people complain that the teaching of Thich Nhat Hanh is simplistic, arguing that surely there must be more to do than just breathe and smile. People long for something more mysterious and metaphysical. Yet this simple practice of mindfulness, of staying in the present moment, being clear and aware, has the power to help us find our way through all difficulties.

Therapists of many schools have their ways and wisdom. And many know that the symptom has to be respected and understood rather than avoided. Yet a therapist who practices mindfulness may have an enhanced ability to stay fully present with difficulties, and to avoid running from them. It is so easy otherwise to end up colluding with our patients' desire to ignore painful realities!

Mindfulness means acknowledging the truth. It means starting right where we are. And if we are in pain, that means acknowledging we are in pain. Only when we know that we are in pain can we look into the pain and discover the way out. Conversely, when we are happy and mindful, we know that we are happy, and our happiness is thereby multiplied.

THE BALANCE POINT

There is a balance to be struck regarding painful thoughts and feelings. Some patients get stuck in their negative thoughts and feelings. They need us not only to model a capacity to explore these thoughts and feelings without being afraid of them, but also to help put these feelings into perspective, into a larger frame of reference and meaning, so that they do not get stuck there. Other patients push difficult feelings away from them too soon, and need our help to stay with them. Mindfulness is right at the middle of this, right at the balance point. I tell patients that thoughts and feelings are like clouds: they come and go, and we have no control over either their coming or their going. But we are not the clouds. We are the sky. Mindfulness is the art of allowing these mental phenomena to pass through unimpeded and without resistance, neither clinging nor rejecting. This is sometimes called "choiceless awareness."

TEACHING MINDFULNESS TO PATIENTS

I have given a lot of hints about how you, as a therapist, can cultivate greater mindfulness in your life. Only please remember that this is not some heroic task that you are taking on. Living mindfully is simply a way to live with greater peace and joy, a way to be in your life fully and completely rather than miss it.

Many of the exercises so far in this book are also things you may be able to teach your patients. But again, do not rush to give patients exercises to do. Remember above all in therapy sessions to be truly present, open and aware, noticing what is before you. If you are anxious to try to figure out what exercises to prescribe, you may be shutting down on your experience rather than being truly present.

The goal in mindful therapy is to help the patient relate to his emotional life, and all of his experience, in a different way. It is not an attempt, for example, to try to *eliminate* sadness, worry, or anxiety, but to help the patient see these in a different light when they do arise. Thoughts and feelings are not in our control, but come and go on their own. To imagine that thoughts and feelings are controllable only sets us up for failure, removing us even further from the reality of already being a buddha.

Consider this famous thought experiment: You can ask a patient to close her eyes. Then tell her that you are going to give her a very important instruction, that it is essential she follow it very strictly. The instruction is: *No matter what you do, don't think about pink elephants.* Of course, most patients will find themselves thinking about pink elephants immediately, and many will chuckle a little at this absurd instruction. A few will report success, at which point the therapist asks, "How did you know that you were successful?" The patient will have to report knowing this in the only way it is possible to know this: with reference to the very thing they are trying not to think about! In this way, being successful then means they actually were not successful.

Having made this point, the task is to help the patient come to experience that *peace is found, not through repressing experience, but through acceptance of whatever comes up.* This is the only sort of peace that is really possible. It contrasts dramatically with what we may normally do, which is to try to control our inner experience. Yet controlling our inner experience is not only impossible but also self-defeating. Inevitably, being afraid of a certain experience or being unwilling to have it entails getting more of it. If you are afraid of fear, you then have, as it were, fear *squared.* If you allow yourself to experience fear, fear will come and go as a normal part of life. You don't have to be troubled by it. To paraphrase FDR, you don't have to fear fear. It may be unpleasant, uncomfortable, or inconvenient. But when you see the fear as just fear and not a disaster, usually, the fear will subside. But this is a little bit subtle. If you attempt to control fear by *pretending* to be willing to have fear so that you can make it go away, you are back in the old model of attempting to control thoughts and feelings. A lot of the work of mindful therapy is helping patients (and ourselves, for that matter) to know the difference between these.

The therapist can learn a lot by noting how a patient assimilates the practice of mindfulness into their preexisting view of herself and life. The depressive, self-critical patient will tend to assume that mindfulness is a matter of self-critical attention. The self-aggrandizing patient will find more reasons to congratulate himself. Patients who tend to wallow in negative feelings will confuse this with being mindful, while those who ignore negative feelings will justify this in terms of mindfulness of the positive elements of experience. Helping patients become aware of these tendencies is a crucial aspect of the therapist's role, and one that patients have difficulty doing for themselves.

One day, Eric complained to me that he had been meditating for several weeks now, and it "wasn't working." I asked him to explain to me what he meant by this, and he told me that he was still just as sad about his divorce as he had been when he first came in. I pointed out to him that he was acting as though he wanted to control his sadness, but that mindfulness was not about that. Mindfulness was about letting the sadness flow naturally, being willing to have the experience, letting it come when it comes and go when it is ready to go. Then I asked him to breathe in and out mindfully, and describe the battle that was going on in him—the battle in which he was both experiencing sadness and fighting against his sadness. When he finished describing this, I told him that was all very good noticing, and was already mindful.

Eric got the point. By being willing to be with his sadness, he was able to let it come and go. At the end of the session, he even confessed that his initial complaint was not true: he had had a couple of bad days, but overall there was much less sadness. But he saw a little more clearly that mindfulness was not a bargain to try to reinstate an impossible sort of control, but rather, true acceptance.

GOOD DIGESTION

Another way to describe mindfulness is to compare mental life to the process of digestion. Part of what the brain does is digest experience. Occasionally, however, something goes awry with this process. It might be that a particular kind of experience is overwhelming, as seen in post-traumatic stress disorder (PTSD). A person with such an overwhelming experience relives it in dreams and flashbacks because he has not been able to digest it.

A much more common problem is that we get "emotional indigestion" because, when we try to control our experience in some way, we interfere with the natural metabolic process. Since we live in a culture that places a high premium on being happy and optimistic, we attempt to suppress other sorts of feelings, those we refer to as "negative." When we try to do that, it may seem to work for a short time, just as some people may think they are successful in not thinking about pink elephants. But this kind of success requires a lot of energy. It creates a background of tension and anxiety in all that we do. And sometimes, when the suppressed feelings emerge, they emerge with a vengeance.

Mindfulness is a way to overcome emotional indigestion. By allowing our awareness to flow freely and openly with our experience, we gradually digest these difficult experiences and feelings. Then they are assimilated, absorbed, integrated into the rest of life. They take their natural place in the ecology of the psyche. The soldier with PTSD, for example, experiences his memories as happening in the present. What he needs, however, is to find a way to *remember* his war experiences without reliving them, that is, to know that these are just memories. If he can learn to stop the struggle against having this experience, if he can talk about it and bring accepting awareness to the experience again and again, it will gradually lose its power. But once again, he must be willing to have the experience he is actually having, not making a bargain to pretend to be willing in order to eliminate the experience, for that is already unwillingness.

I will say more about metaphors and their use in mindful therapy in chapter nine, but these are offered here as a way to reflect on mindfulness. The basic requirement is to find a way to make it safe to have the experience of the difficult emotions or experiences without being overwhelmed by them. The presence of a mindful therapist provides one element of safety. Another very important element of safety is mindful breathing.

TEACHING MINDFUL BREATHING

The simplest way to begin to teach mindfulness to patients is to teach them mindful breathing in session. By practicing in session, we increase the probability of practice outside of the session. Starting usually with the second meeting, I begin every session with a few moments of this practice. I usually start this at the second session because, very often, people come in anxious to tell their story and ready to talk, and I don't want to impede this important outflowing in any way.

I frame mindful breathing in different ways with different people. I generally will have some clue about how to approach this from my intake form, where I have asked them simply to describe their religion or spirituality and its importance in their life. Sometimes people have sought me out because they know of my interest in mindfulness and Buddhism through my books and talks. With such people, it is very easy to put mindful breathing in the context of Buddhist spirituality. However, with others, I know they may have a different spirituality, or spirituality may be unimportant or even something they reject. Here I tread carefully. I may just couch this as an exercise that helps us calm down and be prepared to do the work of therapy that I have found helpful. This is not an attempt to deceive the patient, since such practices can be framed in different ways that are legitimate.

While the manner in which I introduce mindful breathing will vary given the belief context of the patient, a generic form of introduction may be something like this:

If it is okay, I would like to begin today's session by teaching you something that will help in many ways. It is an exercise known as mindful breathing. Please close your eyes, and sit in the chair comfortably. Sit upright, but not in a rigid or uncomfortable way. It also helps to ground yourself by having both feet flat on the floor.

Begin by just becoming aware of your surroundings, for example, what you hear around you . . . Now notice the feelings in your body . . . For example, the feel of clothing against your skin. The pressure of your body against the chair. Notice how the chair is doing the work of holding you up, how it supports you. Allow it to do the work for you, and let your muscles relax. Just let go, and let them loosen and lengthen, letting go of any tension.

Now notice your body breathing. Allow your awareness to drop down into the abdomen, and from there, become aware of your body breathing in and out, expanding and contracting, breathing naturally without your having to make it go any special way, but just noticing it. Follow each breath all the way in, and all the way out, noting all the sensations of breathing. Perhaps you can see that, when you stop and pay attention, breathing in and out is a pleasure. So just spend a few moments here with me breathing like this, allowing your attention to rest on the breath, not having to figure anything out or solve anything right now, not straining or struggling—not even trying to do this perfectly. And whenever your mind wanders, just notice this, knowing it is completely natural, and bring your attention back to the breath when you are ready.

So let's breathe in and out like this together for a little while.

The amount of time I spend breathing in this way is usually short—perhaps 10 or 20 breaths at most, and with some individuals even less. After the first time, the instructions can be gradually shortened and simplified, until eventually you say something like:

Let's just enjoy a few mindful breaths together . . .

Occasionally, I will return to a fuller instruction to keep the practice sharp and clear. Very few patients complain or refuse to do this practice, though I always honor their request if they do. The vast majority come to look forward to doing our mindful breathing together. Even some who are initially reluctant may feel more comfortable later in therapy when greater trust is established.

Of course, there are always some individuals for whom mindful breathing is not appropriate. The mindful therapist never tries to impose any particular approach on a patient; for the emphasis is always on understanding and presence, and from such awareness, it will generally be obvious which patients need to pass on this exercise. Overall, I am impressed that if this practice introduced gently, in an inviting manner rather than demanding, the vast majority of people will accept it. Very rarely, I encounter someone with so much anxiety that focusing on the breath is not helpful. In such cases, calming imagery or sound can be employed as an alternative, or the attempt can be abandoned. Always in mindful therapy, the relationship is more important than any technique or particular approach. From this base, therapist and patient explore together what will be most helpful.

A special case of individuals who may be resistant are fundamentalist Christians. Such individuals may have fears that this practice is somehow un-Christian. For them, it is helpful to frame the exercise as mindful breathing. If they know something about Christian history, I may remind them that there is a rich Christian tradition of meditation. With such individuals, as well as with those who are anti-religious, I may admit that there is a connection with spiritual traditions, but suggest that they can also legitimately think of it as a form of relaxation and stress reduction. Sometimes with Christians I talk a little about the importance of breath in the Christian tradition, saying that it connects with the Hebrew word *ruach* in the Old Testament and the Greek word *pneuma* in the New

Testament, words meaning both breath and spirit, indicating that there is a connection between breathing and the presence of the Spirit. I invite them to silently evoke God's presence in the therapy room as they breath, if they are so inclined, though, as I psychologist, I will not engage in verbal prayer with them.

OTHER USES OF THE BREATH

Practicing mindful breathing is, in my view, far from just an opening exercise. It may in fact be the most important thing we do in a session. To breathe this way, especially with the emotional support of another person, can be very healing in its own right.

Beyond using breath awareness at the beginning of sessions, I also encourage patients to practice on their own outside of sessions. The instruction for this is simple. I invite them to try to spend a few moments each day doing some mindful breathing, perhaps five or ten minutes to begin with, or even just three or four mindful breaths, gradually extending it as they feel comfortable doing so. Above all, I ask them to approach it as something enjoyable, rather than something that is "good for them" but which they have to force themselves to do. While certain forms of meditative experience only appear after twenty or thirty minutes, I would rather people gradually learn to enjoy and value the process than be overwhelmed by the time demands it places on them. If the time demand feels difficult, they will just see meditation as another chore they have to do.

In the New Testament, Jesus compares the Kingdom of Heaven to some very small things, like a lump of leavening or a grain of mustard, that have sizable effects, spreading through the whole batch of dough or growing to become a sizable bush. This is a hopeful image. Even a small of amount of practice can be helpful, just as those first steps toward assertiveness or toward challenging negative cognitions can ultimately result in a life-changing way of being in the world. To stop doing and rushing and struggling, to just sit and breathe for a while, is a revolutionary act.

I also point out that there are many opportunities to practice mindful breathing that occur naturally in daily life. For example, when you are waiting in one of those long, automated phone queues, why not stop and breathe mindfully? When you come to a red light, when you are standing in line at the store, these are also good opportunities to enjoy mindful breathing. Anything that slows us down during the day—a traffic jam, a big slow RV in the fast lane—becomes an opportunity to do something different. Such exercises, seen from the point of view of mere stress reduction, may be rather trivial, providing perhaps a slight and momentary reduction in heart rate or blood pressure. But their importance is more than that, for by working in this way, patients are learning to connect the attitude of mindfulness—practiced in formal meditation—with their daily life. They are learning to have a different relationship to otherwise annoying experiences, putting them in a different context.

The breath is important in the process of learning to relate to emotions differently. When patients are working on difficult areas of their emotional experience, it is helpful to encourage them to pay attention to their breathing. When they start to breath shallowly or catch the breath in a session, I call their attention to it as soon as I can do so without interrupting their processing, and invite them to breath mindfully, while allowing this difficult material to continue to come up fully and completely, using the breath as a kind of anchor, as something to hold on to so they can experience the difficult emotions without being swept away by them or overwhelmed. If they have also been practicing outside of therapy, this will be very powerful, but it still helps with those who do not.

In this chapter, then, you have been introduced to a wider understanding of what mindfulness is and how to bring mindfulness into your practice of psychotherapy. You have also learned how to begin to teach this to clients in sessions. In the following chapters, I will introduce you to a number of basic Buddhist ideas and how they can provide you with insight into your own life and your work as a mindful therapist.

CHAPTER FOUR

The Stone the Builders Rejected: Suffering and the Way Out

Here, monks, is the noble truth of suffering. Birth is suffering. Old
age is suffering. Sickness is suffering. Death is suffering. Sorrow,
grief, mental anguish, and disturbance are suffering. To be with
those you dislike is suffering. To be separated from those you love is
suffering. Not having what you long for is suffering. In other words,
to grasp the five aggregates . . . is suffering.[24]
—BUDDHA

THE FOUR NOBLE TRUTHS of the Buddha can be summarized quite simply:

1. Suffering is.
2. Suffering has a cause.
3. Suffering can be stopped.
4. There is a way to live that prevents suffering. (The eightfold
   path.)

If you understand the four noble truths deeply, you have the
essence of Buddhism. Not only that, but you then understand

everything you need to know about how to find ultimate peace, how to put an end to all suffering and enter nirvana. The first of the four noble truths, and the cornerstone of the Buddha's teaching, is the truth of *dukkha*—suffering or sorrow. A revealing translation of dukkha is *unsatisfactoriness*. I like this translation because it includes not only great loss and difficulty, but also the minor inconveniences, the hassles of life. We all know that to have someone we love die is dukkha. We know it is dukkha when we find out we have a terrible disease, or even suffer a career setback. But it is also dukkha when we're late for an appointment and can't find a parking place. It is dukkha when we order merchandise on the internet and it arrives broken or defective. It is dukkha when you have three cancellations on the same day. These "trivial" things are also worthy of healing attention.

Sometimes the first noble truth is misleadingly summarized as "everything is suffering." While that is an interpretation that some have made, it is not the only way to understand the Dharma. Thich Nhat Hanh, for example, argues that suffering should not be put on the same level as impermanence and nonself, since impermanence and nonself are "universals," something that applies to all phenomena, whereas suffering is not. A table, he argues, will only cause us to suffer if we attribute permanence or separateness to it.[25] While suffering is an important aspect of our experience, it is also important to recognize that there are many wonderful things in life, and to enjoy them fully. Otherwise, we will not have the strength to deal with dukkha when it arrives. In fact, one way to take the truth of suffering to heart is to dedicate yourself to the full appreciation of the many wonders of life that constantly surround us, but which we fail to notice because they do not stand out as important against the background of our ego- and survival-centered way of seeing. A beautiful flower neither threatens us nor helps us meet our goals for success. Therefore we may rush past it without noticing it.

Yet seeing the flower is one of the best things in life. "Behold the lilies of the field!" Only to see it—to really see it—we have to step outside the narrow attentional confines of our utilitarian framework.

The heart of the difficulty lies not in the nature of things, but in the nature of our perception. When we perceive in a grasping way, then everything becomes a cause of suffering or a potential cause of suffering. Even when good things come our way, seeds of suffering can be sown in us through fear of losing what we have gained. If someone is promoted, he may be happy. But at the same time, already a seed of suffering enters in. He knows that everything comes to an end some day. And what if he is unable to fulfill his new responsibilities? What if he fails? Furthermore, as anyone who has achieved some measure of success knows full well, when you get to the place you thought you wanted to be, it is never quite what you imagined, even if it is very good. And sometimes, of course, it is even a disaster. Alternatively, you may find the love of your life, the one that you had been hoping for. Yet this too contains a seed of suffering. For someday, you will have to let go of this person, whether through his death or your own, whether through divorce or separation, or even just the simple process of change and impermanence.

This may seem a jaundiced view of the world, but that would be an incorrect understanding. Negativity and despair are not the point of the Buddha's first truth. Correctly and thoroughly understood, the truth of suffering is a liberating insight. The true effect of understanding this teaching is joy.

Many Buddhist monks and nuns remind themselves in their daily practice that they will die—part of a practice called the five remembrances. Reciting the five remembrances is a powerful practice.

The Five Remembrances

1. I am of the nature to grow old. There is no way to escape old age.
2. I am of the nature to suffer ill-health. There is no way to escape ill-health.
3. I am of the nature to die. There is no way to escape death.
4. All that is dear to me and everyone I love are of the nature to change. There is no way to escape being separated from them.
5. My actions (karma) are my only true belongings. I cannot escape the consequences of my actions.[26]

To bring these truths home and look into them deeply, you can practice by distilling each remembrance into two brief phrases, then saying them aloud or silently, breathing with them, using the first of each pair (below) to breathe in, the second to breathe out, staying with each point until you begin to feel it deeply or simply as long as you wish.

Old age/no escape
Ill-health/no escape
Death/no escape
Loss/no escape
Actions/true belongings

The effect of this practice is not gloom and doom, as one might fear, but that one lets go of the neurotic clinging, striving, and worrying to which one is otherwise so deeply attached. Suddenly one can see that the world is a beautiful place, filled with flowers and smiling children and many pleasant things. When we cling to life and ignore death, all we can see are the things which either seem to further our goals and purposes—which we believe so very desperately will makes us happy—or which threaten their realization. Flowers and smiling children are hardly noticed.

TAIL-CHASING

Imagine a dog chasing his own tail, reaching a point of severe exhaustion, but still pressing round in tight little circles. The more frustrated he gets, the faster he tries to run, and the faster he tries to run, the more frustrated he gets. But he becomes so used to the running that it no longer occurs to him to stop. This is dukkha.

Now any self-respecting animal, any real dog, would actually not act in such a fashion for very long. At some point, the game stops being fun, instinct intervenes, and the animal will stop the chase abruptly, and, resting with great dignity and self-possession, will suddenly appear as though he had nothing whatsoever to do with something as silly as tail-chasing. If we could imitate it—if we could play our silly tail-chasing games with great sport and fun, and then drop it when it was time to drop it, this would all be well and good. But because of our cognitive capacity, we do not always heed our instinctive wisdom. We do not always have the sense to stop. We keep seeking the unobtainable satisfaction. And even when external considerations force us to stop the chase, we may nonetheless be continuing it internally all the while.

DESPAIR AND NIRVANA

Suffering is a noble truth, or in some languages, a "holy" truth. The concept of suffering and holiness is not completely unfamiliar to us in the West: witness the crucifixion of Christ. We may have become numbed to the point of this image, either through familiarity, or through negative experiences of Christianity, yet the suffering of the crucifixion is at the heart of meaning, redemption, and transformation. There is no resurrection to new life without crucifixion—a point reflected in myths far older than the gospel.

In a certain sense, patients in the throes of darkest despair and depression are also closest to nirvana. They see the vanity of striving and struggling accurately. Unfortunately, we as therapists, members ourselves of a society that denies pain and suffering, may try to convince them otherwise, to show them that human endeavors are important and worthwhile, without acknowledging that there is value in their point of view—because, quite frankly, it may scare the devil out of us to be around such despair. But I often have the sense around such people that if their despair could be tweaked *just a little bit,* if they could actually reach the point of deep acceptance of what they are experiencing, they might be able to enjoy the flowers and the children again, experiencing these phenomena as infinitely precious in their very transience. For depression is actually a halfway state, full of despair, but not going all the way through to acceptance. Depressed people correctly sense the unfulfillment inherent in the tail-chasing game, and if, instead of despairing, they could come to see it exactly for what it is, they could laugh—and be in serious danger of becoming a buddha on the spot! But they have been taught, as we have all been taught, that life is no laughing matter, that life is a very serious business. The truth is quite the opposite: Life is *precisely* a laughing matter—and not some hollow, bitter, laughter, but heartfelt belly laughter. The only difficulty is, of course, that life sometimes *hurts.* But if we can see this hurting, this dukkha, all the way through, we could be liberated, laughing buddhas.

Of course, this laughter is not to be confused with callousness or lack of caring. But I will often tell patients who report suicidal feelings that their suicidal feelings are in fact very important material, and we need to respect these feelings and perceptions, looking into them deeply and patiently. The risk, I add, is that of taking it too literally. Suicidal feelings teach that something about one's way of life is not adequate and needs, in some sense, to die. And what could be more important than that? Yet we often find this process of letting go a very painful business—as dying is. What we as therapists know, and must present with some confidence, is that on the other side of this crucifixion is resurrection. On the other side of this death lies new life. On the other side of dukkha is nirvana.

When we consider that our patients who are in a process of deep transformation are going through a kind of death, it becomes easy to empathize with their fear, to understand why they do not just go ahead and change in the ways it may seem obvious to us they need to change. We know well enough from the crucifixions in our own lives that we are no less anxious than they to avoid suffering. Every time we sit down to breathe mindfully, we can easily see the same process at work in ourselves.

In alchemy, understood as a process of inner transformation, the prime material is placed inside a vessel and covered with a lid. Heat is then applied, and the appalling blackness, ooze, and smoke that emerge—as unappealing as they are—are the very process by which the gold of wisdom is forged. An important aspect here is the lid on the vessel. The lid signifies that there is no escape from this torment. Indeed, if there were, we would all run away from it—and rightly so. But life presents us with puzzles that seem to have no solution—which is the nature of a true life dilemma. We can neither seem to solve the dilemma, nor avoid it. Our job is not to help our clients run away from their life-changing, painful dilemmas, but to help them learn to be in them. Our job is to be the lid.

One sermon the Buddha gave involved the idea that everything is on fire. That is, when we take things in a grasping way, without realizing and accepting that everything is impermanent, trying desperately to hold on to the good and avoid the bad, then everything we see, touch, hear, taste, smell, or think *burns*. We are, in fact, in a kind of hell. However, when we change the nature of our perception, when we recognize the impermanent nature of all things and stop struggling against this bare and basic fact, then it becomes possible to appreciate everything.

When you stop the struggle, your experience becomes like listening to a symphony. Imagine a woman listening to a symphony, but liking only the treble sounds, and hating the bass. When the piccolos and violins are playing, she is ecstatic. When the cellos start up, she gets a little nervous, especially in the lower registers. And when the bassoons and basses are prominent, she is a very unhappy person indeed. If she could, perhaps she would like to rid the orchestra of all the deeper tonalities. The only problem, then, of course, is that the symphony would no longer be a symphony. It would lack the depth, color, and richness that the deeper sounds provide. You would also quickly see that part of what allows you to enjoy the higher notes is the contrast with the lower ones.

As a therapist, you have a front row seat in the symphony of human life. You are in an excellent position to understand why the Buddha made suffering the cornerstone of his teaching. Suffering is of course what brings our patients to us in the first place. We are excellently positioned to see the drama of human suffering, to see how our patients attempt to deal with suffering by not dealing with it, by avoiding it. And yet of course that avoidance cannot work, at least not in the long run, and our job becomes to help the patient learn to stay present to the suffering, the very thing he most wants to escape. Every successful therapy involves someone who has learned to be with their suffering and to approach it in a different way, seeing it in a more satisfactory frame of meaning. And in the most successful cases, learning to deal with one type of pain generalizes into a broader and deeper transformation. It is by being willing to be with that suffering—perhaps only because it became too intense at some point to avoid any longer—that the deepest transformations take place.

Suffering is the door. But it can only open if it is first recognized. Otherwise, we just bang our heads on it.

DON'T RESIST

When the Buddha teaches that there is a way out of suffering, clearly he does not mean that there is a way to escape pain. Pain per se cannot be avoided. But pain does not have to become suffering. Buddhist teacher Shinzen Young clarifies the relationship between pain and suffering with the following equation:[27]

$$SUFFERING = PAIN \times RESISTANCE$$

Pain comes and goes in life. But that is not yet suffering. Suffering is the product of the pain and our resistance to it. If RESISTANCE equals zero then SUFFERING also equals zero. The more we tighten up against pain, the more we suffer. The more we ease up and open out to the pain, softening to it, allowing and experiencing it, the less we suffer.

To bring mindfulness to our pain means to stop resisting, to stop struggling, to accept it, and through accepting it, to stop the suffering. I recall one occasion when, as a child, I pursued a baseball popfly and stumbled on a rise in our backyard, tumbling head over heels. I was not injured. I was not injured not only because I was young and flexible, but also because, as I child, I did not know I should have been afraid of getting hurt. I was not afraid, and did not tighten up. When we tighten up, we get hurt. We suffer.

The ancient Taoist sage Chuang Tze makes the same point in this wonderful, humorous passage:

A drunken man who falls out of a cart, though he may suffer, does not die. His bones are the same as other people's; but he meets the accident in a different way. His spirit is in a condition of security. He is not conscious of riding in the cart; neither is he conscious of falling out of it. Ideas of life, death, and fear cannot penetrate his breast; and so he does not suffer from contact with objective existences. And if such security is to be got from wine, how much more is it to be got from Spontaneity.[28]

Like physical pain, our emotional pain is just emotional pain. It is an experience we may prefer not to have, but it does not, in itself, need to be problematic. If there is a sad feeling in us, it is just a sad feeling. But when we tighten up, we create real misery and suffering. We say in effect, not only "I notice a sad feeling rising up in me," but also, "That's terrible! This must not be! This means my life is completely awful." And we may even go so far as to add, "This will always be this way." Worse still, if we have been under the care of a mental health professional, we can add in to the mix a view of ourselves as a *depressed person.* Then I have a disease called depression instead of just being a person experiencing a sad feeling or mood.

Both Buddhism and psychology agree that suffering is a matter of perception rather than something objective about reality. What the reality is, we don't really know, because we don't deal with *just this*—just what is happening—but are busy drawing out the implications. Yet the implications for events are seldom knowable. Another classic Taoist story illustrates this problem wonderfully:

A farmer's horse runs away. All the neighbors agree this is a piece of bad luck. "Maybe," says the farmer. But then the horse returns with six wild horses. What a stroke of good fortune, the neighbors say. But again the farmer says, "Maybe." Then his son breaks his leg trying to tame the horses. How terrible, say the neighbors. "Maybe," says the farmer. Then the army comes into the village looking for conscripts, and because the son's leg is broken, they leave him alone. "What good luck," say the neighbors. And, by now, you know what the farmer said: "Maybe."[29]

A FOUR-STEP PROGRAM TO END SUFFERING

We can usefully frame the four noble truths as a kind of "four-step program." These steps are interrelated in such a way that to understand one is to already understand the others, and to understand the others deepens our understanding of any one. Using the four noble truths as a four-step program is what the Buddhist would call "expedient means"—simply a useful way of working, and not any kind of ultimate truth in itself. The risk of doing this is the same as the risk of meditation or any other method, that we might reify the approach and end up being used by it rather than using it for our healing and liberation. The end of suffering is a process rather than a discrete event, a process that, in the Buddhist tradition, may take many lifetimes to complete. But I have found working with the four noble truths this way very helpful.

Step 1: Recognize that this is suffering.

We have become so used to putting a spin on things, that for many of us, it is already a quantum leap to recognize when we are suffering. For many, suffering must be so extreme before it is recognized as suffering, that it is often very difficult to do something about it by that point. We are like the person who ignores the growing symptoms of disease, putting off going to the doctor until the remedy is a severe one or may be ineffective.

When was the last time you asked how someone was doing, and that person told you bluntly, "I am suffering"? For many of us in this culture, putting a positive spin on things is almost a reflex. It becomes second nature not to say that we were fired when we were fired, but to say that we decided to try our hand at something new. If someone calls early in the morning and wakes us from a sound sleep, and then asks, "Did I wake you?" even in our sleepy state we reflexively say no, as though to admit that we were human beings who require rest were a rather shameful business. When things in our life get really bad, we might go so far as to say we are "hanging in there." In a culture of optimism and success, we are very far from the frank admission of the first noble truth.

This can go so far that not only are we preserving some sort of inhuman public self or persona, but also that we ourselves no longer know the truth. Often it feels unsafe to acknowledge our suffering, even to ourselves, when actually it is far riskier not to. If we fail to acknowledge our suffering, how will we find the way out? And that is the essence of why suffering is so important: by paying attention to it, we can find the way out. Without acknowledging suffering, we may end up staying in jobs, careers, relationships, and other situations that are terribly destructive— destructive not only of our mental and emotional well-being but also ultimately of our physical well-being. Yet we would leave these situations in a heartbeat if only we allowed ourselves to see and know the truth.

Most suffering does not take the form of exterior events. In fact, the essence of suffering lies, as I have said, in our thinking and perceptions. We can see this directly in meditation. It may be a wonderful day, the sun is shining, and nothing troubling at all is occurring as we sit, but we nonetheless notice that much of the thinking that draws us away from our breath or other focus of meditation has a dukkha aspect. Perhaps we find ourselves planning the day ahead, but this planning has an anxious quality about it as you sort through the various matters that require attention, hoping things will go a certain way while at the same time fearing they will go some other way. This also is dukkha. The part of us that plans and prepares is a useful part, but when it gets out of hand, when it runs in an unmindful and unconscious way, it is quite unpleasant. Alternatively, you may find yourself thinking about something in the past with longing regret. Once again, remembering can be useful. But when we not mindful, when we become lost in our remembering, so that we confuse memory with reality, it can easily develop a painful quality. That also is dukkha. Furthermore, our thinking sometimes reflects an inner struggle, a painful ambivalence. We want something, but do not want it at the same time. This, too, is dukkha. It is only when we learn to step back from the ambivalence, bring calm awareness to it and let it be, that we find relief. By bringing mindfulness to it, we pour cooling water on the flame of our inner struggle.

Brian was a classical guitarist. Others envied his talent as well as his ability to earn a living by playing music. But Brian did not enjoy playing the guitar. There was too much bitterness and pain surrounding the instrument from too many long, enforced hours of practice. He was constantly in an inward fight between the part of him that said he should practice and the part of him that wanted to run from the instrument and do something, do anything but practice again. But since he made his living by playing guitar, this profound ambivalence was too threatening to face. The inner struggle continued in an unconscious way that perpetuated itself, and that even may have been manifesting in physical symptoms of joint pain that precluded practice.

The ambivalence was evident in a repetitive dream in which Brian lost his guitar. Brian said he had had that kind of dream for as many years as he could remember. Suspecting this to be a wish-fulfillment dream, expressing an aspect of him that would just as soon lose his guitar, but knowing that he had positive feelings about the instrument as well, I led him in an empty-chair exercise (see page 225), giving him ample opportunity to express both sides of his feelings about the guitar, including especially the negative aspects. This allowed Brian to bring deeper awareness to his inner conflict. The healing power of this increased awareness was soon apparent. The dreams stopped immediately, the pain in his joints was reduced, and Brian was, at least sometimes, able to play guitar with joy.

Of course, not all cases are as quick and clear as this one. Sometimes facing our pain, in this case the pain of ambivalence, will only resolve itself after repeated efforts to bring awareness to it, perhaps over months or even years depending on the nature of the suffering. Yet while ultimate resolution may elude us for some time, often there is at least some relief right away. Facing the truth of our suffering brings immediate relief. The moment we breathe and acknowledge our suffering as suffering, we already feel better. Mindfulness teaches us that things do not have to be fixed right now. We can appreciate the change that occurs the moment we come to the breath.

If we as therapists are to assist others in acknowledging their pain, it helps if we can do it ourselves. It helps if we are people who are aware of what hurts in our own lives, admitting it frankly to ourselves and to those close to us. If we cannot admit this in our own lives, then we are caught in an illusion. We may be trying to be somehow superior to our patients, keeping them and their suffering at arm's length. But the wounded healer knows her pain.

It may be only rarely appropriate for us to reveal this to our patients, not because we are trying to conceal our humanity, but because it may distract from the work at hand. The usual caveats apply to this kind of self-disclosure. It should be done, when appropriate, briefly, in a way that facilitates the patient's own processing without refocusing attention on ourselves. It should be done only if it will not reduce the patient's sense of safety in our capacity to be with them and available to them. And of course it should be largely avoided with some individuals who have a personality disorder, especially of the narcissistic variety, for both your own protection and theirs. Otherwise, when we tell the narcissistic client something that would normally create sympathy we will experience his arrogance instead and we may be burdened with disruptive countertransferential feelings.

In light of these caveats, statements to patients about our own suffering have a limited, infrequent—though not to say unimportant—place in therapy. It is the pinch of spice in the dish. In any case, though, the limitation on self-disclosure should not stem from a need to maintain a false view of ourselves. People who are ready for psychotherapy are aware of their suffering and willing to acknowledge it. In this way, the door to transformation is open. Some patients are in such pain that emergency palliatives must be applied before meaningful work can be done. But many others come into therapy and try to play the same part they have played their whole life long, trying to appear better than they are in order to be liked and respected by the therapist, or trying to appear overly helpless to solicit sympathy, just as they do in the rest of their lives. And indeed, if a patient is not open to his pain, and if we cannot help him be open to it, then therapy, however much it may be a pleasant and supportive experience, will lack the power of deep transformation.

Only when we know our suffering as suffering, and can admit it to ourselves and others, can we see the mark of nirvana upon dukkha. Only then can suffering become release, transformation, and healing. Acknowledging that what we are experiencing is a form of suffering should not be underestimated; it is often the largest and most difficult part of ending suffering.

Step 2: Recognize the cause of the suffering.

Step Two is intimately connected with Step One. Once you have recognized your suffering as suffering, you are already beginning to see the causes and conditions that create it. The main cause of suffering is always internal. It is our distorted perception of reality that hurts, not reality itself.

Consider this example: If we are driving on the interstate, and find that a feeling of irritation arises in us because of an aggressive driver, we could easily get caught in our blame and anger, emotions pointing out and away from ourselves. We could then fan these feelings into flame, and end up worse off than we were before we gave that driver our attention, before we acknowledged our suffering. But the reality is that as long as there are automobiles, there will be aggressive drivers. We should know when we go on the highway that we will likely encounter some of these, and be prepared to do this in a way that does not shatter our peace. If we cannot do this, perhaps we do not belong on the road that day.

Another kind of inner cause is our limited kindness and compassion. If we saw more deeply, we would understand that someone driving aggressively is trapped in dukkha. The aggressive driver is a teacher, showing us that we need to increase our kindness, compassion, and understanding. If I can increase these sufficiently, I will not suffer from the encounter with such drivers. If my compassion is large enough, it can easily encompass this kind of experience. Practicing compassion in this way allows us to express what Buddhists call *kshanti paramita*, the perfection of inclusiveness or forbearance. We can accept whatever comes up, as the mountains accept the rain or the sun, the heat or the cold without struggle.

In Buddhism, the senses play an important part in our suffering.* The senses are not neutral in Buddhist understanding, but have a kind of stickiness about them. We do not notice all things equally, but are drawn toward certain kinds of things. We are

---

*In Buddhist psychology, there are said to be six senses: seeing, hearing, smelling, tasting, the feeling body, and the thinking mind. The discussion of this chapter illustrates how the thinking sense causes suffering.

drawn to phenomena that stir our desire and longing, on the one hand, or our pain and fear on the other, whichever is more congruent with our mood and our preconceptions. In our culture we are easily drawn, for example, to beautiful human forms, particularly those that are the object of sexual longing. When we encounter such forms mindfully, this is perfectly safe. We can say to ourselves, "Ah, how lovely!"—and enjoy the beautiful form fully and completely. But if longing enters in, there may already be dukkha involved, the pain and sadness of wanting and not having.

In *The Human Adventure,* Catholic monk William McNamara recounts a visit from three Jehovah's Witnesses. One of the callers was a breathtakingly beautiful young woman, and McNamara fully enjoyed her beauty. "Gosh, you're beautiful!" he said. However, McNamara was not caught in longing and desire, and therefore did not experience suffering. He was free to contemplate this beautiful form. In a way, it is a kind of sacrilege *not* to experience and appreciate beauty. The Jehovah's Witnesses, prepared for many kinds of responses, were unprepared for this, and left.[30] A Zen story illustrates the same point. Two traveling monks came to a river, where they encountered a woman needing help to cross. One of the monks offered to carry her, she accepted, and he did. Several miles down the road, his companion confronted him. "How could you do that, when we monks are not even supposed to touch a woman?" The monk who had carried the woman responded, "I left the woman at the river. Are you still carrying her?"

The beautiful woman in the first story presented no difficulty to McNamara. In fact, he enjoyed her more fully than a man who would have seen her with longing. The monk who carried the woman across the river in the second story had no problem in doing so. He did not let the rules of monastic life interfere with being helpful. But for the Jehovah's Witnesses and the monk's companion, these incidents were problems, sources of confusion and difficulty.

It is not just longing and desire which generate suffering, however. Sometimes we suffer because our senses are drawn to things which annoy or irritate or otherwise cause us to suffer. Have you ever noticed that when you are in a very good mood, you are less disturbed by bad driving than otherwise? Why do you think that is? It is because we are drawn to things that are mood congruent, which therefore keep us stuck in a mood or even amplify it. This is the aspect of dukkha generated by the stickiness of our senses. Thus when we encounter, say, a rude and unhelpful person at the end of a long telephone queue, one aspect of our suffering is that our attention is held captive by that person. Why is that? Maybe it is because we have not taken good enough care of our own mind/body, so that we are drawn to things which are congruent with the state of mild irritation we are already in. Maybe we would do well to spend some time breathing and smiling mindfully, cultivating calmness, kindness, and compassion before making the next phone call.

I do not mean to say that there are no external reasons for our suffering, though, as we shall see, Buddhism teaches us to question the neat separation between internal and external. But in terms of this sometimes expedient division of reality, we can say that there really was a driver there who really was driving in an aggressive manner. However, even in this sense, there is no enemy, and no one to blame. Because if we look deeply, we know that such a person is caught in suffering. Rudeness is a symptom of dukkha. As such, it is a neutral fact, the result of causes and conditions as much as a storm, an earthquake, or the flow of electricity. Imagine getting all upset because of the way electrons flow in circuits!

Again we can turn to Chuang Tze for concise expression:

Suppose a boat is crossing a river and another boat, an empty one, is about to collide with it. Even an irritable man would not lose his temper. But suppose there was someone in the second boat. Then the occupant of the first would shout to him to keep clear. And if he did not hear the first time, nor even when he called to three times, bad language would inevitably follow. In the first case, there was no anger, in the second there was—because in the first case the boat was empty, in the second it was occupied. And so it is with man. If he could only pass empty through life, who would be able to injure him?[31]

We suffer, then, because we see enemies where none exist. We personalize what is not personal. And because our senses, when not used mindfully, lead us around, so to speak, by the nose.

Working with Step Two
Healing insight into the cause of our suffering is not just a cognitive matter. Intellectual insight is not enough. Liberating insight into the cause of suffering involves our whole being—intellect and emotions, heart and mind—everything. In the language of psychotherapy, it is the process of "working through," of continuing to bring accepting awareness to problems as they recycle through a series of clinical sessions.

The process of working through may be compared to untying a knot. To be effective in untying a knot, it helps to have an attitude of calm and patience. One must not be in a hurry. Some knots are small and simple. A pull here, a tug there, and *voilá*, the knot is untied. A larger knot will require much more time and patience. It may well not be untied in one sitting, but will call for a patient process of returning to it again and again, tugging a little bit here, pulling a little bit there. Eventually it will yield. Eventually, everything yields to the gentle power of mindfulness.

Sarah came into therapy with a deep sadness resulting from a failed relationship. At first, she was full of anger and blame: How could he! How dare he! Slowly she began to talk more about her choices and less about how awful her former partner was. She came to see that she was attracted to men who were "bad boys," who treated women poorly, but who somehow seemed exciting. She connected this with her father, whom she loved so much, but who had often neglected her. She came to see that she had made this kind of choice repeatedly. Over time, she started to see this deeply, and to understand, with a more than intellectual understanding, the pain that this pattern caused her.

It took a while. Her attraction to such men did not immediately change with the first emergence of her insight. But gradually she started to notice men who had previously been invisible to her and see them as interesting and attractive.

It bears repeating that looking into the causes of suffering in accord with Step Two is something that occurs at more levels than the cognitive. The cognitive level of understanding is just the beginning. While important, it is only the entry level to deeper understanding, to life-changing wisdom. People in therapy need a lot of encouragement in this process. Some may terminate prematurely out of impatience, when, if they had been patient with the process of working through, they may have gained the needed level of insight to result in change. This can happen, but at least let's not let it happen because we as therapists contribute to this process. Let us be sure, from our side, to bring patience to the process.

In *Zen Buddhism and Psychoanalysis*, Buddhist scholar D.T. Suzuki cites the example of native people in the south Pacific being visited by American scientists. When they heard it said that the Americans thought with their heads, the people thought the Americans must be crazy. They said that they of course think with their *abdomens*. People in China and Japan also, when confronted with a difficult problem, will advise one to "ask one's belly." "The belly," comments Suzuki, "stands for the totality of one's being, while the head, which is the latest-developed portion of the body, represents intellection."[32]

One way to put Step Two into practice which you can use for yourself and teach to clients is the art of simply holding a problem in awareness while you breathe in and out from the belly, examining the problem's many facets in a patient way, noting their interrelationships, and adopting a non-goal-oriented attitude. In other words, this is the practice of *sitting with* a problem.

Just hold the whole matter in mind patiently, not expecting an instant solution of any kind, and not pressing for one—just being with the whole matter about such and such, for as many sessions of meditation as it may take. All of a sudden, you may find yourself acting in new ways that are effective in avoiding the kinds of difficulties you used to have, without even always knowing quite what it was that you figured out.

I sometimes introduce patients to this practice in a therapy session. While I do not interrupt when their words are pouring out from them, when they reach a pause, I may ask them to return to the mindful breathing established at the beginning of the session, and hold "all that about the such-and-such problem" in mind, stepping back from the difficulty just enough to touch it without getting lost in it, telling them that insight may or may not come, but the important thing is to just be present to their global sense of the problem, without trying to force any special thing to happen.

Effective, deep insight is like insight about touching a hot stove. Perhaps at one time, when you were a small child, you had to be taught not to do this. If your parents told you not to touch the stove, there may have been a struggle in you about whether to comply, or to fulfill your curiosity and touch it anyway. But once you have been burned, you have a new level of insight. There is no longer a struggle in you about touching the hot stove. You do not have to fight with yourself to get yourself to avoid touching it. This is true understanding.

Therapy is a kind of meditation *à deux*. The therapist role in this process of untangling can be very helpful—even crucial—in preventing patients from falling into the same old difficulties under a new name, providing patience and encouragement, helping the client reach true understanding, and so forth. We help those who come to us a great deal simply by taking the same sort of patient but caring attitude toward their problems that we want them to have.

Step 3: See the way out of suffering.

One aspect of our problems in living is the fact that short-term consequences are more potent in determining our behavior than long-term ones. Just as a hungry laboratory rat will be reinforced for lever-pressing when the food falls within a fairly short time of the behavior, but not if the food falls hours later, so it is with us. This is part of why we may engage in destructive behaviors such as excessive drinking: the short-term consequences are pleasant, though the long-term ones are severely negative. The job of the therapist in such cases is to help the patient bring mindfulness to her experiences in a way that makes the longer term consequences more salient, and the shorter term consequences less important.

An approach that gently keeps the patient aware of the negative consequences, accompanied by repeated working through, including staying with the patient through the all but inevitable learning process of slips and errors and relapses, can eventually succeed where other approaches fail.[33] This is not a matter telling the patient what the important consequences are, but of drawing them out of the patient. Thus, for example, you may think your patient should quit smoking because of the risk of lung cancer, but your patient is frankly more concerned about the unattractive nicotine stains on her hand. The wise therapist will let go of his agenda, and help the patient focus on what she is concerned about.

In other words, a lot of the mindful therapist's job involves working with what is already there rather than imposing what we want to be there. The Chinese word *li,* a central Taoist teaching, illustrates the point. Li is the grain in the wood, the pattern of flowing water or moving clouds or pebbles on the beach. It is an uncontrived, non-mechanical, natural kind of order—the very footprint of the ultimately indefinable Tao. To accord with li is to go with the flow, to swim with the current, to follow the path of least resistance. It is the art of judo, in which little force need be exerted to bring the opponent to the ground because you use the force of gravity and the energy of your opponent. Good psychotherapy is like this. It defeats our most difficult problems—not by exerting a strong counterforce, but by this gentle, calm awareness or mindfulness. Thus, when you enter a therapy session with a patient, li teaches us to ask ourselves, what is the psyche up to here? Where is this problem leading this person? Or perhaps, if the patient has a theistic orientation, what is God up to in this person's life? Li teaches us to observe and respect the unfolding of this person's life energy, rather than imposing some pre-conceived goal onto the patient.

Step 4: Follow the path that leads away from suffering.

Step Four is a matter of what we could call lifestyle. There are certain ways of living that are simply not conducive to ending suffering, that in fact only make it worse, while other ways of living reduce suffering.

Some ways of living that create suffering, such as substance abuse, or an inordinate preoccupation with money, power, or sex, are obvious enough. We can readily understand how such things are destructive. Yet even more instructive are the seemingly innocuous actions that can trigger chains of destructive consequences. A simple thing such as hitting the snooze button too many times on a work morning, while seemingly minor, may not be minor in its consequences. Because of this, we are then impelled to rush through the morning. Members of our household become mere obstacles in our way, which of course seldom helps the quality of our relationship with them. Also as a consequence of this simple thing, we lack the time for meditation, a little inspirational reading, or anything that might prepare us to live deeply and mindfully that day. This leaves us vulnerable, beginning right at the top of the day. After such a beginning, everything affects us more deeply. By the time we arrive at work, we can already feel used up, empty, and exhausted, just from the commute. But at this point, of course, the work day has just begun. We are like someone who goes out into the pouring rain without a rain coat because he didn't have time to put one on.

The Buddha offers a drastic image—a cow with no skin, who rubs up next to a wall or the bark of a tree. All the parasites come and suck the poor animal's blood, since she is so unprotected, so vulnerable. In this way, something as simple as sleeping too late can have major consequences, and set your day on a course that creates a lot of dukkha.[34]

A note of caution must be struck at this point, however, for all of us brought up with a Western religious sensibility. Even if we have rejected our religious heritage, we can easily get confused, and think all this is a matter of being good or moral. But once we trigger that side of the polarity, once we feel that we are being *told* to be good, it is again the natural human response that we become all the more motivated to rebel. So it is very important that we Westerners do not confuse this point. One is not *bad* because one hits the snooze button. And one certainly is not *good* if one doesn't. It is just simply a matter of fact that by doing so, one sets oneself up for a more difficult time. And what is more, these difficulties can become self-perpetuating, creating a series of problems. A moralistic perspective is misleading, and can as often create rebellion as compliance.

One way to say it is: everything depends on how you brush your teeth in the morning. Not *whether* you brush your teeth but *how* you brush your teeth. If you can do a simple thing such as toothbrushing in a calm, present, relaxed, mindful way, then you have generated just that much momentum in the direction of peace, of liberation from suffering. But if you are not truly present while you are brushing your teeth, if while you are brushing you are already planning and worrying about the day ahead, if you are preoccupied with your many problems and worries, then you are generating momentum in the direction of suffering.[35]

In this spirit, then, we could add, it all depends on how you drink your coffee, how you eat your lunch, how you walk out to the mailbox. Do you do these things with awareness? Are you practicing breathing and smiling? Do you notice how blue the sky is, that a dog is barking or a bird is singing? It all depends on this. Just as dukkha can be a matter of minor daily hassles, so anti-dukkha, the antidote to dukkha, can also consist of simple, non-heroic approaches to daily life, just being fully open and aware of the many positive elements that we normally fail to notice.

The fourth noble truth in Buddhism is the famous eightfold path: right view, right thinking, right speech, right action, right livelihood, right diligence, right mindfulness, and right concentration. The keyword here is *right,* the traditional translation of the Pali word *samma* or the Sanskrit word *samyak.* The idea is not so much "right" in the moralistic sense, but in the very pragmatic sense of being a correct antidote to dukkha.

Dukkha is the great teacher. Dukkha shows us how to live. It is not a matter of making a cult out of our suffering. There are far too many unhealthy religious examples of that sort of thing. It is simply that, to live correctly, to live in harmony with reality, means to live in a way that leads to liberation from dukkha. So dukkha is like the North Star helping one to walk south. It is not so much "if it feels good, do it," but "if it causes suffering, change direction." In ways great and small suffering reflects back to us that something about the way we are living, or the way we are viewing our lives, is out of harmony with reality. It is a feedback system, like touching the hot stove. Only if we live mindfully, however, will we be able to discern the lesson. If we are asleep, how can we learn? If we are not present, how will we understand?

Four-Step Exercise

Below is a form that frames the Four Noble Truths as a four-step exercise. You are free to copy it for your own use and your work with patients. I have found this a very helpful tool. Please try it yourself before you give it to patients, so you are familiar with it.

Step 1 (Recognize that this is suffering): On a piece of paper, describe in a sentence one aspect of your life that is difficult and causes you suffering.

Step 2 (Recognize the cause of the suffering): Begin by cultivating calmness in yourself. Pay attention to the breath, perhaps dwelling with a simple word such as "calm" as you breathe in and out. Ask yourself, "What are the causes of my suffering in regard to this situation?" Then continue your meditation by simply holding an awareness of this issue and its causes in your awareness, without trying to analyze or figure anything out, just being with the question. Tell yourself, "Just being present with all this," and repeat this to yourself whenever you drift too far way. Continue this for a few minutes, ideally around ten or even more, without trying to come up with answers or solutions. Only then consider the following questions, and record your insights. But remember: you are not trying to force a solution, or to force answers to these questions. It is the process of gentle, sustained awareness that matters. Then simply use the questions as a framework to record any insights that may have occurred to you, if any.

1. Is there something I have done, or routinely do, that may have contributed to this suffering?
2. Is there something that I could have done that might have been helpful regarding this suffering, but didn't do?
3. Is there something that I said, or routinely say, that may have contributed to this suffering?
4. Is there something I could have said that would have been helpful?
5. Is there something about how I view myself, or how I view others, that may have contributed to this suffering?
6. Is there something about the way I view the situation that contributes to my suffering? Am I seeing this situation in a way that is exaggerated, distorted, or too black and white?
7. Is there something about my overall beliefs or view of life that may contribute to this suffering?
8. Is there something about the kinds of choices I have made that could helpfully be reconsidered?
9. Am I resisting reality rather than following it and harmonizing with it?

If you find yourself engaging in excessive guilt and self-blame, meditate on yourself as a beautiful, vulnerable young child of preschool age. What happened to you that contributed toward your making this kind of error? How do your errors and unproductive actions reflect pain and suffering in you? Try to get to the place where you can see this the same way you see a storm or Chuang Tzu's empty boat. Record your insights, however small they may seem.

If you view the problem as the fault of another person, ask yourself how the hurtful words or actions of that person reveal the suffering in them. Again, reflect on the individual involved as a beautiful young child, and imagine what kind of suffering could have caused that person's present actions, trying to see it like the storm or the empty boat. Record your insights.

After you have reflected on these questions, return again to meditation on the problem as above, ideally for another ten minutes or more, without analyzing or pressing for solutions. Then see if more insight ripens regarding the above questions, and add to your answers. Adopt a process orientation toward this work, allowing it to unfold according to its own timetable, without forcing it. Honor whatever insight you get for now, even if it is only a small part of the solution. Remember: the process of mindful attention is more important than the answer. If you have allowed yourself to bring mindfulness to a life issue, that is already a kind of healing.

Step 3 (See the way out of suffering): Based on insights gleaned from Step Two, record any changes you would like to make. Be specific. Conclude by closing your eyes and imagining yourself successfully instituting these changes. Let yourself experience just how good this feels.

Step 4 (Follow the path that leads away from suffering): Based on the above insights, consider whether there are general lifestyle changes that could increase your resilience to this kind of suffering. Write these down, and again meditate briefly, clearly imagining yourself putting these into action. Finally, solidify these insights by sharing them with another person.

THE LESSONS OF DUKKHA

By learning the lessons of dukkha, we learn what we need to do, how we need to do it, with what attitude we need to do it, and what we need not to do. Thich Nhat Hanh summarizes the Buddha's insight in these words: "When a wise person suffers, she asks herself, 'What can I do to be free from this suffering? Who can help me? What have I done to free myself from this suffering?' But when a foolish person suffers, she asks herself, 'Who has wronged me? How can I show others that I am the victim of wrongdoing? How can I punish those who have caused my suffering?'"[36]

The path that leads out of suffering and into peace and liberation, as indicated in the four noble truths, is to know and acknowledge suffering when it arises, look deeply into its cause to find the way out, and learn to live in such a way that we suffer less. The path involves facing what hurts with bold honesty, learning to abide in the experience of our pain without evasion, calming and clarifying until insight unfolds, and we know what to do and what not to do.

Before discussing more about the specifics of the eightfold path in chapter seven, we will turn now, in the next two chapters, to teachings of the "three poisons" and their antidotes, and the "three dharma seals," both of which can deepen our insight into the nature of suffering and how to reduce it in psychotherapy.

CHAPTER FIVE

Discover the Jewel in Your Pocket: The Antidotes to Suffering

To the extent that we try to master the environment or be effective with it, to that extent do we cut the possibility of full, objective, detached, non-interfering cognition. Only if we let it be, can we perceive fully. Again, to cite psychotherapeutic experience, the more eager we are to make a diagnosis and a plan of action, the less helpful do we become. The more eager we are to cure, the longer it takes. Every psychiatric researcher has to learn not to try to cure, not to be impatient. In this and in many other situations, to give in is to overcome, to be humble is to succeed.[37]
—ABRAHAM MASLOW

WHAT IF I TOLD YOU that you had at your disposal wondrous, magical, mystical powers to bring healing to your patients?

In fact, you do have such powers. Only, they are powers that you may tend to overlook or underestimate. You overlook them because you are like the king's son in the Lotus Sutra, who wandered the world as a beggar, not knowing that precious gems, capable of meeting all of his needs easily and abundantly, had been sewn into the lining of his own clothes. You have within you all that you need to be happy, to find your way out of suffering and become a free, joyful, enlightened human being.

EXAMINING OUR ASSUMPTIONS

Psychology, like other disciplines, suffers from temporal chauvinism. We can be so wed to the myth of progress, that we become myopic regarding the past. We imagine that all good and valid things must have been written in the past ten years. In fact, a psychology professor told me that his students do not want to read anything more than ten or twelve years old. Under such circumstances, the discipline of psychology, rather than progressing, resembles a patient with Korsakoff's syndrome, lacking in long-term memory: we must continually re-learn what we already knew.

We forget that much that is happening in psychology today is fad and fashion, just as much as many of the things of yesterday were fad and fashion. Twenty years ago, behavioral psychologists snapped themselves with rubber bands to punish unwanted negative cognitions. They did this with utter seriousness and a conviction that this was reasonable and scientific. Why do we no longer see people doing this? Many such things change, not because they have been disproved, but because they have fallen out of fashion. We have simply moved on—thank heaven!

Much of what passes for progress concerns the more refined tools we have to play with. We may not be really much better at understanding human beings than we were in the past, but we do have more sophisticated tools and methods. Fifty years ago, the predominant theory of schizophrenia was the psychogenic theory of the absent father and dominating mother in combination with an appropriate diathesis or vulnerability. Now we talk about dopamine levels and structural differences in the brain.

But is this *progress,* or is it just different? How much of the change in our point of view is the result of a *better* understanding, and how much is just the result of having tools to look at the problem at a *different* level of analysis, one that seems inherently more "scientific"?

It may be unfair to say that such changes are entirely a matter of fashion, tools, and methods, but it is at least partly due to such factors, and probably a larger part than we normally like to admit. To my knowledge, the psychogenic theory of schizophrenia was not rejected because of research findings, but simply put aside in the face of biological findings. Yet again and again, when I have encountered the families of schizophrenics, I see the pattern of the controlling mother and absent father. Why is that? One should certainly consider that the direction of causality might be the reverse of what was thought, and that individuals who become schizophrenic, being difficult to deal with as children, tend to elicit maternal controllingness, and tend to have fathers who in frustration cede their involvement altogether. That is quite possible. But it is mere prejudice to dismiss older theories because evidence at a different level becomes available.

Perhaps the new theories about schizophrenia are more correct. It would certainly be difficult to deny the utility of antipsychotic medication, for example. But we should in no event be fooled into believing that people in times past were less intelligent than we are because they lacked MRIs or electron microscopes. And just because we have a new kind of evidence does not necessarily mean the old evidence is invalid.

A lot of research with our new toys shows that mental events and differences between individuals have correlates in brain structure and activity. Is anyone really surprised by this? Of course this is the case! What *is* surprising is that we assume this to be a demonstration of causality. Some Buddhists suggest the reverse, that mind is primary rather than brain.[38] They do not have any difficulty acknowledging that mental events correlate with brain activity: they simply dispute our assumption of material cause as primary. This point of view should not be lightly dismissed because of our prejudice against "mentalism," as though by giving a position a pejorative name we have defeated it.

We know that serotonin is implicated in mood. Yet we tend to forget that we can change serotonin levels by changing how we think. If you sit in a dark room, rehearsing negative thoughts, even if you are blessed with an optimistic temperament, your serotonin levels will drop along with your mood. Continue this long enough, and the lowered level of serotonin becomes chronic. Of course, you can affect the process by taking medications that block the reuptake of serotonin, increasing the available quantity of the neurotransmitter. But since our thinking also affects these changes, it could also reasonably be argued that mind affects brain.

In considering the possibility that people in the past were intelligent, sometimes even wise, and might continue to have something to offer us, let's take a look at some wisdom that is truly old, not just from twenty years ago, but from the ancient past—the Buddhist theory of why people suffer.

THE THREE POISONS

Buddhism offers the analysis that our suffering results from one or more of what are called *the three poisons*.[39] These are: greed (*lobha,* in Sanskrit), hatred *(dosa),* and delusion or ignorance *(moha).**

---

*The terms as translated here are generally ego-dystonic: one seldom experiences oneself as greedy, full of hate, or deluded. To understand how these operate in ourselves, we can understand greed as the desire to grasp, to have for oneself, or even simply, to move toward some desired object. Hatred is connected with anger, often an anger we feel is justified. It is the recognition of some object as aversive, the desire to avoid and move away from such things. Of them all, delusion may be the hardest to recognize in ourselves. We often do not realize we were deluded until some cherished dream collapses—the romance ends suddenly and painfully, the hard-sought degree does not change one's life, and so on.

When we hear the English translations of these terms, for many of us a barrier arises. It is helpful to remember that the Buddha is often called the Great Physician. Greed, hatred, and delusion may sound bad in a moralistic sense rather than a diagnostic one. But in using these terms, the Buddha is simply diagnosing the problem. Viewing these moralistically often just makes it worse by leading to repression and denial. If it is bad in the moral sense to feel greedy, but greed is nonetheless the name for what I am experiencing, then what can I do? My knowing that greed is bad does not prevent my feeling greedy. At best, I can only delude myself, perhaps suppressing the feeling of greed, or failing to acknowledge that greed is an accurate label for the kind of experience I am having.

We are left with the problem that seems ubiquitous in religious and moral teaching. We may be told to love our neighbor, and in the warmth and comfort of a religious service we may even imagine ourselves capable of doing so, but this does not mean that we will be able to be loving, especially when people are rude or frustrating or unkind to us in some way. In fact, the consequence of the split between religious teaching and how we actually live is likely to be such that either we conclude these two things have little to do with each other, or we distort our awareness in some way to eliminate the dissonance we feel. And in this way, our lives become inharmonious and disunified, and we may conclude, as many have, that we are better off without religion or spirituality.

In light of the previous chapter, it should be clear that repressing is not helpful. The first step in healing our suffering is acknowledging that it is there. If we stand a chance of learning to love our neighbors, we first have to know it when we are angry at them. Or envious. Or disdainful. Or any of a host of other attitudes and judgments. The same applies in the case of the three poisons of greed, hatred, and delusion. To be able to work with these, we must learn to acknowledge when they are present, calming the mind until we can come to see things differently, more realistically.

So let's look deeply into these poisons to see how they cause suffering, and thereby, glimpse the way out.

HOW GREED HURTS

Greed is the desire to have all good for myself. From this point of view, every time someone else gains something that I want for myself but do not have, I suffer. Every time I lose something that I want, I suffer. Every time I see a television commercial for something I do not own and cannot afford, I suffer. I may be on the vacation of a lifetime, but I still may suffer a little bit when I notice that the first class airline passengers get better treatment than I do.

Fundamental to an understanding of suffering lies the insight that suffering, at its base, is a form of delusion or ignorance. Greed is based on the idea of being a separate self, such that my welfare is then something independent of the welfare of other beings. The mindful therapist, however, informed by the Dharma, knows this is incorrect. In the course of our development as children, we learn to separate objects out from their background and to distinguish them from other objects, seeing them as separate and distinct, and seeing ourselves also as something separate. Language reifies and strengthens this perception of separateness. As Alan Watts pointed out, because of the conventions of language, requiring that every sentence have a subject and a verb in English, we have such absurd sentences as, "The wind blows." But could you have a wind without the blowing? Could you have blowing without wind? Or isn't it in fact the case that what we mean by wind is exactly the blowing, and vice versa?[40]

In other words, only in language and thought can we ultimately play the game of dividing reality up into bits. When there is knowing, there is both a knower and an object known; but you never can really have one without the other. When breathing is occurring, there is both air and a breather; but you cannot have one without the other. One without the other is an abstraction that does not exist in reality. In this sense, when you look at a flower, you could say that you and the flower are one. But that is not quite right either. What is really there is something like: human-being-seeing-flower—an inseparable linkage of noun-verb-object.

Thus we can come to imagine that the good fortune of our friend is something separate from ourselves. Even without any metaphysical belief of non-duality, however, we can easily see that the happiness of our friend affects our own happiness. If our friend is an unhappy person, his unhappiness will affect us, as will his happiness. This is why after a therapy hour with a profoundly depressed person, one feels drained: for we are not nearly so separate as we generally think. From a practical point of view, we can readily distinguish one person from another, and since my good fortune may well affect me more directly and immediately than my friend's good fortune, I may be inclined to think of it as something separate. But there is no ultimate separation. For my friend now has a happy companion in me, and so long as he does not buy into the mythology of ultimate separateness—of happiness as a zero-sum game in which someone else's increase detracts from mine and vice versa—then his happiness can also increase. For this reason, Zen Buddhists especially describe reality as "not two" rather than as "all one." "All one" is a poetic expression that evokes a sense of this reality of interconnection. But *not-two* is more precise, since *one* already implies *two*. And the nature of the universe is such that things deeply interpenetrate each other.

This insight demonstrates why countries repeat the same mistakes over and over again in international relations. Countries still act as though they can gain unilateral benefit without considering the interconnectedness of the global community.

We think we can adopt friendly relationships with oil-rich Arab nations, for example, and ignore the conditions of their people as being their own business, and that we can thereby have the separate benefit of an assured, cheap supply of oil. But this is, as many have begun to see, a short-sighted point of view. Where our country is on friendly terms with an oppressive regime, we are then seen by the people of that nation as oppressors. And we then become the objects of their hatred and terrorist tactics. If a revolution arises in such countries, as it did in Iran in 1979 for example, we suddenly find ourselves on the outside. In all of this we create a lot of suffering, a lot of bad karma, all deriving from the delusion that our well-being is separate from that of others. Reality—not as a matter of philosophical belief but of direct perception once the mind is calm enough to see clearly—is a matter of profound interpenetration and interconnectedness, where everything affects everything else and is at the same time affected by everything else.

The perception of interconnectedness does not necessarily mean that one must always sacrifice one's own good, for it operates in both directions: our happiness or unhappiness affects others as much as theirs affects us. For this reason, if we give up too much too soon out of some ethic of self-sacrifice, and thereby become unhappy, then we suffer, and our suffering likewise can spill over to others. This is one area where religion all too easily becomes neurotic: My pretending to be selfless may only drive my selfishness underground, thereby making me a twisted being, whereas, if I could own my selfishness as a starting place, I am at least straightforward and direct, and stand a better chance of modifying it. But you cannot modify what you refuse to acknowledge.

Everyone has probably had the experience of knowing some self-sacrificing pseudo-saint who feels bitter and unappreciated. In the therapy setting, for example, we know that our work is very difficult to do. The better we are at doing it, the easier we make it look, but we know it is not easy. So if we agree too readily to a reduced fee, but end up feeling badly about it, we have then planted seeds of resentment in ourselves. By reducing our happiness, we may thereby reduce our effectiveness with the patient. It would be more helpful to acknowledge our true feelings and work out a compromise that does not leave us or our patients with ill feeling. Greed means being solely pre-occupied with our own welfare. This is a cause of suffering because it doesn't work, and it doesn't work because we are far more deeply interconnected with others than we imagine. But it is important to note that this does not mean it is somehow wrong to consider our own happiness and benefit along with that of others. Our happiness is as relevant as anyone's, and if we try too hard to be good, to be generous, it may backfire.

The universe is benevolent. It seeks to bless us and be generous with us. Based on this principle, many people practice prayers and visualizations to increase wealth, to find love, and so forth. That is all well and good as far as it goes, but there is a danger. If the effect of such practices is to increase our preoccupation with what we lack, we may end up unhappier than we were before we undertook them. This is like keeping a journal in which you only record your unfulfilled needs and desires, and then read and re-read it, focusing increasingly on what is missing. Presented so baldly, this is obviously a rather foolish thing to do. But it is at the same time not that far from the way we sometimes live. The point is, focusing only on what we lack only stimulates greed. And this is unfortunate, not because of some abstract notion that greed is bad, but because it leaves us more desperate, more unhappy, and more frustrated than we were to begin with.

Jeff had enjoyed a fabulous career as a lawyer, making millions of dollars annually, but spending every bit as much. He somehow never anticipated that this could come to an end, and that he

*would come to be, through many health problems, disabled and
unable to continue his law practice in the same manner. He now
earned a bit over $100,000 per year, through whatever part-time
work he could find from old colleagues and clients. Although he
talked endlessly about how poor he was, he also planned to buy a
new Lexus—a car well beyond many people's means. Our work
together consisted largely of helping Jeff experience his pain, recognizing that, while many would be happy with his income, for
him it was a long drop from a high place, while at the same time
he could learn to acknowledge that there were still many conditions for happiness in his life.*

In light of this analysis of greed, we can understand how lotteries, for instance, cause suffering. Very few actually win an
amount sufficient to bring any significant financial relief. But by
feeding people's greed, by feeding their vain hopes, lotteries
become an invitation to despair. We may enjoy the fantasy of win-
ning, but unless we are careful to approach it in a detached and
realistic way, it may result in our being more dissatisfied with our
present lives than ever. It can also prevent us from making realistic plans to solve our financial difficulties.

In our work, greed can take the form of preoccupation with
money. Of course we want to do well. Of course we want to earn
a good living, and those who do the difficult work of psychotherapy deserve to prosper. But the whole area of money in therapy
can create a lot of frustration in us, unless the patient's welfare is
at least as important to us. Otherwise, when patients try to find
ways out of their bills, when insurance companies find trivial reasons to deny claims, and so on, we will be very unhappy. We will
suffer.

Once I had a therapy session (as a patient) with a therapist
who spent the first thirty minutes of a fifty minute session discussing how I would pay the bill. I am not exaggerating. I

noticed quite precisely how much time had gone by. Perhaps the therapist was concerned I could not pay him, since I was a student at the time. Perhaps he'd recently been cheated of payment for some of his services. I like to think there may have been some such extenuating circumstance. But I paid him in full—and never returned again. Whatever the issue, something was badly out of balance.

Please hear this clearly: It is not bad to want abundance. It is simply human to do so. But unless you are careful, if you become too focused on this aspect of life, you will only be frustrated. You will suffer more. That is the point.

All three poisons have a self-perpetuating aspect, but this is perhaps most clear with regard to greed. Greed can never be satisfied. Once we get to the level that we once imagined would satisfy us completely, we find it no longer does so. Even John D. Rockefeller, the tycoon who established the family fortune, when asked how much money was enough, admitted he always needed a little bit more. Greed leaves us perpetually restless and unfilled, trying to quench our thirst with salt water.

HOW HATRED HURTS

If greed means wanting all good only for myself, hatred is the desire to have others suffer. When we are trapped into the point of view of ignorance, of separateness, we sometimes see others as the cause of our suffering. From that point of view, we can have the mistaken belief that striking out at someone whom we see as causing us to suffer will bring us relief. Except perhaps in the very short run, this is simply not the case. Hatred is an attempt to defend ourselves from pain, but an ineffective one. In the long run, it never brings the satisfaction we imagine it will. A patient of mine once told me a saying that hatred was like taking poison and expecting the other person to suffer.

Hatred, and its related affect of anger, are destructive forces. We know clearly that anger releases the costly hormones of epinephrine, norepinephrine, and cortisol. While these hormones do a good job at preparing us to deal with an emergency, their regular presence in the body in significant amounts destroys our organs and our well-being. We now know, for example, that it is the hostility component of the Type A personality that most contributes to heart disease rather than rushing or impatience.[41]

Anger and its cousin, hatred, like all three poisons, creates negative effects in two ways: through its effects on our environment, and through its direct effects on ourselves. Anger creates anger. As we approach others with anger in our hearts, we do angry things, which in turn cause others to harbor ill will toward us. If others in turn act on this ill will and cause us pain, we get even more angry, or may even come to hate them. So anger first of all causes us to suffer through its effect on our environment, which then reflects more hatred back to us. Secondly, by rehearsing angry thoughts and acting on them, we create a habit of being angry. The more we think such thoughts and act in such ways, the more anger increases in us, the more our health and well-being suffer.

Just as greed holds the illusion of happiness, so hatred has its own way of deluding us. When we are full of anger or hatred, one of the by-products is a feeling of power. This is seductive, as I have often seen with patients whose focus of treatment is anger. While they can readily see the destructive aspects of their anger, at least intellectually, it is still difficult for them to reach the level of effective insight, since anger also makes them feel powerful. The short-term consequences are positive in the same way that the short-term consequences of addiction are positive, and it can take a lot of work to help them see the longer term consequences as more salient.

Some of our patients carry anger or hatred toward their parents. Many people in therapy are there in part because their parents were, to say the least, less than ideal. And in some cases, they were even severely neglectful, violent, or otherwise destructive. It is useful, of course, for patients to see that their difficulties are not their *fault,* that they are the result of suffering created in part by the ignorant actions of others. That way, at least, the hate is not turned on themselves. Yet at the same time, if they do not come to see those who have wronged them in this very same light, knowing that those people's actions were ultimately the result of similar causes and conditions, of treatment they received from others in turn, then the work of healing is incomplete. Such patients may not hate themselves, but will still carry a lot of hatred toward others.

Sometimes when a patient becomes frustrated with herself for not being able to change as she would like, I will, with great caution, remind her that this is the result of many years of experience, habit, and conditioning, and help her see her failure to change sympathetically. Then, with even greater caution, I may take a further step, and suggest that this is true also of the people she is angry at. If such remarks are well timed, she may accept them. But again, initial acceptance may be only intellectual, and need to be deepened through the ongoing therapy. The work of healing is not complete until one sees both oneself and others with this kind of insight. This kind of insight is called compassion.

HOW DELUSION HURTS

The essence of delusion is a turning away from reality, insisting that reality be the way we want it to be rather than the way it is. Greed, hatred, and delusion overlap. For example, the false hope of the lottery ticket could be called a kind of delusion, a tax on the statistically impaired, as well as a kind of greed. If the fantasy of instant wealth, and thereby of an instant solution to all one's problems, while innocent enough as far as it goes, is too strong, then it can result in serious disappointment, and even financial drain.

Delusion comes in many forms. One form of delusion is the myth of specialness. We can easily see this myth at work in some of our patients, particularly those with narcissistic tendencies. This should not be unfamiliar to us. If we are honest, we can recognize that we too can suffer at times from this form of delusion, one which is particularly seductive for therapists who have a transpersonal or "spiritual" orientation. The belief of the narcissist that the rules do not apply to him creates a lot of suffering, both for him and, sometimes more obviously, for those in his life. The belief that he is so special, that obviously he will be lifted up above the normal life trials suffered by mere mortals, has ruined many lives. The individual who drops out of school convinced that he will become a big Hollywood star or top NBA player will, for the overwhelming most part, suffer great disappointment. Yet the media feeds this painful delusion. After all, some ultra-successful individuals did just that. But those infected with the virus of specialness fail to comprehend the odds and fail to comprehend the staggering number of lives ruined by such delusions. American optimism tells us to go for our dreams against all odds. Our culture holds up many shining examples of people who were successful doing just that, who refused to take no for an answer, who persevered and emerged victorious. We do not talk much about the many more who took foolish risks and paid significant consequences. The reality of life teaches a more nuanced message than just following one's dream, a message of knowing oneself. Do I really have the talent to make it as a movie star or Major League Baseball player? And if so, do I have also the tenacity to develop that talent, and persist when all the doors seem to be closed? If I can say a realistic yes to these questions, based on a solid, undeluded view of myself and my abilities, than optimism is appropriate. But if I never did well in Little League, I may be better off not feeding my dream of becoming the next Babe Ruth. Knowing when to go all out, and when to be realistic, is a decision that must be founded on the wisdom of self knowledge.

Steve was a forty-five year old man with a history of severe drug abuse and many emotional difficulties. He had had only one significant relationship, and generally had been unable to sustain much closeness in his life. He lived alone. His pattern in therapy exemplified this theme, coming for a few sessions once every year or two, but then dropping out again, as though he could not allow me to get too close.

Steve was an intelligent man, but because of his difficulties and poor work history, generally had to take jobs below his abilities. When he returned to therapy on this occasion, he had not gone in to work for six weeks at his lower-level factory job. His employer had been quite patient with him, but Steve was obviously at risk for termination.

To try to keep him in therapy a little longer, treatment had to proceed particularly slowly and gently, patiently titrating in an awareness of his pattern. Steve's aspirations were grandiose. He wanted to be an artist, but could not accept anything less than his work hanging in the Guggenheim. Feeling special and entitled, he was unable to accept the limitations of the employment he could have, or endure the compromise of "keeping his day-job" while he pursued his artistic dreams in his free time. Through gentle application of awareness to this theme, he gradually came to accept a more realistic view of himself, seeing that he did not need to see himself in such grandiose terms to feel like a valuable person, and more able to make the kind of sensible compromises his life required.

The myth of specialness can also take more mundane forms. If we feel that because we are special, we do not have to pay attention to our finances, we may be shocked when our checks are overdrawn, or when we discover that we have passed the deadline for our taxes. We become at risk for the many ways in which neglect is risky, neglecting maintenance of our homes, our cars, or our love relationship and friendships. We can find ourselves more aggravated than we need to be from petty annoyances, when getting a parking ticket or being unable to find a parking space conflicts with our entitlement. Specialness is designed to protect us from blows to the ego, but actually creates a greater vulnerability to them, since reality simply refuses, in ways great and small, to cooperate with our sense of entitlement.

A particular type of delusion is the special relationship. Ours is a culture with little room for the transcendent or spiritual. One of the few places this dimension is permitted to enter our lives is in the area of romantic love. When we fall in love, we permit ourselves to experience *ecstasy,* literally standing outside the normally tight confines of our own egos. In this way, romance must often bear the total weight of our need for such experiences.

It is not that we need to become sour or close ourselves off from the ideal of romantic love. In its place within the total constellation of a human life, it can be a source of joy and an opening of the heart to love someone else beyond ourselves. However, when romantic love is called upon to meet our total need for transcendence and ecstasy, it is unsuited for this purpose. It simply cannot bear that much weight. Also, when someone falls in love, it can be a kind of disaster in a person's life. Every therapist has witnessed how someone who is deeply involved in her inner work, however difficult, shuts down completely on this process and drops out of therapy, imagining that all her problems have been solved now because she has fallen in love.

A lot of suffering results from this. If we view our relationship as too special, we may be unwilling to invest the kind of down-to-earth effort that makes relationships work in daily life. Minor difficulties are then perceived as major flaws. We also fail to appreciate the concrete human being in her specific humanity, seeing her only as one who fulfills, or frustrates, our need. Romanticism of this kind is the precursor of divorce.

Related to the delusion of the special relationship is that of the external rescuer. This is the belief that, while I myself have no wisdom, someone else does. And if I merely attach myself to that person, all will be well. Some patients view the therapist this way, though this may be more commonly observed in the overzealous denial of the therapist's importance than in any direct way. In any case, the Dharma offers us an antidote to this problem. Near the end of his life, the Buddha taught that one must be a lamp unto oneself. No one can give us what we seek unless we learn to find it within ourselves.

The mirror image of specialness is seen in patients who feel they are uniquely *awful* in some way. The suffering of these individuals is obvious. What's worse, they may not be motivated to do much about it. After all why should a person of such little value try to take better care of herself?

It is easy to sympathize with the person who feels bad about herself, and more difficult to do so with the person who feels special or grandiose. But if we see deeply, we will know that both suffer equally. Both are equally caught in delusion. Neither has a view of self grounded in wisdom.

An important kind of delusion in therapy is transference, both positive and negative. When patients see us in an overly negative light, perhaps as their bad father or mother, it will be difficult for us to create the kind of trust that will allow us to be of help. But also, patients who idealize us will suffer when they come to see we do not have magical solutions to all their problems. Delusions of a positive or a negative nature are ultimately equal ailments.

Before considering the antidotes, let's consider the Three Poisons in light of two clinical cases.

Harold is a businessman, owner of a chain of successful stores. Harold's net worth is measured in tens of millions of dollars. He has been working at the same business since he was a child, initially in a store belonging to his father, now for many years in his own store. Harold is 72 years old. He has no other interests than his work. His marriage is unhappy.

Harold's son Scott works for him in the family business, running one of the stores for him. Harold and Scott's relationship is close but highly conflicted. Their conflict centers around a sales manager that Scott has a lot of faith in, but whom Harold despises. Harold's hatred of this employee serves the purpose of keeping him involved in the business. Underneath all of this is a keen fear of death, which like all inordinate fears of this kind, is in the end a measure of his unlived life.

Financially, Harold could retire, but this presents tremendous emotional obstacles for him. One of these is a total absence of leisure skills or interests other than work. The other is that he equates retirement with death. The hated employee traps him in his delusion that he will live forever if he only keeps working, convincing him that his ongoing involvement is necessary to the health of the business. Who else would keep an eye on this employee, about whom his son is so naïve? For the same reason, Harold is extremely litigious. He continues to throw money after lost legal causes because they at least distract him from the pain of choosing what to do with the time remaining to him.

There is an element of greed in his clinging to his business: he simply does not want to let go, or allow his son or that hated employee to reap the benefits of his lifelong work. Harold has a lot of anger and even hatred toward the employee, as well as an unexamined belief, a kind of delusion, that work will somehow keep him immortal. Hatred, greed, and delusion conspire together to keep Harold trapped. Though he feels he would be unhappy if he retired, he fails to appreciate how unhappy he is now.

In the course of therapy, Harold's preoccupation with his son and the hated employee gradually abated—not because I talked him out of it, but because of the "three antidotes" discussed below. As he experienced the understanding of the therapist as love and compassion, and as he gradually came to see the wisdom of letting go to at least some extent, he was slowly able to reduce his involvement with the business and adopt other interests, though never able to retire altogether.

Cathy is a woman in her late thirties with a history of anorexia. Her eating disorder is currently in check, but still evident in her preoccupation with food, eating, weight, and appearance. Like many with her disorder, she has a great deal of difficult feeling the reality of her life and her emotions. She has two main operating principles: (1) everything is fine, and (2) everything will be okay if I just stop eating. She is a woman who lives entirely on the surface of things, a living embodiment of the Billy Crystal character who maintained that it is "better to look good than feel good."

Of course, despite her first operating principle, not everything is fine in Cathy's life. Aware of the ticking of her biological clock, and highly desirous of having children, she desperately wants her current relationship to move into marriage and a family. However, this pain is muted by her overriding principles. Her preoccupation with eating and her view that everything is fine conspire against her feeling her needs with clarity.

In the course of therapy, Cathy discussed the future of her relationship with her partner. Though I told her that this may need to be an ongoing conversation rather than a one-time discussion, she only managed to bring it up with him once. His response not being much in line with what she wished, she was terrified of raising the issue again. Cathy dropped out of therapy early, to date unwilling to discuss where her relationship is going, and unable to confront the widening discrepancy between how her life is and how she would like it to be. She is choosing delusion, rather than looking into her suffering deeply enough to discover its roots and find a way out.

Cathy is a pleasant, likeable person, and suffers neither from greed nor anger. Her suffering is the result of a delusion, based on a deep-seated conviction that she must always be happy and see the bright side of things and never acknowledge anything other than the most positive of feelings.

THE THREE ANTIDOTES

To this point, then, I have shown how a mindful therapist understands the origins of suffering in our greed, hatred, and delusion or ignorance. Properly understood, these are not moralistic judgments, but diagnostic and etiological ones. I have shown through examples how this sheds light on clinical cases. With this established, we are now ready to understand the antidotes to these ills. Like the poisons, the antidotes are indeed powerful.

Put simply, greed is the desire to have all good for myself alone and none for others. The antidote to greed, anti-greed, is *love.* Hatred is the desire to have others suffer. Therefore the antidote to hatred, anti-hatred, is *compassion,* the desire for the suffering of others to end. Finally, if the source of our suffering is delusion, a deluded way of seeing, the antidote, anti-ignorance, is *wisdom.*

Does this trinity of love, compassion, and wisdom not seem a little familiar to you? The antidotes we have been seeking, the magical ingredients of successful and potent psychotherapy, love, compassion, and wisdom, may be familiar because they resemble what Carl Rogers described as the necessary and sufficient conditions for change—unconditional positive regard (love), empathy (compassion), and congruence (wisdom). Greed involves trying to hold on tightly to the other person. But when you practice unconditional positive regard, you allow the other to be as he is. Hatred involves pushing others away and rejecting them. Empathy is the opposite because it involves understanding the other deeply, and is therefore the opposite of aversion. The deluded person if full of doubt, confusion, and deception, while a person who is congruent knows who she is without concealment or disguise, willing to be with the flow of her organism from moment to moment.

THE NATURE OF MIRACLES

Love, compassion, and wisdom are miraculous medicines. But why then do we as therapists often undervalue them? Why do we have the feeling that these are not, contrary to Rogers, sufficient, even if they are necessary? Certainly, we would not submit a treatment plan to a managed care organization that read, "I will give this person lots of love and compassion; I will give them large doses of authentic interactions and wisdom." But just why wouldn't we do that? Why do we have difficulty acknowledging these miraculous components of healing?

One reason may be a lack of a real understanding of the miraculous. Normally, we only acknowledge something as *miraculous* if it occurs instantaneously. If too much time has lapsed in the unfolding of a miracle, we may miss it. The apple bud blossoms into a beautiful flower and then an apple. The body heals itself of cuts, bruises, illness, and injury, as the mind heals itself of trauma. We do not see the miracle, however, *because it happens over time.* Yet if we are not trapped by time, we can see that it is still miraculous. The enlightened person, freed from the limitations of time and space, is not deceived by this.

It is said that Saint Francis of Assisi stood before an almond tree and asked it to tell him of God, at which point, the tree blossomed. Perhaps this was a miracle in the usual sense of happening instantaneously. But perhaps also it was a miracle in that Francis could *perceive* the blossoms as already present. The miracle of the blossoms was already there, requiring only one additional ingredient—time—to become manifest. Either way, the appearance of beautiful blossoms is miraculous.

The three antidotes are miraculous—sometimes working with dramatic speed but more often through their steady application over time. There may be a role for other techniques and methods of change, but the therapist who knows less of these, and more about love, compassion, and wisdom, is the one with the greatest capacity to effect miraculous change. The main value of our techniques that we have accumulated so carefully may actually be to give both us and our patients hope that there is something to do, while love, compassion, and wisdom do the real work.

THE COMPONENTS OF HEALING

Love is an attitude of friendliness. It is composed of a substance called understanding. When we understand, we love. Love is the wish for the happiness and well-being of the other.

Love also contains respect. We know that the person before us is multifaceted and not just a patient, just as we are many things besides being a therapist. We know that the person before us has Buddha nature.

In Buddhism, there is a bodhisattva named Never Disparaging. This bodhisattva told everyone he met that he would never disparage them, because he saw in each person a future buddha. Some individuals reacted negatively to his saying this, and assumed that Never Disparaging was poking fun at them. He wasn't. And as he persisted, people began to understand the value of this point of view. To love someone therapeutically is to love them with awareness of the wisdom and potential wisdom present in that person, despite whatever error is present now. Every day, I hear statements from my patients that teach me, and I remember that therapists have no monopoly on helpful insight. In fact, it may be far more important for us to nourish the wisdom in the patient than to try to give them our own.

Compassion is the desire to end another's suffering. It too is composed of a substance called understanding, for when we understand, we of course want to help relieve the suffering of the other person. Both love and compassion must be tempered by equanimity. That is, we must know that we cannot change reality for this person, or preclude the sometimes painful process of learning that he must undergo. Patience and acceptance are our greatest allies, so that we do not push too soon for change that the person is not yet ready for or capable of. Equanimity is essential to healing. Without equanimity, we easily become frustrated, and our love and compassion are transformed into anger.

I mentioned that we therapists can be like the man who was unaware of the precious gems in his own coat. We are suspicious of words like love, compassion, and wisdom. They have an old-fashioned ring to them. They sound more like words to hear from the pulpit than words to encounter in a book about psychotherapy.

This reaction may be based more on conditioning than substance. Yet I think that we could do much to help our clients, and our profession, if we could heal and reinvigorate these terms. It may be the case that part of our reluctance is that we want to offer something *real,* something based on hard evidence, on fact. We may want, like the physician, to offer something real and substantive, something equivalent to a shot or a pill. And words like love and compassion and wisdom may seem to reek of soft and muddled thinking.

Our understanding of these terms need not be muddled, however. While our English word "love" is complicated by its many meanings, the (Sanskrit) word Buddhists use *(metta)* is not muddled at all, but something very clear. It means the intention or wish for the object of our love to be happy. Sometimes it is translated as loving-kindness, to distinguish it from romantic attachments and other kinds of love. Likewise, the Buddhist word for compassion *(karuna)* means a clear intention or wish to help relieve the suffering of another person. The practice of compassion inevitably involves the practice of wisdom at the same time, making us aware that many of our attempts to be helpful can fail to be so or even be destructive without deep insight into what is needed. Compassion and love, in this sense, have an emotional component, but are also something more than emotion, signifying something both practical and intentional.

It only takes a moment's reflection to see that a therapist without love and compassion, as defined here, will not be a very good therapist. Who would want to see a psychotherapist that lacked these critical qualities? These, rather than injections or pills, are the stuff by which our therapeutic efforts stand or fall. The mindful therapist always remembers that when a patient comes in whose life is falling apart because of a crippling depression, it is not "just another case of depression" to the patient. To her, it is her *very world* that is falling apart.

Our job, however, is not so much to *teach* the value of love and compassion to our patients (though there is a role even for that, as I will discuss presently) as it is to administer and embody them. Clearly, we do not go about the business of helping our clients by telling them, "Your problem is that you are too greedy. You have to let go. You need to be more loving." This analysis may be correct, but it is not skillful. And in Buddhism, as in psychotherapy, it is important to be skillful. Right intention is not enough. To simply talk about love and compassion would be like a physician talking about an injection rather than administering one.

In the Sutra of One Hundred Parables, there is a story about a man who is ill. In one version of the story, the doctor tells him only pheasant can cure him. So the patient begins to repeat the word *pheasant* over and over. He doesn't feel any better though. A friend comes and sees his error. He draws him a picture of a pheasant, and tells him this is what he needs. So the poor man eats the drawing, and when he feels no better, hires an artist to make him many such drawings. But no matter how many drawings he eats, he still does not improve. Finally, the doctor comes by, and has compassion on the man in his mistaken approach. He takes him to the market, where they buy a pair of pheasants, bring them home and cook them for dinner. Then the patient improves.[42] Our patients do not need us to talk about love and kindness as much as they need us to administer them.

ADMINISTERING LOVE AND COMPASSION

How then, can we cultivate loving-kindness in ourselves, and learn to administer it more effectively, more skillfully?

To embody love and compassion, it is first of all important to exercise these capacities toward ourselves. Therefore, all the strategies for taking care of ourselves discussed in earlier chapters are not at all incidental to our work as therapists, but are in fact crucial. The more loving-kindness we have toward ourselves, the more we have to give to others. The more compassion we have for ourselves, the more we have to give away. For love and compassion are one capacity, and it is simply not the case that we have specific capacities of love and compassion for ourselves separate from love and compassion for others.

The way to keep our intention to be loving and compassionate alive is to practice understanding. Love and compassion are made of understanding and rooted in understanding. As irritation arises in us, we can begin by practicing love and compassion toward ourselves. *Poor me. Here I am, wanting to be a loving person, but feeling irritated. I suffer with this feeling, and then suffer more because I try to resist having it.* In other words, we begin by giving understanding to ourselves. Understanding, as a more cognitive element, is something that we can practice. And then, likewise, we can administer the same remedy regarding the other person. Seeing more deeply, more mindfully, we know that the other person must have pain and suffering in her. The clerk in the store who was ill-tempered with us may be suffering from a recent loss; the person who cut us off on the road may be deeply depressed and facing many difficulties. People do not act this way unless they are suffering. When patients create suffering in you as a therapist, what the psychoanalysts call countertransference or projective identification, it is because there is suffering in them. For people who are happy, joyful, and at peace do not cause suffering in others: people who have pain and suffering in them do. When we realize that this is the case, we become full of understanding.

These are the factors that Carl Rogers clarified so well as accurate empathy. While we cannot force ourselves to agree with our clients or manufacture warm feelings toward them, when we *understand* them deeply, and see them as full of suffering—when we see it from their point of view even if we know that it contains a lot of error, even if we disagree with them—love and compassion, unconditional positive regard and empathy, are already present.[43] We don't need to force ourselves to feel something we do not feel. We simply need to cultivate understanding, which is the same thing as mindfulness. In fact, we could simplify even further and say that, instead of needing two things, one called love and one called compassion, all we need is mindfulness. Mindfulness, applied to human beings, can engender the willingness to understand. We practice understanding toward ourselves when our patients, as people in pain, are not always pleasant to be with, and may trigger pain in us. We practice understanding toward our patients, and not only does this help them, but it at the same time protects us, so that we suffer less even during difficult sessions, and can continue to be present with them.

Perhaps you've had similar experiences: When I meet people and they learn that I am a psychologist, some people get nervous, as though I had the power to read their mind and already knew a lot of things about them they would rather I didn't know. Others open up, and begin to tell me a lot about their suffering and their difficulties—sometimes inappropriately so. But others want to know why in the world someone would want to do what I do: *Doesn't it bother you when you are with someone who is in a lot of pain, and who sometimes, because of it, is not very pleasant? Don't you worry about them, and take this pain with you even when you leave the office?*

Some therapists may in fact become preoccupied with their patients and worry too much about them, or carry painful feelings into the rest of their lives to a problematic degree. These need to cultivate equanimity, and greater trust in the human capacity to find one's own way. Other therapists, however, claim they *never* think about patients outside of therapy. If that is not just overstatement, it seems to me to be a problem in its own right. If therapy is a real human encounter, *of course* you will think about your patients from time to time. I will sometimes have an insight about a patient while I am walking or making coffee or showering, or find insight about them in a dream. The boundary between patient and therapist must be neither too permeable nor too rigid.

Love and compassion are what allow us to find the balance between obsession and indifference. If I do not have enough love and compassion in me, I will suffer doing the work that I do. I will experience my patients with irritation and frustration. Therefore, to be able to do this work and not suffer too much, I must cultivate love and compassion in myself. The very thing which provides the healing to the patient protects me as well.

How fortunate we are to have work that involves the practice of love and compassion! How different it is, for example, from the commodities broker on the floor of the exchange, a phone in each ear, yelling and gesticulating, face contorted with stress. People who work in difficult jobs involving aggressive competition during the day will be more exhausted by it than a therapist who cultivates love and compassion by means of understanding toward herself and her patients all day long.

The insight of the three poisons and their antidotes is familiar. Yet just because of this familiarity, we must take care not to discount it. In fact, one cannot overestimate its importance. The important thing is to embody love and compassion through the vehicle of understanding. This is a very direct treatment. And at times, we can also teach this to appropriate patients.

THE ANTIDOTE OF WISDOM

Wisdom is not only a matter of deep spiritual insight, but also practical. Often our patients need the latter more than the former. They have some mistaken ideas about how the world works—ideas which are reasonably easy to see from the outside—and they require information about this. So while it is important for us to embody wisdom of both kinds as best we can, and while the emphasis in therapy remains on this embodiment, there is a also a place for giving hints and suggestions, for imparting wisdom, including discussing the way the world works. Indeed, how could we be loving and compassionate if we withheld what we know about this?

In certain Buddhist traditions, a person must ask three times before the teacher accepts someone as a student or answers a question. This is a very telling ritual, and far from a mere formality. It reminds us that we should not be too ready to speak to those unprepared for the answers, and that a person must be serious about wanting to know before they will be ready to listen to answers.

In the New Testament, we find a similar sentiment expressed when Christ tells his disciples not to cast pearls before swine. Since we presumably do not like to think of our patients as "swine," this is to be understood as a dramatic way of talking. Functionally speaking, "swine" here means those who are unprepared to receive a teaching. Not casting our pearls before swine means not answering people who are not ready to receive. This protects us from feeling unvalued, and increases the perceived value of whatever we do offer. Interpreting and advising are gifts, and gifts must not be overdone or they become devalued and inflationary.

Though I would not apply this rigidly in psychotherapy, it might be a helpful to consider letting a person ask for a solution to their difficulties a couple of times before providing whatever answer or partial answer we may have to offer. A patient of mine recently discussed an expensive trip he was considering, and asked me whether I thought he should do it. I told him, I really did not know. I was not being evasive: I genuinely did not know. I reflected back to him that I saw him light up when he spoke about this trip, but that he knew much more about his overall life situation than I did, so only he could tell how this piece fit in with everything else, including his financial needs.

Sometimes I have an opinion about what a patient should do. Yet even in this case, I think it is important I do not respond hastily. For one thing, my opinion might be wrong. For another, even if it is right, if I offer it prematurely it might as well be wrong. So instead of answering immediately I might respond the first time with a reflection: "You really want to know what to do about this." Then I might ask what they have thought of or tried already. This not only functions like the reluctant teacher above, but also avoids some pitfalls. Otherwise, when you give your advice, you may get in reply, "Oh, I already tried that. It didn't work." It is also fascinating how many patients stop asking for an answer and begin to process answers of their own when not given one, perhaps realizing that the best answers could only really be found by themselves. But when a patient seems ready, I will offer what insight I have, though the patient will often come up with the best answers.

I mentioned above that I genuinely did not know what the answer was to my patient's question about the trip. An attitude of *not knowing* is, I believe, extremely valuable for the mindful therapist, as it is in Buddhist practice. When you think you know, you stop being open. Not knowing helps us not only avoid offering premature advice, but also helps us remain open to the patient before us, seeing this person as a unique individual in a unique situation rather than another "case" of depression, or anxiety, or marital difficulties. Not knowing, while the opposite attitude from what we learned in our education, is our best friend in the therapy room. The wise therapist respects not knowing, is comfortable with it, and even cultivates it. We cannot understand if we think we already know. And to know you don't know, taught Confucius, is the beginning of knowing.[44]

You might like to try actively reminding yourself before a session, "I do not really know what this person needs. Let me just be calm, and see what the psyche (or the universe, or reality, etc.) is up to here." Often when we can do this, patients come up with much better answers than we could have, and, more importantly, learn to connect with their own internal wisdom.

Yet, with these caveats in mind, there may be a time to offer insight, and even to talk a little about love and compassion. Since the focus in therapy is the well-being of the patient, I couch this teaching in those terms, emphasizing that the first thing about love and compassion is that they are good for the one who gives them. As the antidote to harmful feelings of deprivation (a therapeutic reframe for "greed") or anger (hatred), they can immediately cool the flames within us. With some patients, I may mention, depending on their spiritual framework, the experience of the Dalai Lama, whom many see as an extremely kind and compassionate person, who has said that he always feels he is the main beneficiary of his practice of kindness and compassion, and that only secondarily does it spill over to the other person. In other words, in a prepared patient, you may be able to offer in some form the insight that the loving, compassionate person *suffers less*.

EXERCISES

These practices may be helpful to both you and your patients.

Young Child Meditation

Buddhist teaching promises the following benefits from having greater love and compassion: (1) we sleep better, (2) upon waking we feel well and light in heart, (3) we do not have nightmares, (4) we are liked by many people and at ease with everyone, (5) we become dear to nonhuman species both visible and invisible, (6) we are supported by gods and goddesses, (7) we are protected from dangers, (8) we reach meditative concentration easily, (9) our face becomes bright and clear, (10) our minds are clear at the time of death, and (11) we are reborn in the Brahma Heaven, where we can continue the practice.[45] The Bible teaches to love neighbor as self, and Buddhist meditations regarding love traditionally begin with oneself. The Buddha taught that there is no one more worthy of love in the whole universe than oneself.[46] So cultivating love toward oneself is often a good place to start, and often easier to do than cultivating love for another person. Beginning with love of oneself, we can gently expand to include others.

In the West, we sometimes encounter a unique difficulty with this approach. Here, there are many people, including some of our patients, who find it difficult to love themselves or who even hate themselves. One way around this is to ask the patient whom she really does love, whom she can easily summon up loving feelings toward. It may be a child, a partner, or even a pet. With such people, I suggest they start there, and when they can do this successfully, only then cultivate love toward themselves.

Thich Nhat Hanh suggests that you meditate on yourself as a five-year-old child—so precious, so beautiful, but also so vulnerable, capable of being hurt by a harsh look or a single unkind or thoughtless word. Reflect on your life as a small child, on how your very tender feelings were often hurt or disappointed, how sometimes, even if you were very fortunate and had very loving parents, they did not understand what you needed, how other children could be cruel, how scary it was to start school, and to gradually learn the painful lesson that you were not always the most popular, athletic, or academically gifted. To make this concrete, you can meditate with a photograph from that time, if one is available. In this practice, you can begin by meditating on yourself like this for a period of time, until you feel a changed attitude toward yourself, a deeper love and an understanding of how your needs for love went unfulfilled by the people around you.

The second part of this practice is to meditate on another person. Thich Nhat Hanh recommends we do this with our parents, seeing our mother and father as young children, equally beautiful and equally vulnerable. But it also helps to do this with other people in our lives, such as our partners, friends, coworkers, or someone with whom we are having difficulty. Therapists may like to try this practice for a client, perhaps especially one that is difficult in some way. Continue for a meditation period or a number of meditation periods until you feel a change in your attitude toward the other person.

Defusing Anger

When anger arises, picture where you and the person you are angry at will be in 100 years or longer. Perhaps your flesh will have rotted away, and only the bones will remain. Maybe they are scattered about. Maybe they are already dust, and have already blown away. When you realize the impermanence of both yourself and the person you are angry at, you may find it is possible to let go of your anger, to see that both of you are precious and temporary manifestations of the ground of being, that what you are angry about is in fact small compared to this realization.

Like all such practices, it will be effective in proportion to the depth and clarity of your envisioning. So continue this visualization long enough and deep enough that you begin to feel your anger blowing away with the skeletal dust.

CHAPTER SIX
Look Deeply at the Nature of Reality:
The Three Dharma Seals

*Mankind are nothing but a bundle or collection of different
perceptions, which succeed each other with an inconceivable
rapidity and are in perpetual flux and movement.*[47]
—DAVID HUME

THE PURPOSE OF PSYCHOTHERAPY is the transformation
of suffering. It is the same purpose that the Buddha had in
seeking liberation for himself and others. After all, if one is liberated, one is liberated from something. And that something, for
the Buddha, was suffering or dukkha. At the end of his life, the
Buddha maintained that he had taught nothing but suffering and
the end of suffering. The Buddha is thus our elder brother in the
business of transforming suffering. In our time, we could imagine he might as easily have been a psychotherapist as a spiritual
teacher, and we can view him from our vantage point as either of
these. But however we view him, his insights have a lot to teach
us, and nothing can be more urgent for us than to try to understand them.

The traditional story of the Buddha's early life may be somewhat stylized, but no doubt it contains a distillation of much of the essential truth. The young prince Siddhartha Gautama grew up in the lap of luxury. Like many of us in the industrialized Western world of today, he was protected from many of the harsh realities of life. When he journeyed out into the world he encountered for the first time an old person, a sick person, and a dead person. He was shaken. He suffered what we might call today an existential crisis, his mind reeling to comprehend the awful reality of these stark facts of human existence. For the dilemma of human life is precisely that we are life aware of itself, and therefore, aware of our mortality. By virtue of our awareness, we transcend to some degree the limitations of our human, mortal condition, while still being caught in it nonetheless. It was this very dilemma that motivated Gautama's quest.

On his fourth journey from his palace out into the world, the Buddha encountered a *sadhu*—a holy man, an ascetic, a person dedicated to spiritual enlightenment. He saw in this person the potential answer to the dilemma of sickness, old age, and death. He vowed to become such a person himself—and left his family, his palace, and his comfortable life to live in the forest and seek a solution. One day, after years of mastering various spiritual disciplines and seeing their limitations, he sat beneath the bodhi tree, and as the sutras tell us, the universe shook at its foundations as he realized the answer to his questions. He became the Buddha, one who is awake, an enlightened person.[48]

Just what kind of answer was it? What insight did the Buddha experience in his breakthrough to enlightenment? Whatever it was, it satisfied his need to understand old age, disease, and death. Not just a temporary inspiration, it resulted in a way for him to live his entire life in psychological balance and equilibrium. It was an insight profound enough to draw others to him in large numbers. That his experience was an intuitive grasping of the nature of reality and of human life with his whole being is clear from the way he spoke and taught. Since he always stressed that there was nothing particularly sacrosanct about himself or the way he clothed his insight in words, when we approach Buddhist teachings, our job is to listen *behind* the words for the reality they point to, and not get fascinated with the categories and concepts, a little like listening to the reality of pain behind a patient's denial.

Knowing the difficulties of trying to express his insight in words, at first the Buddha was uncertain whether to try to explain it to anyone. He knew very well that words alone could never convey what he had come to know and understand, and that in fact, people would distort his teaching, seeing in it what they already believed or feared, enshrining the words themselves, or debating about them, rather than looking at the reality to which they point. He would later say that hearing the Dharma—his teachings—was like picking up a snake, requiring great care lest one be worse off, in the end, than one was at the start.[49]

But ultimately he decided that sharing his insight might do, overall, more good than harm.

The words he chose are daring, provocative words, words that are designed to break up one's normal way of seeing the world. They are not a philosophy per se nor a religion per se. To treat them as a philosophy or a religion tames and domesticates them, makes them into something to venerate or debate. The teachings are fresh, wild, radical, even iconoclastic. They are nothing less than a way of seeing that leads out of suffering. That is the reason he spoke them in the first place—the only reason.

The Buddha lived a long and fruitful life as a teacher, and thus had the opportunity to express his truth in many different ways, in accord with the situation and the need of his listeners. But for many Buddhists, the "three dharma seals" contain a vital essence of what the Buddha wanted us to understand—so much so that teachings which do not contain these three elements are not considered true teachings of the Buddha. These three elements, as presented in the teaching of Thich Nhat Hahn, are impermanence, non-self, and nirvana.[50]

IMPERMANENCE

The Buddha is of course not alone in having observed the impermanent nature of all phenomena. The pre-Socratic Greek philosophers concerned themselves largely with determining what the basic stuff or material of the universe is. And whereas some said it was fire or water or earth or air, Heraclitus famously observed that "everything flows," or as we might put it, that the basic stuff of the universe is this flowing and changing. The ancient Chinese sage Kung-tzu, whom we commonly call by his romanized name, Confucius, made the same observation. One day as he crossed a bridge over a flowing stream, he said, "Flowing like this day and night." Intriguingly, these other thinkers lived in roughly the same era as the Buddha.

In the teachings of the Buddha, we see this uncomfortable fact of transience laid down as the cornerstone of a whole way of life geared toward the cessation of suffering. The genius of the Buddha was in seeing that the way out of suffering lay in seeing it all the way through, in looking directly into the face of reality. And what he discovered is that when you do so, contrary to what one might expect, the painful facts of reality become the very door of liberation.

What the Buddha understood is that we do not suffer because everything is impermanent; rather, we suffer because we *resist* this fact, because we delude ourselves into believing that everything is, or should be, permanent. And therefore we are continually shocked by it. We of course recognize with some acceptance that *other* people, and the things *other* people cherish, are impermanent. So when an eighty-five-year-old person dies, we console ourselves that he at least lived a long, full life. But when it comes to *ourselves* and the things and people in our own lives that we cherish dearly, when it comes to all we rely upon for comfort and support, we are always shocked at these losses. It is as though, deep down, we expect that somehow we ourselves will be given a free pass. Even though we know that everyone who has ever lived has died, we have an unexamined, deep belief that somehow or other we will be the first ones not to.

But impermanence is not necessarily a negative reality. It is simply what is. It has positive as well as negative aspects. Without impermanence, our suffering would have no ending. Pain would continue forever. Tyrants would rule for eternity. Our children would never grow and mature. Any task undertaken would go on forever without end. The barking dog would never stop.

We like impermanence with regard to certain things but rail against it with regard to others. And it is this very picking and choosing that creates our difficulties. Our real choice is not whether we will have to face impermanence—it's inescapable— but whether we will come to terms with it. Reality does not change at our convenience. But if we fail to live in harmony with reality, we simply suffer more. We may act as though there were something noble in resisting going gentle into that good night, but resist or not, go we will. Freedom lies in the radical acceptance of the nature of things.

As a mere philosophy, our reaction to the teaching of impermanence may be, "Oh yes, of course, I see that. So what?" And then we go about our business. But the Buddha invites us to look deeply into the nature of impermanence, into the heart of darkness itself as it may seem, to reflect on it, to live with it, to befriend it, to note the impermanent nature of everything and everyone we encounter in daily life, seeing the impermanence of things in meditation and in life over and over again until the mind becomes accustomed to it and stops fighting against it. When this happens, contrary to what you might expect, one achieves a state of deep peace, acceptance, and joy.

From a medical mental health perspective, the people we work with are sick. If they have, for example, an unusual degree of sadness, and if that persists over a longer than expected period of time, we diagnose them as depressed, as though something were wrong with them. But some people are depressed because they actually sense the nature of reality a little more deeply than many who seem adjusted to our impermanence-denying culture. They have seen into the nature of reality more than others, but have not seen it *all the way through*. They have not seen it with calmness, clarity, and acceptance. In the language of transpersonal psychology, these people may be better thought of as in a condition of spiritual emergency rather than a clinical crisis in the usual sense. Some of the people who see a little more deeply, and are disturbed by their vision, become celebrated writers and artists. But many seemingly ordinary individuals have caught a glimpse of the true nature of things also, and are reeling just as much. But lacking an artistic mode of expression to help them find release, they are left in the thick of the basic human dilemma with no known way out.

From the perspective of adjustment not just to culture but to the nature of reality, some people suffer because they are more perspicacious than others rather than less so. With such individuals, it is a profound mistake to merely treat them as sick and help them adjust to a culture that is sick. For there is a razor's edge between despair and enlightenment. Seeing impermanence with resistance is darkness and depression; seeing it with acceptance is joy and peace.

Knowing this can help us see our patients in a new light, less as sick, and more for what they are—buddhas and bodhisattvas to be. It teaches us that merely to help them adjust to a sick culture and send them back out into it is at best insufficient and at worst even harmful, and that our job, at least with those who are prepared for it, may be the deeper task of helping them see their despair-inducing insight all the way through to some degree of peace and wisdom.

This is where the goals of the mindful therapist and the goals of traditional psychotherapy part ways. Traditional psychotherapists have the more limited goal of adjustment. They help make patients more functional in the patient's cultural context, no matter what that may be. The mindful therapist clearly has a larger goal than that—to harmonize the person's essential being with the essential nature of reality. To some extent, every therapist must be aware of these issues. But since we are not yet buddhas ourselves, we may easily underestimate how sick our own culture really is. The Buddha gave us his perspective on this when he said bluntly, "All worldlings are deranged."[51] If we are to re-envision our work as therapists in the context of healers, shamans, and gurus, then it requires at least some sense that this may in fact be so.

The basic fact, then, is that when the impermanent nature of all phenomena is seen deeply and all the way through, with acceptance rather than resistance, there is nothing but joy. There is nothing to get upset about. Our true job, if we can say we have one, is to enjoy the swirling dance of life, and dance along with it joyfully. And we come to this point through mindfulness, by mindfully observing again and again and yet again that when we take the opposite tack and try to resist impermanence, we only create suffering.

It is like the fabled flower that blooms only briefly one night every hundred years. Taken superficially, it might lead to indifference or despair: Why should I care about a flower I may never even get to see? Taken deeply, however, we will know that, when that flower blooms, it is even more precious for its impermanence, for the brevity of its manifestation. When we live with deep insight into impermanence, we can learn to experience each moment, each person, each experience as precious.

NO-SELF

Even if you picked up this book just a moment ago, and began reading at this very sentence, you are not the same person you were when you started reading it. By tracking my words, the color of your thought is a little bit different, to name the most obvious thing. But your body is different too. You have exchanged gas molecules with the environment around you. Cells are in this very moment coming into being, while others are dying. Your emotions, too, change subtly from moment to moment, even if your overall mood seems more or less the same.

When Buddhists speak of no-self, this is what they mean. When you are look deeply into the river of yourself, there is nothing to hold on to, nothing permanent and unchanging. Your body, your feelings, your thoughts, your perceptions—all are flowing and changing from moment to moment. What you really are is a part of the whole cosmos, deeply interconnected with all that is. You are that flowing reality. You are life without boundaries. And just as you do not feel inclined to be sad and hold a funeral when one of your cells dies, so, at the macro level, we can learn to see things the same way. To understand this is to eliminate fear.

No-self does not mean that you are not real, but rather, that what you are is something quite different from what you think you are. We normally think of ourselves as some sort of underlying, unchanging entity that moves through space and time, accumulating different experiences, but remaining somehow the same. But Buddhist teaching invites you to reflect on what exactly this unchanging something is. And indeed, once you begin to look, you will not find anything solid there to hold on to that you can call a self.

Once when I presented this idea to a group of psychologists, one of them responded that the self is that which is doing the observing.

And this is a good insight. However, one must ask, what happens when we stop observing? Does this observer self then cease to exist? If the self is something that comes into and out of existence, then it is something quite different than what we normally assume when we talk about self. It is something more like a process—which is once again the point the Buddha is making.

Here again, the Buddha offers us an uncomfortable insight, and one that we may want to resist. It is really the same insight as impermanence, only in this case, it is impermanence with regard to the self. Since everything changes, including ourselves, what is it that we mean by "self"? Yet here too, as with the idea of impermanence in general, this seemingly difficult teaching is an invitation to see reality in a different way, to realize that the universe is something quite different, and we ourselves are something quite different, from what we normally assume. When you realize the truth of no-self, you can relax in a new way. What is there to hold on to so tightly, to defend so anxiously? What is there to worry about? We are this flowing and changing. Why should we upset ourselves about anything?

We can try to resist this flowing and changing, but we will not succeed. We will not succeed because this is the nature of what is real, and what is real always wins out over fantasy. And while it sounds frightening, once we accustom ourselves to this reality, paradoxically, we can relax and enjoy what human life offers us. In fact, it only then becomes possible to really enjoy life, for only then do we stop fighting and defending and struggling and worrying, only then can we be sufficiently open and calm and clear to appreciate the wonder of the nature of things.

Imagine two people sitting by a river, watching it flow. One sits contentedly, watching, listening, enjoying the flowing of the river. The other struggles against it. He wishes the river would stop all this flowing and changing. He becomes frustrated, angry, and upset. None of this, however, changes the river.

In fact, the image of the river can give us another way of looking at no-self. We may call a river the Rio Grande or the Mississippi, and think of it as the same river from day to day. But when we look into this idea, we know that the river is never the same. The molecules of water in it are constantly changing. One day, the river may be quite low; another time, it may flood its banks. Over longer courses of time, even the location of the riverbed changes. Eventually, rivers may disappear altogether. So just what is it that we are calling the Rio Grande or the Mississippi?

You are the river. The molecules in your body are completely different than the ones in your body ten years ago or so. You think very differently than you did when you were a child. So what is it that you are calling Tom, or Jane, or Sally?

Changing perspectives, consider this: Under different circumstances, making different kinds of observations, physicists can describe light as either waves or particles. Looked at from a certain perspective, light seems to be something solid—particles called photons. Looked at another way, they seem to be an activity—a wave. Are photons waves or particles, a solid something, or an activity? To say it another way: Are the basic elements of the universe nouns or verbs? Perhaps these elements are really neither waves nor particles, but something like both at the same time, and depending on the question being asked, they will appear more like one or more like the other.

All other forms of spirituality besides Buddhist spirituality are noun/particle forms of spirituality rather than wave/process forms of spirituality. That is, in many religions you talk about entities: God, spirit, soul, and so on. But Buddhist teaching brings out a different aspect. Buddhism emphasizes the process or wave aspect of reality. It brings out the truth that there are no fixed, unchanging entities, including an entity called self, but that what there really is is a kind of activity, a swirling river of flow and change.

The nature of the basic parts of reality may be something that is neither wave nor particle, or both wave and particle, depending on our point of view. But if you want to understand the nature of things, it is helpful to know this. It is helpful to know that reality may be described as a process. Being open to seeing things this way reveals unique aspects of the nature of things. It can be a stretch for those of us who are used to entity spirituality to see things from this point of view, and to do so without making the mistake of elevating no-self to any kind of rigid dogma in place of entity thinking. But to be honest, let's admit that there is something about no-self that causes us to recoil. We have an idea that a self exists. We seem real enough to ourselves. We have a deeply ingrained habit of viewing life as the dramatic involvement of ourselves, the protagonist, getting entangled with other characters, confronting obstacles and difficulties, but always remaining, somehow, the same "I." It is difficult—even frightening—to let go of seeing things in this familiar, comfortable way. But when we examine it closely, what we call a self is a thought. And like other thoughts, it comes and goes.

None of this actually means that you are *not* real. You are not an illusion in that sense. When you stub your toe, there is a real experience of pain. Only, when we know that we are more than this idea of ours of being a permanent and unchanging self, when we know that we are, in a sense, the whole thing, we can experience the pain with a different attitude. The concept of no-self is not a nihilistc teaching. It is not a new concept to clutch and defend. It is an anti-concept to inoculate us against concepts in general. It is a way of seeing.

Rather than meaning that you are nothing, no-self means instead that you are *no thing*. You are not an object of some kind. You are a process. When we look at a table, we know that what we are seeing is nothing so solid as what we imagine. Ultimately it is composed of molecules in motion. What we call table is really a name for a process that we cannot see clearly enough, because it is too small and too quick for our eyes. Looking at the table at the subatomic level, we know that it is really mostly space. The solid matter of the atom—if we can speak of it that way for a moment—is, relatively speaking, the size of a baseball in Yankee Stadium. What we are really seeing is the process of molecules and sub-atomic particles interacting. Yet this fact does not scare us. We know that we can still place the process called "cup of coffee" onto the process called "wooden table," and our coffee will not be spilled. Although our habitual way of seeing is not ultimately correct, it does have a certain practical utility.

Having an idea of self is like that. It is a kind of convenient fiction. It just happens to also be the case that this convenient fiction is the source of a lot of suffering. And this suffering becomes a process of its own. Like the process of inertial action that causes objects to remain at rest or keep moving in the same direction unless they encounter an opposing force, the process of suffering tends to continue on and on, unless we bring a different kind of awareness to it, unless we bring mindfulness to it.

We do not have to continue today on the path of suffering we were on yesterday. We are free to start again. We do not have to lug all that heavy baggage, all that habit and conditioning along with us. In this very moment, we can start fresh. We can step into the reality of our Buddha nature. When we sit down with a patient, while we do not forget what we knew about that person from our prior meeting, we do not have to keep that person trapped in a set of expectations from that meeting, or from his diagnostic label. We know the force of habit may be very strong, but we also know it is quite possible for this person to become much more free and happy.

For if what we are is not some unchanging substance, but the process itself—if, as Buddhism also teaches, the part contains the whole as the whole contains the part, than what you really are is *the whole thing,* the flowing and changing and evolving universe itself. And thus ideas of alienation and separation are fundamentally erroneous, a basic misunderstanding of the nature of reality. We are not some separate little fragment, lost and adrift in a hostile universe. We are *It.*

Now this kind of thinking, when attached to so poor and transient a vessel as a human being, is prone to obvious dangers of self-inflation and grandiosity. And for this reason, some spiritual traditions steer away from the boldness of such a statement. But properly understood, this is really the same as no-self.

Deciding between noun/particle spirituality and activity/wave spirituality is determined by the nature of the question one is asking and what kind of medicine is needed. Both the teaching of no-self, and the teaching that the part is the whole, are in themselves concepts, words. These words are there to point us in the direction of reality—not to replace reality. And sometimes, one of these concepts will be more useful than the other.

Janice is a needy, dependent individual. She has no difficulty attracting partners but she has a great deal of difficulty keeping them. Once she is in a relationship, she does not allow her partner any space. Whenever her partner goes to work, or wants to be with friends, or wants to do anything at all apart from Janice, Janice becomes afraid. She feels rejected, and her pain is so great that she can launch herself into a deep depression lasting days simply because her partner had lunch with a friend.

This has set up a repeating pattern in her life, in which she attracts men, gets involved with them, but suffocates them to the point that the relationship has another explosive, angry ending. And her view that she is always rejected and abandoned is then reconfirmed. At that point, she feels all alone and depressed, and suffers terribly until she meets the next man, whereupon the cycle begins again. Something similar happened in therapy with me when I held her accountable for missed appointments after this had occurred several times. Unable to deal with the feelings of rejection this engendered, she devalued our work and stopped coming to therapy, triggering in myself a taste of her own painful experience.

Traditional psychology might say that Janice lacked a "sense of self." But one could also say that Janice was caught in a self, in viewing everything in terms of herself as an unchanging entity that needs and needs and wants and wants, rather as an interrelated part of the activity of the universe. She believed that her happiness had to come in a certain form—in the form of a partner who would be there for her always.

I never spoke to Janice about no-self and impermanence. I doubt she would have found this teaching very compassionate regarding her pain. Instead, out of a no-self and impermanence viewpoint, I simply gave her understanding and empathy, and called attention to her own experiencing, to the process that she called herself. When she talked about being too clinging, this insight only gave her another reason to be depressed, and the net result was no change in her behavior. I called her attention, therefore, to process, to the what of her experience.

I pointed to the times when she was actively engaged with her own life and interests, and contrasted this with the pain she felt when her partner was away or when she had no partner. I told her that "not being clinging" was not a useful concept because there was no way to change that. "Clinging" was just something she was, or something she has, like a disease. (This is related to the poison of greed, which all of us are subject to.) "Clinging" does not provide a way out. What provides a way out is paying attention to her own experience, noting that she is happier when she gets involved with her own interests and follows up on these, and that this myth of happiness coming through a partner only continued to cause her pain, even though she understood through our work how this had originated in her childhood experiences.

Janice had made progress by the time she left therapy, despite her devaluing, angry statements. My job was not to get hooked into the drama and play the expected counter role, the role that complements hers, by seeking after her to come back. Instead, I communicated that if she wanted to come back at some point, she was welcome.

Since Janice left therapy so abruptly, I could easily have become trapped in the view that her case was a failure. One could argue it either way, however. While she made devaluing statements at the end, there were many indicators that she was doing better. So I could also trap myself into a defensive point of view, arguing that she had indeed been helped. The truth is, as in many situations we face as therapists, one simply cannot say for sure. But this not knowing comes with the nature of our work.

If clinging to self is bad, then clinging to no-self is even worse. Clinging to no-self brings the danger of darkness, nihilism, and despair. It also involves a certain kind of mental rigidity. People who cling to no-self become allergic to using the word *self*. They reprimand other Buddhists who use the word as though they had committed some deep dogmatic error.

In truth, you can use the word *self* quite freely. I certainly do in the process of psychotherapy, talking to clients about caring for themselves, loving themselves, freeing themselves, becoming an individuated self, and the like. The use of language in Buddhism has the same intention as the use of language in psychotherapy. Unlike language in an academic context, the correct use of language in psychotherapeutic and spiritual contexts is to evoke healing and transformation. You do not somehow get extra points for being more precise or more technically correct, particularly if this only confuses your patient.

Please do not hesitate to use the language of self when that is expedient. Like the Buddha, be pragmatic. When the language of self makes the point, use it. And when the language of no-self makes the point, then use that.

NIRVANA

Some scholars explain that the word nirvana comes from a root meaning to extinguish or blow out. This has been interpreted in many ways, but the interpretation I like best is that nirvana is the extinguishing of concepts. When we no longer see reality through concepts, it reveals itself for what it is: wonderful.

Recently, as I walked around my neighborhood in the morning, enjoying the trees, enjoying the many plants and flowers my neighbors have planted and cared for, I also noticed lots of weeds. In New Mexico, we have many incredibly resilient species of weed, one dramatic version of which is the tumbleweed. These weeds are survivors, able to thrive without human care in the harsh desert environment. Anyone who gardens here knows that there are the early spring weeds, the late spring weeds, the early summer weeds, and so on, and can watch them come along in waves as the warm weather weeks roll by. As a gardener, there is a tendency for me to see weeds as the enemy of my precious tomato plants and lettuce. But this particular morning I saw a tall weed backlit by the rising sun. *And I saw that it was beautiful.* I realized I have a wrong perception, dividing up the world into "plants" and "weeds," the one being liked and desired, the weed being a hated enemy. And now I can often appreciate the "weeds" as well as the "plants" on my walk.

Of course, the idea that "weed" is simply a concept that arbitrarily divides different plants is not a new one. What makes an experience an opening into the extinguishing of concepts is that it is experienced rather than merely understood intellectually. Intellectual understanding is important as a first step, and is not to be denigrated: but a true opening is a matter of changed perception.

But just because we can see the world in this way, does not mean that we lose the faculty of discrimination. I still know that some plants that I see are what people call *weeds,* and others are what people call *plants.* But I can see a little bit more clearly, a little more free of concepts. I am just a little bit more like the child who really sees the ball rolling, rather than the adult who merely confirms knowledge that of course balls roll.

Having reified concepts in general, and having a reified concept of self in particular, is what most interferes with the clear, joyful perception of being that is nirvana. "Everything has been nirvanized from the non-beginning," says Thich Nhat Hanh.[52] Yet spiritual teachings sometimes make the path of "unselfing," of impermanence and no-self, seem negative and painful. It is far more the case that this process is one of joy and liberation. Every step you take in the direction of impermanence and no-self is a step toward freedom, peace, and ease of well-being. Seeing this gives you the energy needed to keep on the path.

Hindu sage Ramana Maharshi says it well:

. . . [W]hen your heart has expanded so much that it embraces the whole of creation, you will certainly not feel like giving up this or that. You will simply drop off from secular life as a ripe fruit drops from the branch of a tree. You will feel that the whole world is your home.[53]

Whenever you go about making a change in your life, there will be positive and negative aspects. If you want to give up smoking cigarettes, you know that there will be times when you want a cigarette, but must nonetheless forego having one. There will be times when you will feel irritable and unhappy because your body is adjusting to the absence of nicotine and other chemicals acquired through smoking. Yet you will not be successful if you do not also envision clearly the positive aspects of making this kind of change. If you can envision yourself as having more energy and not getting out of breath, as remaining healthy and free of lung cancer, as living longer and enjoying life, both for yourself and for the sake of those who love you—if you can envision yourself as finding a new freedom from the perennial need to keep track of how many cigarettes you have left and when and where you will get your next opportunity to light up, you will have a greater chance of being successful. Envisioning yourself in a new way is a no-self/impermanence teaching in that you start to let go of the illusion that "I am a smoker" as though this were some static, unchanging, and unchangeable reality.

The world seen through self and permanence is a place of great suffering. But the world seen through nirvana is the Garden restored. Everything shines with an inner radiance. In fact, looking at everything that way, as though shining with inner light, is a wonderful way to practice nirvana. You may feel that you are just imagining it at first, but imagining is always a part of coming to a new way of seeing, in the same sense that we had to imagine going to the moon before we could get there.

I have visited the Museum of Folk Art in Santa Fe several times. And each time, I was struck by the ever-present motif of skeletons and death in Mexican folk art. This is all the more striking because Mexican culture is so full of passion and life. Similarly, many people say that the traditional culture of India is world-denying. Yet visitors there are often struck by the vibrant colors, the joyful festivals, the sense of joy in living of these so-called world-deniers. This kind of paradox should not surprise us. It is the presence of death (impermanence) that teaches us to value and celebrate life. It is our suffering that ultimately shows the way to bliss.

Practicing no-self and impermanence, you will find that every step takes you toward nirvana, toward a realm where you are completely safe, happy, and at home, a world full of buddhas and bodhisattvas, of wonderful flowers and trees and amazing animals, a world of love and peace. Precisely what makes this perception possible is that you stop clinging to what cannot be clung to. You stop trying to damn the river. You join the dance.

Impermanence in Daily Life

For several days, spend some time with a focused intention of looking at everything as flow and process. For instance, when you see a beautiful flower, know it is only the manifestation of a cycle of growth and decay. You know that the flower is a temporary configuration of molecules that is changing moment by moment. You know that the molecules are composed mostly of space. When you see a young child, see her as becoming a young woman, going through adult joys and difficulties, growing old, and one day dying. Or see an old man, and look at him so that you can see the young man in him, the boy, the infant, even his parents and ancestors. Look at your teacher, and see in her all her spiritual ancestors, perhaps all the way back to the Buddha. Familiarize your mind with this point of view, and realize it applies ultimately to yourself and other people as well. This is a practice of realizing no-self.

No-Self in Daily Life

Every time you take a breath, you can practice no-self by considering that molecules of air that a moment ago were self are no longer self, and molecules that were not self, that previously were in the atmosphere, and before that in a plant or an animal, are now "self." Every time you take a bite of food or a sip of water, every time you perspire or excrete waste, you have the same opportunity. You know that the trees are your lungs, for their work creates the oxygen you need to live. And if you know this deeply, you quite naturally wince when someone hurts a tree. You know that the happiness of others is your own happiness as well, and that by taking care of them, you at the same time care for your nonself.

In mindful therapy, when you see your patients from this point of view, you still have a realistic perception of their habits, conditioning, and personality tendencies. But you also know that they are a process of change, and that none of this need be permanent.

Impermanence and No-Self in Psychotherapy

The essence of impermanence and no-self is a shift in awareness from thing to process. This is an important practice for therapists. It is especially important, however, for relative novices, who can be caught up in judgments about themselves and their own performance, as well as evaluating their patients. Without fighting against these judgments and perceptions, merely noting them and letting them be without giving them a lot of energy, see about shifting your attention to process. What is happening now? When you shift your attention to process, a sense of self can sometimes disappear or at least weaken. To the extent this happens, you may realize that your self-consciousness is unnecessary, and find it dropping off from you like a garment when you change clothes. Or, perhaps more likely, you may find it is still there but it just ceases to matter so much.

And if this is an important way of looking for beginners, remember: we are all beginners.

Subjects for Contemplation

Spend some time breathing in and out, and contemplating the following statements, holding each gently in your awareness, without debate or analysis.

1. The more I cling to life, the more unhappy I become.
2. The more I try to defend myself, the more closed off I become.
3. The more I let go and let be, the happier I am.
4. If I let go a little, I have a little happiness and peace. If I let go a lot, I have a lot of happiness and peace.
5. The more I see myself as a separate fragment, the more anxious I become.
6. The more I live in the future, the more impatient and unhappy I become.
7. The more I dwell in the past, the more I experience sadness and regret.
8. The more I can dwell in the present moment, the more happiness I experience.
9. The more I know myself to be the ultimate reality, the more I feel at peace.
10. If I am not now living in the present moment, when shall I do so?
11. There is in fact no other moment than the present moment.

CHAPTER SEVEN
Walk the Path of Joy, Peace, and Liberation

The idea at the bottom of this ideal [of individuation] is that
right action comes from right thinking, and that there is no
cure and no improving of the world that does not begin with
the individual himself.[54]
—CARL JUNG

IMPLICIT IN EVERY DESCRIPTION of pathology is a vision
of well-being. When we diagnose patients, we imply they are
in some way out of balance, somehow outside a state of wellness.
When we diagnose someone as *depressed*, for instance, we do not
mean that a well-functioning person does not experience sadness,
but we mean something about the degree and kind of the sadness
involved, about its persistence and depth. If we diagnose someone
as having *bipolar disorder*, we mean that his mood swings exceed
what is normally expectable in a human life, which will have ups
and downs in the best of circumstances and in the most resilient
of individuals. When we speak of a relationship as *enmeshed*, on
the one hand, or as *disconnected*, on the other, we likewise have in

mind a state of relatedness to others that is in balance, that lies somewhere between all-consuming and estranged.

THE QUESTION

In this chapter, we will consider the Buddha's answer to the question of what well-being is like, and what it may mean for us as individuals and practitioners of mindful therapy. At the same time, we must remember that the Buddha's viewpoint goes beyond mental health as we normally use the term.

Before we consider the Buddha's view of well-being in detail, I invite you to conduct a thought experiment with me. Imagine if you will that you are a perfect buddha, a totally enlightened being. You abide in a state of perfect psychological equilibrium, full of peace, wisdom, kindness, compassion, and joy. It is a state independent of circumstance. You are filled with a kind of knowingness about which you can only hint to others, because it is a knowingness beyond verbal knowledge and intellectual concepts. Being compassionate, you want to help those around you who suffer. At the same time, you know that anything you say will be distorted and misused. So you hesitate to teach at all. In fact, under the circumstances, you consider remaining silent a perfectly reasonable option. Yet suppose you decide nonetheless to try to give an accounting of your new state. And suppose further, that someone asks you how to live so as to leave suffering behind as you have done, how to live a life of peace and enlightenment.

If you enter into this experiment, you quickly realize that what you say will be in continual danger of reification. Human nature being what it is, you know many will take your words literally, and become more concerned with your words than with the reality they point to. You know you can only point people in the right direction. You know that this is the most that is possible. Yet, inescapably, some will take your words too rigidly, too literally, while others will reject them altogether, and whichever of these is the case, people may even be worse off than they were before.

A humorous example of this dilemma occurs in the rock opera *Tommy*. *Tommy* is the story of a traumatized kid who becomes enlightened by playing pinball. When people gather around him, he teaches pinball as the path of enlightenment. He starts laying down rules. Pretty soon, the new religion has become the same as the old religion people had rejected, telling people what to do and what not to do. The followers rebel, repeatedly muttering, "We're not gonna take it." So in the end they are back to the beginning, without a path to follow.

A Zen koan penetrates the heart of this dilemma: A monk is hanging by his teeth from a branch high up in a tree. He cannot reach the branches above with his hands. He cannot touch the branches below with his feet. On the ground, someone asks him to tell him the highest truth of Buddhism. If he doesn't speak, he is derelict in his duty to help living beings; if he does, he may be killed. What should he do?

Suppose then, that you, a buddha, with all these misgivings, decide to teach nonetheless, and someone asks you what the good life looks like. How should we live? How can we find the peace and balance you have? And you, as the Bible puts it, open your mouth and start to teach, describing as best you can how to live so as to become liberated from suffering. What do you say?

THE BUDDHA'S ANSWER

The Buddha's answer, as we described in part in chapter four, was to begin with the most striking aspect of human existence first. He placed the greatest difficulty right at the center. He advocated looking deeply into the nature of suffering. Then, in the fourth noble truth, he describes what such a life would look like, using what is now known as the *noble eightfold path,* the path of eight limbs or practices. These are: right view, right thinking, right speech, right action, right livelihood, right mindfulness, right diligence, and right concentration.

The first and most important thing to know about this path is what the Buddha meant by the term *right.* While the Sanskrit term underlying this *(samyak)* may have something of a moral flavor to us, it is not primarily that, and certainly not moralistic. The Buddha is not trying to lay down rules or laws. He is trying to answer the question: What does the way of life look like that leads to liberation? Such an answer is not only prescriptive, but descriptive. It describes a way of life that is at the same time the thing in itself. Put another way, if you can live this way fully, then you are living the enlightened life. The eightfold path provides a map. It points the way, rather than being some sort of list of rules. *Samyak,* in other words, does not mean morally right as opposed to evil, or even correct as opposed to incorrect, but completed, perfect, effective in bringing about the end that is sought, the termination of suffering and sorrow. This is in fact the same concept found in Christ's teaching that "You must be *perfect,* as your heavenly Father is *perfect.*" The Greek word *teleios* clearly does not mean "perfect" in the sense of never making a mistake, but like the Sanskrit *samyak*—complete, full, whole. The Buddha's *samyak* means right in the sense of conducive to the ending of sorrow. The meaning is to end sorrow. If you want to stop suffering, then adopt a view of life, a way of thinking, acting, and speaking, and so forth, that is effective in bringing this about. Cut off the nutriments that feed the suffering. Stop the struggle. Stop imagining that your striving will bring about happiness. For struggling and striving are themselves suffering, and suffering only engenders more suffering. Only peace brings peace.

So it is of first importance, then, to escape the moralistic view. The moralistic view is one of anxiety and worry. It leads only to frustration and rebellion. We always wonder, "Am I doing it *right?*" (In fact, this is one of the first concerns people have about meditating, as if they naturally want to put it in the category of the moralistic). It is also full of anger. We can find ourselves threatened, thinking, "*Those* people are not doing things like me. They must be bad, wrong," and so on. Our anxiety and fear create a need to repudiate those who are different. Moralism constricts us, whereas a truly spiritual path opens us up—to life, to other people, to everyday reality, to ultimate reality, and to everyday reality as ultimate reality. Thus, the spiritual person does not love other people because that is some kind of rule, but because she knows the deep interconnectedness of all beings, and sees deeply that it makes no sense to do otherwise. She does not just avoid lying, but is rooted in truth. She does not just avoid violence, but is rooted in peace.

The eightfold path then asks us to consider this: Is my view of life complete and effective in leading me toward peace, or does it create more suffering in me? Does the way I think about things liberate me, or does it narrow the confines of my life? Do my actions, my way of speaking, my way of earning a living, all move together harmoniously in the direction of liberation? Or do they sow seeds of future sorrow? Am I scattered and unaware, or concentrated and mindful, so that I do not miss my life? And am I trying too hard, so that my very efforts only create more worry and anxiety, or not hard enough? In what follows, I draw freely from teachings the Buddha gave, as well as my own sense of what it might mean in the context of mindful therapy. This is not meant to be an exhaustive presentation, but simply some places where one might begin to explore the functioning of the Buddha's eightfold path.

Right View

Right view means first of all that you have some faith that the end of suffering is possible. Stated minimally, all you need at first is some doubt that you have to go on suffering as you do now, some hope that there is another way.

Buddhist teachings do not invoke blind faith in anything. It is not enough to believe suffering can end because the Buddha said so. True faith accepts this *provisionally,* as a working hypothesis, but then seeks out whether it is so. Try the teaching out for yourself, and see if it doesn't begin to reduce your suffering and increase your peace. Once this process starts, you have greater faith that the teachings are effective.

Right view also means seeing things in the light of no-self and impermanence. For every difficulty in life, you know that it too will pass. You also know this for every joy, and this awareness teaches you to take delight in it while it is there without clinging. When the present joy ends, you release it, and you tune in to what is joyful in the new situation.

When a difficult situation arises, you acknowledge the difficulty but you do not personalize it. You do not add in to the mix a feeling of "Why is it always me?" You don't take a hurricane personally as though the storm sought you out. Similarly, you can come to view the acts of others in a less personal way. You know that the actions of others are also the results of impersonal forces, just like a hurricane. You see in each harmful act the suffering of the person who does it, including the suffering of parents and others who have contributed to the suffering in that person. What is more, you adopt the same attitude toward your own actions. When you look back on your life, and see some of your actions and choices as mistakes, you know that you were doing the best you could with the limited understanding you had at that time, and with all the suffering that was within you. To get angry at yourself or at someone else only prolongs and exacerbates this situation.

It is easy to see, in the case of patients who have problems with anger, that their actions continue the very difficulties they ostensibly want to end. Each time they rehearse an angry thought, or act in an angry fashion, they reinforce the habit of being angry, strengthening all the relevant neural or karmic connections. Further, angry actions create consequences in the world, engendering further situations that in turn trigger anger, and so on. In this way anger reproduces itself, creating more anger, more difficulty, more opportunity for suffering.

The same is true with patients who become angry at themselves, who become sad or are burdened with feelings of shame. The net result of these feelings is as conservative in preserving the state of suffering as those resulting from anger. Upsetting oneself in this way actually *evades* responsibility for change: How could I possibly change, when I am so upset? Getting upset in a sad, self-punishing way has the same results as anger—nothing improves, nothing changes except that the negative habit is strengthened, and the situation intensifies.

Negative actions flow from an ignorant point of view, from a point of view that is out of touch with the nature of reality. Out of this kind of ignorance, the world is not seen and appreciated for what it is, but confirms only what we already believe. The world becomes our own personal Rorschach blot.

Clinically, a good question to hold in the back of your mind while listening to a patient, is how does this person view the world? What are her implicit and explicit ideas about how the world works? It is all too common for us to assume that others see things roughly the same as we do, and radically underestimate how differently others actually do see things. Of course, this is not simply a matter of identifying patients' mistakes and just informing them. That is unlikely to be effective. But if we know their point of view, we will have greater understanding of their pain, and an increased capacity to help.

Right Thinking

Thinking is the speech of the mind. Part of what right thinking may mean is bringing the mind back to the body, for example through mindful breathing, so that mind and body are reunified. It means also calming our thinking, changing the quality of it gradually and slowly and patiently, so that we become less scattered. When our thinking is scattered, when it is not calm and focused on what is at hand, there is a lot of room for error to creep in. Where there is scatter there is Mara, the Buddhist personification of ignorance—if you will, Satan.

Right thinking is thinking that is not caught in concepts. Cognitive psychology informs us concerning the distortion when a depressed person tells himself, "I always fail." This is off-center, global, and exaggerated. All that is needed is one disconfirming instance to prove it false. If this person has had at least one thing at some point in his life at which he did not fail, the statement that he always fails is false. This is the inner dialog of a person caught in concepts. The concept of unending failure has divorced itself from experience and taken on a life of its own. Now instead of a concept that is an attempt to convey the reality of the experience, we have experience dominated by the concept.

Comedian Steven Wright, known for his short bits that push concepts to their absurd extreme, says he has a map of the world that is life-sized. "The scale reads," he says, "One mile = one mile." We can take this to remind us not to confuse our map of reality with reality, no matter how large the scale or how great the accuracy. Maps can be useful, but only if we know they are maps, and see them for what they are, without confusing them with the real thing.

In a therapy context we must always remind ourselves not to invest too much in our concepts, diagnoses, formulations, and hypotheses. The introduction to the *Diagnostic and Statistical Manual of Mental Disorders* (DSM-IV) makes this point, saying that we should be careful to speak of a person having schizophrenia rather than a "schizophrenic"—though I suspect this point is easily lost as one proceeds to read and use such a manual.

While the analysis of the cognitive approach is helpful, the mindful therapist is cautious about challenging distortions in thinking. The danger in this procedure is that, by fighting against certain kinds of thoughts, you may give them more energy and entangle yourself in them more deeply. In the mind as elsewhere in the universe, every action has an equal and opposite reaction. Simple mindfulness can handle this more gently, advising us to just bring clear, calm awareness to this kind of thinking, and letting it come and go of its own, without any particular effort or resistance.

Practicing right thinking in mindful therapy will bring our attention out of the clouds and back into what is going on right now. Much of our perception is distorted, and not incidentally so, but profoundly so—and therefore we must be careful. In particular, our interpretation of others' words and behavior is prone to great distortion, since we often interpret in keeping with our own schemas or complexes, our favored way of seeing others and ourselves, rather than contemplating what is there.

Mindfulness teaches us to acknowledge the truth without evasion. If what we are feeling is a painful thought or emotion, we must always begin with *knowing* that this is happening. Meditation teacher Sylvia Boorstein recounts that at a retreat with a highly-regarded teacher, she asked him about his recent bout with cancer. She was afraid that he would try to sugarcoat the experience in some way, but her fears were allayed when instead he frankly admitted, "It was *terrible!*" It is a relief to acknowledge the truth.

Right Speech

As thinking flows from our general view of life, so speech flows from our thinking. Right speech is first of all loving speech. A classic Buddhist instruction on the matter expresses it this way:

Before admonishing another one should reflect thus . . .
In due season will I speak, not out of season.
In truth will I speak, not in falsehood
For his benefit will I speak, not his loss.
Gently will I speak, not harshly.
In kindness will I speak, not anger.[55]

Right speech, then, is speech that is "in season"—speech that is appropriately timed. Appropriate timing in our personal life means, for example, that we do not raise a difficult issue with someone when they are all but out the door, or when they first return from a tiring day at work. We look for a time when the person may be able to hear us in a calm way. If we are angry, we may have to wait until the force of our anger has abated, caring for ourselves with sitting and walking meditation until we are calm enough to speak. At the same time, it means that we must speak nonetheless, and we should not let the issue get too remote so that we risk forgetting it. In a therapy session, it means we express our insight skillfully, in an understanding and non-blaming manner.

Right speech is honest. We do not knowingly exaggerate or distort—there will be enough of that simply because, as unenlightened beings, everything we say will be skewed by our own egocentric point of view. We certainly do not need to add to this.

Right speech is for the benefit of the other person. In psychology, we talk about being *assertive,* meaning that we speak and act so that there is balance between our own needs and the needs of the other person, seeing both as valid. Therefore we might translate this teaching into the therapy context by saying that, while our speech will of course be for our own benefit, and that is probably one reason we are talking in the first place, we also want our speech to benefit the other person and not harm her. And since we cannot overestimate the degree to which our perceptions are distorted by our own needs and fears, we may even take special care that what we say is for the benefit of the other.

Right speech is gentle. This means, we have to take care not only with our choice of words, but with our tone and manner. It is not enough to use gentle words if we say them with a sarcastic edge or with an angry tone.

Another aspect of Buddhist teaching on right speech is that we should refrain from frivolous talk. This is a difficult one in our cultural context. We are often in situations in our extraverted world where we have to "make conversation." But one way to honor this teaching is to always seek ways to deepen the quality of our interactions, doing our best to speak from our own center directly to the center of the other person. In therapy, certainly, this is especially important. If we create an atmosphere of casual chitchat, it will be hard for our clients to experience the consulting room as *temenos* or sacred space.

There are many Western insights that are in keeping with the spirit of right speech. One example is to ask for what we want directly (rather than to complain about what we are not getting). Another is to talk about our own feelings and perceptions *as* feelings and perceptions rather than ultimate truth, the proverbial "I-statements." When we speak of our thoughts and feelings as just that and only that, we give others some freedom of movement. We do not trap them. We avoid saying things in a way that puts the other person on the defensive or offensive. We want to avoid hooking their fight-or-flight wiring, because if we do not, then positive communication is at an end. These ideas are useful amplifications of the traditional notion of right speech.

Right speech is patient and kind, as Paul says of love in the famous New Testament passage (I Corinthians 13). With patience, we know better than to expect to resolve someone's difficult life issue in one or two sessions, whatever the demands placed upon us by third-party payers. If we have that kind of expectation, we may push too hard, and make matters worse.

Right speech in therapy is reflective. We are above all intent on hearing the other person and conveying that we are doing our best to understand, even when we do not succeed. As one of my teachers used to say, patients will forgive your not understanding. But they will not forgive your not *trying* to understand.

Right speech also involves knowing when to be silent. And when is that? The answer is, "a lot more than you think." When Carl Rogers and others tried to specify what he was doing in a session, they talked about something called "reflection" or "active listening," a process of checking your understanding of what the client is saying. What this does not tell you is how often to do this. Should you stop and reflect every single thought, every single sentence? Most would agree that this would be excessive. But just how often, then, do we reflect back what we are hearing?

Perhaps the answer is: reflect often enough to facilitate the patient's processing, but not so often that you risk interfering with it. We must not mistake a patient's silence for an absence of processing, trying to fill every pause with reflection. Sometimes the most valuable parts of a therapy session occur in these fertile silences.

Occasionally also, we may offer some guidance to patients about how their use of speech may interfere with their establishing positive relationships in their lives, or even in the therapeutic relationship. Mindful of the delicate balance between talk and silence, and mindful, too, of how easily this can be experienced by patients as judgmental rather than helpful, care must be taken here. As with all such teaching, we need to evaluate whether rapport is sufficiently established and whether the person is ready to hear what we offer. It is helpful to be sure that we are speaking for their benefit in such a case. And often, we are better off saying less rather than more, giving hints rather than a full dissertation. Most of us know people who are willing to give us casual advice, the vast majority of which is simplistic and inappropriate for our situation. So if you feel it is time for you to give advice, at least do it in a different manner. See if you can say it in a single sentence, or at most two. If not, consider breaking it into smaller bits, and leaving the rest for another day.

Right Action

Right action, like right speech, is based on the principle of kindness. One way to cultivate right action is, again, to remember impermanence and nonself. If you can plant a deep perception of the fleeting and impermanent nature of life, if you can, for example, visualize clearly where your current difficulties will be in a hundred years, your action will be on target. You will not be so tempted to react unreflectively to a trivial situation. If you remember the truth of interconnection, then you will remember that ultimately to injure another injures oneself, in the same way that, since we ourselves are mostly water, we pollute ourselves when we pollute our oceans and streams.

Most often, right action is not dramatic. While there are circumstances that may require dramatic action, right action is mostly about things like turning the water off while you brush your teeth, accelerating more slowly in your car so you use less fuel, or being kind and polite on the phone. As Mother Teresa taught, there are no great acts, only small acts done with great love. We can put great love into preparing a cup of tea for someone, into the way we drive, into the simple act of listening.

When we fail to act in this way, we strengthen the habit of unkind action. Thus when we act in anger we are practicing being an angry person, strengthening the anger habit. Secondly, our misdeeds have a way of coming back to us. It is easy to see that if someone acts in a vengeful way, others may be motivated to act in kind. But beyond such a simple, linear model, given the profoundly interconnected, interpenetrating nature of reality, it can also come back at us in ways we cannot imagine, even when it appears safe.

An example of possible nonlinear interconnection occurred recently as I was working at increasing the size of my practice. I of course let everyone I could think of know about my increased availability, and my practice grew fairly quickly. However, the strange aspect of this is that very few of the referrals I received came from the people I had spoken to. A lot of referrals seemed to come in from nowhere—from people I hadn't had contact with for years, from people I didn't even know, and so on. So too can we expect anger and other negative things to come back at us in non-linear ways.

Ultimately, right action is action that leads in the direction of non-suffering. If we see deeply, when someone acts in an unkind way toward other beings, we might well ask, "Why is she hurting herself like that?"

The concept of right action overlaps considerably with a behavioral understanding of psychological disorders in Western psychology. When a depressed person isolates himself, removing himself from the natural reinforcers of life, he only adds to his suffering. When the alcoholic tries to deal with her pain through the over-practiced, faulty coping mechanism of drinking, nothing good will follow in the wake of the short-term relief this provides. The simple act of monitoring behaviors that are targeted for change can easily be understood as a kind of mindfulness practice in itself.

From a therapist, right action is the simple everyday things we do. Keeping our appointments without asking our patients to wait an unreasonable period of time. Preventing dual relationships. Keeping good records. Protecting confidentiality. Doing our best for this person. Listening deeply. Understanding.

As with right speech, so also right action involves knowing what not to do. For a therapist, right action may mean not trying *too* hard in a session, not taking on *too* much. You know you are working too hard not only because you are exhausted at the end of the day but also because you tend to elicit reactivity rather than change from your patients. At heart, we offer our clear presence, our understanding, our kindness and compassion. We very much need to remember that these are our stock in trade, and that they do the healing work. Ultimately we remember that our efforts are in themselves nothing special, that in a sense, it is not we who bring the healing, but the degree of mindfulness and compassion in us.

Once again, the Dharma is not passive. Western audiences always need to be reminded of this, which tells us more about our fears than about Buddhism. Passivity is a caricature of the Buddhist attitude. Right action, as well as right non-action, flow from right mindfulness.

Unlike Ajahn Chah's student who practiced not clinging by not repairing the roof, when you are in touch with reality, with your cold, wet body dripping under your damaged roof, you repair it. When you are in touch with your patient, you know what to do—even if it sometimes is outside of how you normally do things. With right action, we do not make the mistake of imposing our philosophy rigidly on any situation, but let our clear and mindful perception teach us what to do. Of course, sometimes we will make mistakes in this regard. We will inevitably misread some things, and fail to empathize adequately, and so on. That is okay, and maybe even ultimately helpful, so long as we get in touch with our mistake and its consequences, so that we act appropriately to repair the situation, just as we would repair our roof. If a self-oriented point of view comes into play, however, we may get caught in defending our actions rather than correcting them.

Right Livelihood
If you remember that "right" means moving in the direction of non-suffering, then you will get the point of right livelihood

quite easily. Some ways of earning a living harm others. There are obvious enough examples of work that does harm, such as working in a munitions factory, but most are more subtle. If you earn your living selling athletic equipment, your work may benefit other beings. If you earn your living selling candy in a society with growing problems with diabetes and obesity, you may be a contributing cause to suffering.

Where I practice in New Mexico, many people are employed at one of the national laboratories or at the local Air Force base, doing "defense work," as we have come to call it. But the reality behind this phrase is, of course, that they are involved in designing, manufacturing, and deploying weapons. Again, even these words sound sanitary enough. But I never forget that it means people dying and children losing limbs or covered with horrible burns. Somehow, I do not see many people employed in this kind of work in my practice. But when I do, I do not lecture them. Therapy may not be completely value-free, but I know it would be out of bounds to moralize about this. When I help such people, am I also contributing to the means of war? Perhaps. But I ultimately believe that increasing the amount of peace and well-being in the world person by person is the best contribution to world peace, and the most enduring.

At first glance, patients involved in this form of livelihood may not appear to suffer from it. But looking at it more deeply, I think they do. They suffer because they have to distort their perceptions to believe that what they are doing is something positive. They often seem to have to harden their point of view. They become prey to questionable political ideas and leadership. The human form, with its many sensitive nerve-endings, is designed to be in touch with the world, to be sensitive, open, and appreciative. Whenever we have to close ourselves off or harden ourselves in some way, we suffer, and those we interact with suffer—even if we are not aware of this.

One patient I worked with many years ago was employed in the defense industry. Being a sensitive, artistic soul, she was appalled by the attitudes of her coworkers. Some of them spoke graphically about how much they enjoyed using their new high-powered rifles on the weekends to explode the heads of prairie dogs. Another, a devout Christian, told her seriously that he thought the whole Middle East was such a mess that we should simply nuke the whole place and then ask God for forgiveness! Since my patient was understandably disturbed by such talk, I had an open door to discussing right livelihood with her.

Another person I knew worked in this same industry as a scientist, and developed obsessive-compulsive disorder. I visited his house, and discovered that his whole large garage was piled high with neatly organized boxes of the things he could never stand to throw out, some of it useful, most of it sheer junk. Such disorders, as is well known, are rooted in anxiety, and may have a biological or genetic basis. But I also see anxiety as arising from repressing things we cannot face, and I could not help wondering whether part of the roots of his problem were not also to be found in right-livelihood issues.

While the basic idea of right livelihood is simple enough, in real life it is often not so simple. My artistic patient was dealing with issues of right livelihood primarily in that her work environment caused suffering in herself—an important aspect of right livelihood to consider. But should she leave her job, where she'd invested so many years toward retirement? That is not a simple question. Of course, if she resigns, someone else will do the work she was doing, maybe someone with less sensitivity, and this may create an even worse situation. And she may have to take on work that is lower in pay and benefits, causing more suffering for herself and her family. As philosopher Martin Buber has pointed out, goodness is a direction, not an end point. This is clearly the case with right livelihood.

For the most part, therapists are fortunate with regard to livelihood. It is easy to feel good about the work we do, especially on those days when we can clearly perceive our helpfulness to others. But this does not mean we do not have issues of right livelihood. We are in many ways a part of a system that contributes to suffering. If we accept contracts with HMOs that limit sessions and are in some cases harmful to the well-being of our patients, we are a part of a system of suffering. And yet, if we refuse such contracts, we may not have a practice, and may not be able to be helpful to anyone. Since the number of people we can work with effectively is limited, our fees must be high enough to support ourselves and our families. Yet these high fees can be a burden to people. Conversely, seeds of suffering have been sown in me when I have accepted patients at a very low fee, only to discover that I am thereby underwriting payments for their expensive new cars, while I still drove my old rustbucket, or worse still, in the end not getting paid at all.

Right livelihood is a direction. There is no perfect way to practice it. We can only do our best. We can only walk in the right direction.

Right Mindfulness

How do we get from mindfulness to a discussion of morals (in the sense defined here of living so as to reduce suffering)? Mindfulness is central here because when we are mindful, we see what needs to be done and left undone. We know what needs to be said and left unsaid. We are in touch with how our work affects ourselves and others.

Humanistic psychologist Abraham Maslow describes this relationship, having to invent language to do so:

Facts create oughts! The more clearly something is seen or known, and the more true and unmistakable something becomes, the more ought-quality it acquires. The more "is" something becomes, the more "ought" it becomes—the more requiredness it acquires, the louder it "calls for" particular action . . .

In essence, what this means is that when anything is clear enough or certain enough, true enough, real enough, beyond the point of doubt, then that something raises within itself its own requiredness, its own demand-character, its own suitabilities. It "calls for" certain kinds of action rather than others. If we define ethics, morals, and values as guides to action, then the easiest and best guides to the most decisive actions are very facty facts; the more facty they are, the better guides to action they are.[56]

In other words, clear awareness or mindfulness shows us what is required. When we pay deep attention, we know what to do. This is not some arbitrary *should* or *ought* slapped on from outside; it is something that grows naturally out of the concreteness of the situation, like a skier making adjustments to the contours of the hill.

Right Diligence

Given the reality of suffering, what kind of diligence, what kind of effort should we be making? On the one hand, our situation is one of some urgency. Who wants to continue to suffer, when we can cross over to the other shore? Buddhist teaching emphasizes that human life is a precious opportunity to awaken.

Right diligence is middle-way diligence. If we do not make an effort, how will we hope to change? Yet we can try too hard, with too much strain and struggle. But strain and struggle are ineffective. Strain and struggle do not create peace; they only create strain and struggle.

The Thai meditation master Ajahn Chah admits, for this reason, that he is afraid of very diligent disciples:

> I'm afraid that they're too serious. They try too hard, without wisdom, pushing themselves into unnecessary suffering. Some of you have determined to become enlightened. You grit your teeth and struggle all the time. You're just trying too hard . . . Simply watch and don't cling.[57]

We can see the problem of right diligence in our patients. Some of them do not seem to comprehend the urgency of the need for change. They are not willing to work between sessions, to meditate, to keep a journal, to record dreams, and so on. They are too lax. But at the same time, there are others who strain and fret. You gently ask for a dream, and they struggle to bring one forth. And the more they struggle, the more they shut down on their receptivity—the less capable of remembering they become.

Our own efforts as therapists require this kind of balance also. Sometimes we want too much to be helpful. We want to say helpful things, we want to do helpful things. We may also want to be appreciated for our helpfulness and be seen as someone who is wise. We are not helping in a no-self way, and so we strain to produce some sage advice, some wise interpretation. Then we risk producing too many of these, so that the economy of our comments becomes inflationary and they lose value. On the other hand, we can be too comfortable. We can lapse into being merely conversational in the most superficial sense. We can become too relaxed. As the Buddha said to a musician, the string must be tightened to just the right degree to produce the pleasing sound. Too slack, and no sound is produced; too taut, and it breaks.[58]

The right balance for us is to focus on listening, on understanding, on being open and receptive, interested, and alert, but patiently allowing the work to unfold. My own journey has been about rebalancing by learning that less is more, that I do not have to strain and struggle to be helpful, that in fact such straining and struggling is unhelpful, and that when I let go and let be, and simply try to understand deeply and calmly, good things seem to happen of their own accord. It is not that I am uninvolved, but that my actions do not seem exceptional, since they grow out of a calm appreciation of the situation. I suspect that many therapists need rebalancing in this same direction, though perhaps for some others, the necessary rebalancing may be toward being more active and involved.

There is a particular kind of receptive/active balance needed with each patient. With one patient I got nowhere with my usual style. It was only when I jumped in actively with counterarguments to his arguments, cut him off at times in mid-sentence just as he did to me (though not as frequently), that there was energy and movement in the consulting room. It took several months for me to catch on to this, to realize that this was what was needed with this particular person.

Right Concentration

Right concentration concerns, first of all, how we approach meditation. Personally, I don't like the word "concentration" very much. It connotes to me something far too effortful. The Sanskrit word *samadhi* underlying this term may also arguably be translated as "calm abiding" or "calming." I like that better. The image is one of letting things be, like letting the sediment in a container of water settle out of its own accord. If we struggle with it, we only stir it up more, making the situation more muddied, less clear.

Concentration, in the sense of calming, is the way we need to listen. It is not straining, but opening, softening, containing, becoming receptive, letting the patient's words and presence take their own precise outline in our awareness.

The Eightfold Path as Diagnosis

When we (or our patients) are suffering, one way to look deeply into the nature of this suffering, and identify its originating and maintaining factors, is to consider the elements of the eightfold path. Contemplating this material, for ourselves and for our patients, can yield insight. We can ask ourselves the following questions (which I will express here in the first person, though keep in mind that it applies to our patients also). The following questions (and my comments on them) are informed by my understanding of the eightfold path, and insights from cognitive-behavioral psychotherapy.

1. Is my view of life distorted or one-sided in some way?
   Often we suffer because our view of life is distorted or one-sided. We may, in other words, need to see the current difficulty as the result of impersonal forces at work, even if they are at work in people. Carl Jung said, in fact, that he'd never had a patient past the age of 35 or so be cured whose solution was not a spiritual one.[59] In a similar vein, the analyst Robert Johnson said that if we refuse to come to the spirit, the spirit comes to us as neurosis.

2. Is my thinking distorted or exaggerated?
   This is somewhat the same idea as the first question, only more specific. Often we suffer because we are exaggerating negative aspects of a situation and minimizing positive ones. Check for this kind of distortion.

3. Is my way of speaking creating love and harmony, or misunderstanding?

   I may have kind intentions, but still need to find a skillful way of expressing what I want to say, using words that heal rather than hurt, that build up rather than tear down. Also, I may be speaking too much. Perhaps I am teasing too much, engaging in humor at the other's expense, or gossiping in order to fit in and have a sense of belonging. Perhaps I am not speaking "in season," that is, my timing is inappropriate, and so on.

4. *Is there some aspect of my behavior that is contributing to this suffering?*
Are my actions compatible with my wish to transform suffering into well-being? Am I caring for my body and mind appropriately? If not, let me continue to bring mindfulness to these areas until I see clearly so that I can change my behavior, until the factiness results in oughtiness (as Maslow put it).

5. *Is there something about my work that is causing me to suffer?*
Maybe I need to change jobs, and earn a living in a way that is less harmful to myself, or to others, or both. Am I gaining the world and losing my soul?

6. *Am I living mindfully and deeply?*
Or am I letting precious moments of life go by unnoticed, as though I were going to live forever and could afford to throw many of my moments away, as though they were superfluous?

7. *Am I trying too hard? Not hard enough? Am I trying in a way that finds a balance between these?*
Athletes know about this. When they are trying too hard, bearing down, trying to force things to happen, things don't go well. Often if they just become mindful, get with the flow of the game and enjoy it, letting the game come to them, things go much better.

8. *Am I too scattered, not concentrated?*
Perhaps I need to calm down and practice enjoying the present moment, even if it is "just" brushing my teeth, drinking my coffee,

dialing a phone number, or entering an appointment time in my calendar.

In all of this, mindfulness is the key. Mindfulness contains the other seven elements of the eightfold path. For if you are calm enough, aware enough, you will have insight about these other areas, without trying to remember all eight at once.

CHAPTER EIGHT
Working with Emotion: Buddhist Psychology

From within or from behind, a light shines through us upon things
and makes us aware that we are nothing, but the light is all.[60]
—RALPH WALDO EMERSON

BUDDHISM IS ARGUABLY THE MOST psycho-
logical of spiritual paths. Authoritative Buddhist texts are
traditionally divided into three parts, called the Tripitaka, or
"triple basket." One of these is the Sutra-pitaka, consisting of the
discourses of the Buddha (which in themselves already have a lot
of psychological content!). The second is the Vinaya-pitaka,
which concerns monastic discipline and regulations. The third is
called the Abidharma-pitaka, which is wholly devoted to an
extension and systematization of the psychology in the sutras. In
this chapter, I will explore mindful therapy in the light of some of
the teachings from the Abhidharma.

According to the Abhidharma, the human psyche can be conceived of in two basic parts. At the base lies *alayavijñana*, or storehouse consciousness. Above it lies *manovijñana*, or mind
consciousness. It is a kind of long-term memory—but not in the
sense that Western psychology uses the term. Storehouse

consciousness contains *bija* (seeds), which are potential mental configurations—thoughts, feelings, and ideas, and beliefs. Some of these seeds are positive or wholesome, such as loving-kindness, mindfulness, peace, or compassion; others are unwholesome or negative, such as anger, envy, fear, worry, and so on. The distinction between wholesome and unwholesome is a matter of what is and is not conducive to enlightenment—not moralistic considerations.

Mind consciousness in Buddhism on the other hand is somewhat like the conscious mind of Western psychology. It is this aspect of consciousness that is immediately accessible. This is shown in figure one.

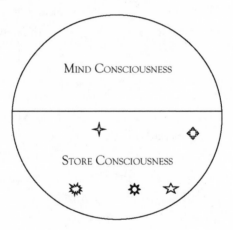

The Example of Anger

We might have a seed of anger, for example, in storehouse consciousness. Perhaps it is a seed that has been there a long time, one planted in us in childhood by some unkind word or unjust action of a parent or a sibling. Once that seed has been planted in us, we continue to have the potential to get angry. Then in our adult, present-day life, someone says or does something unkind to us. The word or action of this person might in some way resemble the original situation that planted the seed. The resemblance may be a very general one, for example, that it is simply another situation in which someone in authority has treated us in a way that we perceive as unjust. At this point, the seed of anger is activated, rising into our conscious awareness, going from the potential state of store consciousness to the zone of mind consciousness. This is shown in figure two.

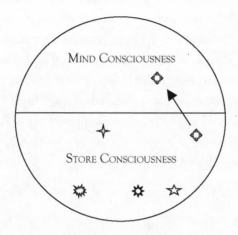

Since anger is an unwholesome emotion, this has become a dangerous situation. If a different kind of seed had been triggered in us, such as a seed of love, joy, peace, understanding, or mindfulness, there would be no danger. But in this case, there is a lot of danger, since anger can threaten our well-being in many ways.

The neutral, almost mechanical quality of this description implies an important point: there is no blame in this model. We are not to blame for the fact that someone has acted in a way that has triggered our anger. This is, in itself, a neutral fact. Nor are the people who trigger anger in us to blame. For they are behaving in terms of the seeds that have been activated in them. The person who is chronically angry is just someone with a seed of anger that manifests readily and powerfully. But though we are not to blame, still everything depends on how we take care of this situation. We may not be to blame, but we are *responsible*. That is, we are capable of making a response. Our job, in the situation of activated anger, is to *take care* of this anger, to heal and transform its energy.

When we act to heal and transform the energy of anger, there are three consequences. In the first place, anger will no longer threaten our own well-being. Secondly, if we have cared for our anger skillfully, the seed in the storehouse consciousness grows smaller. That is, it now has less potential energy, and anger will not arise in us quite so easily as it did before. For this reason, it will be easier to deal with the next time it manifests. Thirdly, since the anger in us does not then spill over to another person, we change our environment as well. The people around us do not have negative seeds triggered, and become less likely to respond to us with anger in the future.

NO ENEMIES

Jesus Christ taught us to love our enemies, but in mindful therapy we can take this a step further. From a Buddhist point of view, there are no external enemies. Seeing someone as an enemy is a misperception, an element of delusion. Such a person would have no power, ultimately, to trigger anger, sadness, envy, or other unwholesome mental state in us, were the potential not already lying in our store consciousness. As Jungian analysis and dream work also shows, it is always a matter of taking care of our own psyche, giving up our projections, refusing the neurotic pleasure of again blaming the harsh father or the unloving mother, reaching the mature realization that, whatever may have gone before, the responsibility for transformation is now ours and ours alone. It is our job now to take care of whatever negative state has arisen in our consciousness. Who else can?

Consider the excellent example set by the Dalai Lama. Despite the brutality endured by his people at the hands of the Chinese, despite their efforts to annihilate Tibetan culture, and despite his own exile, he continues to work at transforming his own anger. He does not choose the path of succumbing to hatred and fear. Of course this seems heroic and admirable. And it is. At the same time, to see this as heroic and admirable in a way misses the point. For the Dalai Lama knows that the first person to suffer when one is angry is oneself, and secondly, the people around us who are now confronted with an angry person. From a Buddhist point of view, this process of seeds being triggered and eventually returning to store consciousness is impersonal, in exactly the sense in which we say to people who are upset that they should not "take it personally." That is, as I have said, the actions of the person who triggered an unhealthy mental state in us are determined by forces comparable to the howling of a hurricane or the eruption of a volcano. All the conditioning (which is one way of understanding the Buddhist term *karma*) of that individual up to this point has pushed her behavior in this direction, just as our conditioning, in the form of seeds, has been triggered by her actions.

ADVANTAGES OF THE MODEL

This approach has advantages over the model of tension build-up and release or "ventilation" prevalent in Western psychology.[61] While both models agree that emotions need to be experienced clearly rather than repressed or denied, the ventilation model, by which we achieve catharsis through the release of emotional energy, particularly if done in an explosive manner, is dangerous. A spark may cleanse a home of leaking natural gas, but it does so by destroying it. If we are not skillful, ventilated emotion can damage our relationships with others, trigger reactions from them that cause additional suffering, and even lead to our own destruction. This is prevented to some extent in a therapy situation by displacing the anger to a pillow, an empty chair, or some other object rather than the individual at whom one is angry. But this does not do enough to eliminate the danger. For there is always the risk that in ventilating a repressed emotion, the individual is in fact *strengthening* the habit of anger, making it more likely that he will respond with anger in new situations. In essence, he is rehearsing being an angry person.[62]

In the West, too, we seem to be reaching an understanding that anger is a destructive force, and that dealing with it is more complex than ventilating would imply. Yet the habits of therapists change slowly, and I find that many therapists still adhere to some version of the ventilation model. Perhaps one reason we are so wed to this idea is that, after a person has beaten a pillow, for instance, we can observe that they reach a state of exhausted relief. This state appears to confirm the ventilation idea, while other consequences remain less immediate, and therefore less apparent, to the therapist. If ventilation makes the patient more inclined to anger, and if this corrodes important relationships, that is less easily observed by the therapist.

Feelings do need to be expressed, explored, and understood. But there is danger when this is done in an explosive or violent manner. If you beat your pillow, you are not mindful. For if you were mindful, you would see that it is a pillow, and you would have no desire to beat it.

The Abidharma model as presented here is easily understood by patients. Explaining this model to patients with anger issues already shifts their perceptions, helping them see the problem as their own tendency toward anger, rather than the external, anger-provoking person or situation. Similarly, with a depressed person, the problem is the potential for sadness within their own consciousness, not just the life situation in which they find themselves. The model inherently implies that all situations are, in a certain sense, neutral, calling for a skillful response rather than a continuing focus on the immediate trigger of the emotion. Of course, if there are aspects of one external situation which require change and can be changed, this is to be encouraged. But too often, focusing on the trigger itself misses the true cause of the difficulty, like the dog sprayed with a hose that bites at the water, while ignoring the individual pointing the hose at him. Patients can also readily understand that acting out the negative emotion only creates more of the problem, since expressing negative emotion unskillfully triggers negative reactions from others. Of course a fully effective level of insight often requires repetition and working through, but the beginning of insight can be felt immediately.

The Abidharma model, in sum, has the advantage of being more in accord with the reality of dealing with difficult emotions like anger, while retaining a clarity that appeals to patients. This model also clarifies an aspect of what nirvana is. When all negative seeds in us are extinguished, we become an enlightened being. We become like Buddhist teacher Dipa Ma who, when asked what was in her mind, replied, "Concentration, loving-kindness, and peace. That is all." At that point, everything and everyone around us now triggers only positive seeds. Our mind consciousness is full of love, compassion, peace, and joy, so that negative seeds cannot gain a foothold in us. While this may seem a distant goal to most of us, it is encouraging, particularly as we come to experience for ourselves how every step in that direction adds to our happiness and frees us from suffering.

CARING FOR NEGATIVE EMOTIONS

If we are not to just encourage our patients to ventilate negative emotion, what then? First of all, if we are practicing mindfulness ourselves, we are already a model for a different way of handling emotions. What is more, we provide a mindful interpersonal context that encourages a more constructive way of dealing with negative thoughts and emotions. Many patients come to a session agitated, and feel calmed by the therapist's non-reactive presence. So once again, if mindful therapy is the practice of deep listening and true presence, this is the most important thing we offer, and in itself will do most of the work of healing, without our needing to explain it.

When patients are ready, however, the therapist can explain this model, and then describe the two basic methods of caring for negative thoughts and emotions that grow out of it. The first of these is simply the practice of bringing calm awareness to the thought or feeling. Just that—just noticing with calmness and clarity. This is the primary way for handling negative mental states. When we simply bring calm, caring, non-interfering aware-ness to a negative emotional state, we gradually decondition our-selves. We are able to metabolize the emotions fully, so that the seed of negative emotional energy diminishes in power. Other-wise, if we struggle directly against the negative feeling, we risk augmenting it. If we are angry and try to deny our anger, if we are sad and try to deny our sadness, we become divided. We struggle within ourselves. This struggle is costly and expends a lot of psy-chological energy. We are then in a state of tension, and peace is unavailable. As Freud taught us, what we deny or repress returns with greater energy and insistence.

What we are unwilling to experience, we get more of.[63] If we are sad, and we think it is terrible to be sad, so that we try to repress the sadness, trying to push it back down into store con-sciousness, our sadness only intensifies. The seed of sadness grows larger. We then suffer from poor emotional circulation, and this is every bit as deadly as blocked arteries. The sadness will eventually come out. It may manifest as a powerful, nearly irre-sistible suicidal impulse. Or if we succeed in repressing it, it may manifest in our physical being, and we may develop a major health problem.

SKY-LIKE AWARENESS

Emotional health means relaxed, open awareness—awareness like the sky. A disturbing thought may manifest, but because we do not fight against it and instead simply notice it and let it be, it need not trouble us. But if the emotion is strong and ego-dystonic—if it does not fit our sense of who we are as a person—and if we therefore try to repress or deny the thought, we create an unnecessary difficulty. We then are in conflict between the energy of the feeling itself, and the energy of repression. When we accumulate many such thoughts and feelings, we develop chronic, free-floating anxiety and worry. It is only when we can open to the feeling, allow it, and let it be, that we can relax. Then we do not have to be on guard. The whole atmosphere of the psyche can naturally calm down, becoming more at ease, solid, and settled.

Sometimes rather than repressing, we become addicted to particular mental states. And even though these states torture us, they are at least familiar. I tell patients these states are like an old shoe: it may have holes, look dirty, and smell bad, but it is *comfortable,* unlike new shoes that often pinch a bit and require breaking in. The addiction to certain mental states parallels drug abuse but the chemicals involved are endogenous rather than introduced from outside. Thus, in some cases we actually seek to perpetuate painful states. We seek out situations that trigger them, and continue the life drama or "games," as Eric Berne called them, to which we have become accustomed. Thus the anger-prone individual is hyper-alert to injustice, reading slights and unfairness into every situation and into the innocent actions of other people. Once the anger is triggered, he amplifies it with mental rehearsal. In similar fashion, the depressed person, who is in this sense addicted to sadness, continues to act in ways that both trigger and perpetuate sadness. She may isolate, sleep too much or too little, eat too much or too little, drink too much alcohol, and so forth. And again, once the negative state has been triggered, she will also mentally rehearse all the reasons for the sadness, so that when someone tries to help her see the distortion and exaggeration in this point of view, pointing out positive elements, she may feel that the other person simply does not understand. By rejecting such input, she defends the stability of her psychological system and biochemical balance at the expense of growth and change.

THE MIDDLE WAY

Treating mental states with mindfulness is the middle way between repression or denial, on the one hand, and perpetuating the addiction to the drama of the negative state, on the other. It is learning that all thoughts and feelings can be allowed to come and go harmlessly. Not only are they uncontrollable, but the effort to control them is part of the problem. When we stop trying to control them and instead learn to let them be, when we learn to respect them as natural facts like a cloud or a stone, without upsetting ourselves over them, then we restore good mental circulation. The negative thought or feeling can assume its natural place in the overall economy of the psyche. Then in fact we have taken hold of the foundation of true peace—not necessarily because there are no clouds in the sky or no stones on our path, but because we have learned to let clouds be clouds and stones be stones, without troubling ourselves.

With this in mind, one can understand why Buddhists practice the five remembrances: recalling the realities of getting sick, growing old, dying, losing everything and everyone you love, and that your deeds (karma) are all you ever truly have. Other practices which drive home the reality of death and change can include meditating in a graphic way on the dissolution of the body, how it turns blue and rots and smells, how eventually nothing but dust is left, and then not even that. When you can look at such things clearly, without evasion, then you have excellent psychic circulation. If you can allow yourself to be aware of such things, then what is there to fear? Anything else that arises in mind consciousness is trivial. And indeed, patients with good ego strength but a lot of worry and anxiety can benefit from these practices immensely. Done correctly, they are life-affirming, helping one to appreciate this present moment for the gift it is.

SOMETIMES IT'S LIKE THAT

In one account, a student was meeting regularly with his meditation teacher. At each meeting, he recounted his struggles and difficulties during meditation. No matter what he said, for a long time all the teacher ever told him was, "Sometimes it's like that." Frustrated as the student was with this constant refrain, it already contained a vast teaching.[64]

Sometimes patients, in the grip of strong emotion, wonder how it is even possible to bring mindfulness to bear on what is happening with them. From their point of view, they are caught in a tidal wave, swept away by powerful forces. To them, the therapist offering mindfulness is like someone in a helicopter throwing down a piece of thread and telling them to climb up. Their mindfulness is as yet too slender to bear much weight.

When patients raise this objection, the first thing to do is to empathize.[65] Most of us have the experience from time to time of being swept away by raging emotion, and we know one can feel powerless in the face of such an overwhelming force. Additionally, it is important to normalize this experience. You can do this by saying something like, "Sometimes it is like that. Don't worry about this, but just focus on the situations that you can bring mindfulness to."

BREAK IT DOWN: DEALING WITH DIFFICULT EMOTIONS

Another practice you can offer patients is to narrow the focus to one aspect of the overwhelming experience. A great emotional flood is composed of bodily sensations, cognitions, and affect. Together, these three make a powerful combination. But if one breaks the experience up into parts, one can often deal separately with an experience that would be overwhelming collectively.

Often the easiest place to begin this narrowing of focus is with sensation in the body. Instruct the patient to breathe and notice the sensations in the body connected with their emotional state as clearly and calmly as possible. One could notice, for example, whether the sensations associated with this emotion are diffuse or localized. If localized, where are they exactly? How would you describe them? Are they a stabbing, a prickling, an ache, a tightness, a heaviness? Is there an image that arises in connection with the sensation? How would you describe the image? Can this image be drawn or painted?

By attending to a single aspect of the experience of strong emotion in this way, and expressing it in a moderate manner, the situation already begins to change and become more bearable. From the bodily sensations, one can then begin to notice what thoughts are involved, just noticing, just bringing bare attention to these, without resistance or argument. What is the nature of these thoughts? What purpose do they serve? And finally, one can bring attention to the emotion itself. How would the patient label these emotions? What are they like? Does the patient have a metaphor for them? and so on.

QUESTION THE PURPOSE: DEALING
WITH DISTURBING THOUGHTS

With disturbing, repetitive thoughts, it can help to ask what their purpose or imperative is. In other words, the thoughts arise in a context that implies that what is must not be or that something else should be. And once we can identify this sense of necessity, we can often ease up and relax. For example, if you are running late and having an anxious thought about arriving to work on time, you might ask yourself what the "have to" behind it is. Immediately one can see that the "have to" is something like: "I have to be at work on time." Just identifying this often brings relief. While the have to is unacknowledged, the vagueness of it cannot be directly addressed. But as soon as you identify it, it automatically sets up another step in the processing of this belief, such as, "As a matter of fact, I am likely to be late, no matter what I think about it." Then you see that, while being late may be undesirable, things are, nonetheless, just exactly as they are.

CHANGING THE PEG

The Buddha offered the image of a carpenter who changes a wooden peg that has rotted by hammering a new peg straight into it rather than first removing the rotted peg.[66] Similarly, we can sometimes change an emotional state by substituting something else for it, rather than struggling to remove it directly.

In terms of the storehouse model of karmic seeds, this means that once a negative seed has been activated, you do not need to struggle against it directly. You do not need to deny or repress. You notice it mindfully, and water a different kind of seed, a positive or wholesome one, so that it sprouts into your consciousness. For example, you can turn your attention to the blue sky, breathe in and out and smile, deeply appreciating it, or you can contemplate a happy child at play so that your delight in the child raises seeds of happiness, love, and joy into your awareness. Then you don't have to do anything directly to address the negative seed. The positive seed will take care of the negative seed, until it returns of itself to store consciousness, transformed and healed. This is a pleasant way to take care of your mind consciousness.

It's possible that changing the peg could more easily be confused with repression or denial, and so it must be approached a little more carefully. In this practice, one must be clear: No effort is made to *squash* the negative feeling. One notices it without adding fear or aversion, but then simply alongside of it one raises another kind of mental energy. It is like noticing that one of the trees in your garden has died, but also noticing that the other trees are flourishing, and so encouraging yourself in a way that is in touch with a wider reality rather than denying the sad aspect.

Therapists familiar with a behavioral approach may see parallels. Changing the peg is what behaviorists call "reciprocal inhibition." That is, you cannot feel both happy and sad, or anxious and relaxed, at the same time. Joseph Wolpe used this approach in systematic desensitization to help people overcome phobias. By teaching patients to relax and then imagine a graded hierarchy of things they fear, they learn to disconnect the feared object from the anxiety, since it is not possible to be both relaxed and fearful at the same time.

Changing the peg parallels the behavioral approach to the treatment of depression. In this approach, depression is understood as *things that people do* (feeling and thinking also are a kind of doing). Depressed people isolate, rehearse negative thoughts, eat poorly, and so on. We can well imagine that if a non-depressed person acted this way, she would eventually become depressed also, no matter how gifted she may be initially with a positive outlook and temperament. Eventually, she too will start producing too little serotonin and other brain chemicals indicated in depression, and might require antidepressant medication. But if it is true that by behaving like a depressed person, one becomes depressed, even altering one's brain chemistry, then the reverse is true also. If the person can begin to act more like a non-depressed person, even if she does not feel like doing so—if she can shower and dress as usual, go to work, eat a good meal, engage in stimulating activities, interact with positive, encouraging people, and so on, the mood will eventually shift. This is very similar. It is the behavioral version of changing the peg.

Zen master Thich Nhat Hanh recommends, in this regard, that if you are angry at someone you love, you can change the peg by considering deeply where the two of you will be in a hundred years. If you can see this vividly, you raise a seed of mindfulness into your store consciousness, in this case, awareness of impermanence, and soon you will no longer be angry. Practices like this can easily be invented with particular patients in their particular situations.

One good way to change the peg is to practice walking meditation, especially if one can get out of doors and do this in a relaxed and natural way, taking time to notice any positive things that are around, such as a tree, the sky, birds, a leaf, or a stone. One can practice walking by timing the steps with the breath, aware of each step, of the contact of the foot with the ground, and stopping to breathe in and out whenever one sees something that attracts your attention in a positive way, taking it in deeply. When thoughts, feelings, and bodily sensations arise, these are noted, neither pushed away nor amplified. Then one returns to the beautiful object or the act of walking.

MOST IN NEED OF LOVE

If you reflect on times when you have been angry or sad, you might be able to see that it is exactly at those times when you were most in need of love and understanding. At the same time, it is on those very occasions when you were least likely to receive it. When you are angry, you do not look very beautiful. You are not very pleasant to be around. Other people may even be afraid of you. So instead of helping you with love and understanding, they may avoid you, or judge and reject you, or even counter your anger with more anger—all of which only make it more difficult for you.

Likewise, when you are sad, you are often not very fun to be around, either. So again, other people may avoid you. They may misunderstand your sadness, thinking that you don't like them or are not interested in them. Once again, the result is the same: the time when you are most in need of love is the time when you are least likely to receive it.

If you can see this deeply, you may reach the level of effective insight, and be able to remember that this is the case with your patient, or your friend or loved one. When you remember how alone you can feel when you are sad or angry or afraid, this can give you the energy to continue to be present to such a person in the time when they are most in need of mindful presence and understanding, instead of giving them even more reason to be upset.

Tibetan Buddhists approach people who are difficult as a particularly wonderful opportunity to practice loving-kindness. Instead of turning away or rejecting them, they remind themselves that such people are in special need, and therefore represent a "great field of merit." They are rare, precious jewels. Raising seeds of mindfulness, kindness, and understanding with troubled people is a powerful and healing practice, and one which, as therapists, we have opportunity to exercise every working day.

A simple way, both for you and appropriate patients, to create a more kind, loving atmosphere, is the practice of saying silently each person you greet, "Hello, my dear friend." If this is done deeply, it can instantly create a different climate around a meeting or a therapy session. Raising seeds of loving-kindness is one of the very best ways to create a wholesomely-toned mind.

SOOTHE YOUR BABY

Thich Nhat Hanh compares handling negative emotions to calming a crying baby.[67] Talking harshly to an infant, telling it to shut up, to grow up, to stop whining and sniveling, and so forth, is, of course, a horrible way to treat a child. Yet often this is exactly how we treat our emotions! As in the punishment paradigm, such treatment creates more of the very thing we are attempting to suppress. When a crying child is treated harshly, when parents say, "Stop that crying, or I'll give you something to cry about!" we have already given the child more reason to cry.

Likewise, we need to treat ourselves kindly. In no event should we treat ourselves harshly. When we are sad, it does not help to tell ourselves, "See, you are a sick person. There you go again, getting depressed. What's the matter with you?" Instead, we need to care gently for our baby.

A friend of mine has an autistic son who works with a behavior therapist. The therapist sticks to her belief that patients need negative consequences for problematic behavior, and tends to apply this principle indiscriminately. My friend, however, knows that this is not always the best thing. He knows that when his son becomes agitated, he needs calming and soothing. He knows that certain objects—especially round ones for some reason—help accomplish this. This approach is much more effective than the therapist's belief in punishment, which only aggravates the autistic child even more, making him even more unreachable. The first step we often need is soothing, calming, before anything else can happen.

All of us on this side of enlightenment are likely to be overwhelmed from time to time. This is not a problem, however, so long as we continue to work with this the best we can, bringing mindfulness the best we can, and practice changing the peg. If we are temporarily overwhelmed and forget to work mindfully, self-recriminations add nothing. We need to soothe ourselves, increasing the chances of regaining our mindfulness as soon as possible, strengthening our intention to continue the practice, remembering always that this very thing in front of us now is the path.

Alex was a retired mechanic who came to see me after his second arrest for drunk driving. Drinking had caused a lot of devastation in his life, and he had an extensive family history of alcoholism. His pattern during the last ten years was one of long periods of abstinence—as long as two years—followed by sudden, dramatic periods of heavy drinking. The triggering event, in this case, was financial concerns, connected with a rankling anger at his ex-wife, who got half of his retirement in their divorce settlement.

Having worked with many people who, like Alex, were in Alcoholics Anonymous, I know that many of them are reluctant to admit to having occasional urges to drink. Clearly, this is a situation of poor mental circulation. The attempt to be safe by repression creates increased danger. I emphasized with Alex that urges to drink are natural. What is more, I told him, they cannot be controlled. They are natural events, like clouds in the sky. As such, they are not something that in themselves means anything good or bad about him or about his progress. In fact, one is better off knowing that an urge is present, so that one can take steps to deal with it. The important thing is what one does when an urge is present, not whether one has an urge.

To make the point that thoughts are not controllable, I used the exercise of asking him to close his eyes and, whatever he did, avoid thinking about pink elephants. Alex tried this, and right away began grinning. He got the point. It took several sessions and several such discussions for this to sink in fully, but soon Alex was reporting that he would actually laugh out loud whenever he noticed an urge, telling himself "pink elephants," and take steps to avoid drinking, such as leaving a situation where alcohol was available, rather than trying to avoid his thoughts.

With this foundation, I began to teach him a mindfulness technique that Professor Alan Marlatt called "urge surfing," in which you actually pay attention to the experience of an urge, noting the bodily sensations, the thoughts and emotions, and watch as they swell, crest, break, and recede like waves on the shore, just riding out the urge, learning to be present with it without drinking. This solidified the point that an urge is a natural phenomenon, and need not result in drinking.

Alex had no skills for taking care of his emotions other than his overpracticed and problematic habit of drinking in response to them. From this new foundation of dealing with urges, however, he could now learn to deal with disturbing thoughts and feelings the same way, thus inoculating himself not only against urges to drink but also against the emotional triggers that create them.

APRANIHITA

To deal with emotions, as we have seen, it is vital to find ways to create a sense of openness, of spaciousness within ourselves, so that we can let them be, neither struggling against them, nor amplifying them by succumbing to the tug of their drama. One Buddhist practice which can help a lot with the creation of this inner spaciousness is the practice of *apranihita*, or "purposelessness."

Purposelessness means not putting anything in front of yourself to run after, but instead remaining rooted in the present moment, being present to what is going on now. For example, in making morning coffee, you can breathe and bring yourself back to what is going on now, the movements of your hands, the sound of water being poured, the aroma of the coffee, and so on, instead of running ahead to the next step, or to drinking the coffee, or whatever you will be doing later in the day. In this way, the moments of your life spent making coffee are valid moments, and not simply a prelude to the rest of your life.

This idea is a difficult one for many Westerners. As I write this, there is a best-selling book entitled, *The Purpose-Driven Life*. To us, being without purpose means being lost. Unaccustomed to this experience, we can even get depressed when we feel no immediate purpose. For this reason, we constantly *invent* purposes, little tasks and errands that "need to be done," feeling always that we cannot rest until we have justified our being with doing. But we can have a different experience.

Alan Watts expressed it this way: "Paradoxical as it may seem, the purposeful life has no content, no point. It hurries on and on, and misses everything. Not hurrying the purposeless life misses nothing, for it is only when there is no goal and no rush that the human senses are fully open to receive the world."[68]

Most of my patients, being good Americans, are far from purposeless. They have, in fact, *so many* purposes—and all of them have to be completed before they are entitled to simply be. This is so pervasive that for many, the "simply being" never actually happens. For one thing, once reaching the point where everything is done that needs doing, they are simply too exhausted to do much but stare at the television or fall asleep. They have no energy left for those most beautiful human activities which are also the most purposeless: praying, meditating, drawing, painting, writing poetry, listening to music, making music, making love, or just sitting in the backyard and watching the leaves fall.

Another way to say it is that the purpose of human life is to be alive, just as the purpose of a flower is to be a flower. But when we become goal-oriented, we lose sight of the fact that we are alive. Thich Nhat Hanh once asked some children what the purpose of eating breakfast was. Some children said things like, so you could have energy for the day, so you would be strong, and so on. But one child said the purpose of eating breakfast was to eat breakfast. The wise old Zen master agreed with this point of view.

Behind our drivenness lies a fundamental distrust of our being. Buddhist practice is about learning to trust our ultimate nature, our Buddha nature. We do not have to treat ourselves as though we would not do anything unless we constantly whipped and drove and bullied ourselves to do so. In fact, it is an interesting experiment to make sometime, and one you can offer your patients. Just sit for a while, until you don't want to sit any more, letting the first impulses toward some activity come and go without acting on them impulsively, until we have a more solid, clear feeling of what we want to do next. Patients who say they cannot meditate may not know it, but if they do this much, they are meditating already!

Of course, having plans and goals is not bad and certainly not evil. Rather, when you are planning, it is good to be aware that you are just planning. You know then that your planning is not the reality, but simply an idea of what you might like to see happen. The danger occurs when you forget this. Every plan, while providing a sense of direction, can also be a danger if you try to impose it on reality, rather than letting your plans evolve in accord with the ever-changing nature of what is.

The majority of my patients are adults over thirty, and they may be more ready for this practice than young people struggling to find themselves and make their way in the world. The ideal patient for the practice of purposelessness is the overdoing, relentlessly perfectionistic person, though at the same time these patients may also be most resistant to it. Like all Buddhist teaching, and all of mindful therapy, apranihita is a remedy, not ultimate truth. But it is in itself a remedy that we Western people in particular could benefit from immensely, creating the space in which we can care for our emotions and learn to be fully aware and alive.

Apranihita simply reveals yet another aspect of being mindful. Apranihita teaches us that something does not have to serve any narrowly utilitarian purpose to be of value. Just to be is holy. Just chopping wood or carrying water, just driving or just eating breakfast, can be of value, in the doing of these tasks and not just in their end state or accomplishment.

In a certain way, therapy is itself an apranihita practice. With the many pressures on therapists today to produce results, with the movement in psychology to rely increasingly heavily on research-driven methods and techniques, and with the limitations from HMOs on sessions, it is difficult to remember that the journey itself is what matters. We are at our best when we remember this.

Patients can become too focused on results. Not too long ago, a man came in facing a major life decision about his marriage and an extramarital relationship he was pursuing. Without telling him what to do, I helped him explore his feelings about these matters, and at the end of the session, asked him about rescheduling. Quick as a shot, he replied, "You mean I have to come back?" A delayed smile came to his face as he realized his question might seem silly, and perhaps wanting to cover the honesty of his remark and create the impression it was a joke. But I knew he was serious. He had genuinely thought that his major life dilemma could be fixed in fifty minutes!

It's our job to help patients settle into the process of psychotherapy, and to have patience with regard to the outcome. When we can do this, the outcome is better as well. But we get that outcome by being fascinated with the process, not pushing for any particular result, but being mindful, being open and aware, and encouraging these same attitudes in our patients. Apranihita is an important practice for therapists. When we try too hard to help, we only create resistance.

The Four Divine Abodes

There are many other practices that we could consider here. And though it would not be possible to mention all of these, I will describe one additional practice that I found very helpful. This is the practice of the four brahamaviharas or divine abodes.

The brahmaviharas are: loving-kindness, compassion, joy,[69] and equanimity. Raising any one of these into mind consciousness creates a climate unreceptive to negative karmic seeds, preventing their activation or at least limiting how long they last. There are many ways to activate these four elements. Tibetan Buddhists, for example, teach us to look at all beings as having been our own mothers (or friends or sons or daughters) at some time in the unimaginable past, helping us to see them with more kindness and compassion. Dwelling on the impermanence of ourselves and all beings around us can help with this also. Or, taking a page from Western contemplative practice, sometimes just dwelling with these words themselves (love, compassion, joy, and peace) can water these seeds in our awareness, since the mind takes on the qualities of whatever it dwells on.

PART III

Daily Work, Daily Life

CHAPTER NINE
Put It to Work

If I wish to treat another individual psychologically at all, I must for better or worse give up all pretensions to superior knowledge, all authority and desire to influence.[70]
—CARL JUNG

I ONCE HEARD IT SAID THAT, before giving a talk, the Dalai Lama looked about him at all the eager, expectant faces, and said, "I've got nothing to give you!"

This is a wonderful lesson in Buddha nature. At one level, of course, the Dalai Lama has *a lot* to give. He has much to say and teach, and his friendly, happy presence is a delight, an encouragement, and an inspiration. So why did he say this? Perhaps he felt that people were hoping for magic, some simple solution to the complex difficulties of living in our time and place. Perhaps he knew that all one can ultimately give is one's presence and one's kindness.

Right before the start of a therapy session I sometimes feel a kind of mild dread. It would have surprised me to know when I started doing therapy that even after so many years, I would still get this feeling. Yet here it is. It is still there because I know that all the people who come in my door harbor a secret wish that I will have some magic to give them, like the man who was surprised to consider that he might need to come more than once to address a major life question. More sophisticated individuals will know better than this intellectually, but emotionally they still fall into this trap. If you ask them, they would of course acknowledge that there are no magical solutions to complex life problems. But deep down, they hope for magic anyway. But alas, poor little me, I have no magic to offer them! So inevitably I know that at some level, each patient will be disappointed. And just as inevitably, I must confront the terror of having nothing to give with courage.

Of course, at another level of analysis, I have a lot to give. I have the experience from over twenty-five years of doing therapy. I have the knowledge of my education and continuing learning. But this does not fully allay the terror of knowing that ultimately, all I have to offer is my mindfulness, my true presence and deep listening, my openness, my understanding.

No wonder, especially at the beginning of a therapy career, we can be so enamored of *technique*. We would love to feel so powerful, so technically capable that we can hide from the terror of the emptiness in meeting this person alone and unarmed, with nothing but our presence. And while we do well to collect our own repertoire of effective techniques, it will never, can never, should never shield us from the human confrontation with the other person, one who has come for you to help them.

While I have discussed technique in passing all along, in this chapter, I would like to give you an idea how a mindful therapist might work regarding specific therapeutic techniques. To do so, the only example I can give you is my own approach. But there are many ways to embody the principles I have outlined in the prior chapters; this is just the way I happen to do it. If you recall our thought experiment about being an enlightened person and contemplating the dangers of teaching, all you learned there applies here. The dangers are legion. Nonetheless, I feel this material and this approach is valuable.

But I want to very clear about what mindful therapy is and isn't: *Mindful therapy is therapy in which the therapist produces true presence and deep listening.* It is not technique-driven. It is not a cookie-cutter approach, where every person gets the same treatment in session one, then the same in session two, and so forth. Many of the techniques I describe here I never use with some patients, while with other patients I use a few of them a great deal. Technique is at the service of mindfulness. It is mindfulness—ultimately the patient's own buddha nature—which does the work of healing.

Please remember this as we discuss technique below.

Like a caring gardener, our job as therapists is to provide the right conditions for growth. We cannot make anything happen, we can only provide the conditions through our mindful presence and listening. We can only do our best to help each plant unfold in accord with its nature, trusting its nature to unfold if we provide the right environment—an environment of acceptance, understanding, unconditional positive regard, and genuineness. Technique should not be employed to force the issue of growth, but as an adjunct, a little extra fertilizer added from time to time.

FROM THE BEGINNING

The first contact is vital. Already the patient gives us hints about what he needs. Already we are revealing something of ourselves as therapists. Most often, a first contact comes by telephone. If you are calling someone back after receiving a voice mail message, this gives you time to take a few mindful breaths, preparing yourself to be available to this person. Right from the first contact, you can communicate that you are present and listening. If possible, make the call when time constraints will not force you to be abrupt. Therapy begins right here.

The next point of contact is the intake form. In accord with the ethics of your profession and applicable law, you must collect data about the patient and give them reasonable information about what to expect from your services. On my own intake form, I indicate that I am open to spirituality as a healing force, that I value meditation, and that I am interested in working with dreams, taking care to do this in a way that does not alienate anyone who is not interested in these things. This is a part of what I tell people on this form:

> *The Nature of Psychotherapy.* I work in a variety of ways to help people solve life problems and grow. I do not believe in one-size-fits-all treatment, but seek to find the best way of working with you as an individual . . . I recommend people keep track of their dreams while in therapy and bring them in. I also recommend meditation . . .
>
> *Spirituality.* In my view, therapy is a process of healing in body, mind, and spirit. I consider your own religious and spiritual beliefs and practices, if any, as a potential source of help and healing in our work. Please feel free to discuss these with me if they are important to you. At the same time, I of course do not try to change any one's religious beliefs. For some people, working at the spiritual level may be vital; for others, it may never come up. I have worked comfortably with both highly religious and spiritual people as well as people who are atheists or agnostics.

I think it is important, if you are spiritually inclined, to reveal this interest right at the beginning, so patients for whom this is also important feel free to tell you about this. I also have a space on the form for people to tell me about their spiritual life and its importance or unimportance to them. I always follow up on this in the first session. In this way, I have an idea about how to incorporate spirituality into my work with this person. At the one extreme, if I am working with someone who is anti-religious, I approach the introduction of religious or spiritual concepts cautiously. At the other extreme, some patients come to me because they have read one of my books, or because they know in some way of my spiritual interests. In this case, I can be more openly spiritual in the language I use.

THE FIRST SESSION

There are several goals to keep in mind for the first session. The primary goal is to *encourage the patient to process*. I try to establish right away (though without necessarily saying so) that therapy is a sacred space for patients, one in which they are learning to pay attention to themselves and their lives, tapping their own wisdom rather than looking to me for answers. It is helpful to avoid trivial conversation. It is helpful to avoid recreating the doctor's office experience, where you fire off questions and receive a series of short answers in return. This medical-style format, so tempting to fall into, communicates the expectation of a passive role for the patient. Open-ended questions (which cannot be answered yes or no) and reflection (re-telling what I understand the patient to have said) help to get people talking and keep them talking, trusting them to tell you what is most important for you to know at their own pace.

In the first meeting one can also begin to get a feel for what approach may be appropriate with this person. The mindful therapist seeks, above all, to be a mindful presence, supporting and guiding the patient's work and exploration. With some problems, though, one may need to work in a concrete, focused way, letting your approach be determined by the needs of the patient. The mindful therapist is careful, however, to allow plenty of space for patients to open up and process other types of concerns, inviting them to use the therapy space to go more deeply. In this way, some who come in for short-term, focused work are later ready to engage in deeper exploration.

Adopting a stance of being ready above all to *listen* rather than argue, advise, and so forth, is a helpful mindset to enter a session with. It corrects for the natural tendency to think that nothing good is happening unless we "fix" the person and the person's situation somehow. However, this does not mean that you should squash yourself into an overly passive mode of interaction. Enter ready to listen, but then allow the nature of the interaction and the needs of the patient to determine what you do.

As I have already mentioned, I begin sessions with a few moments of mindful breathing, with the exception of the first meeting. Quite often, people in the first session are brimming over, ready to spill their story out, and I do not want to impede them from doing so, or imply that any technique, even one so wonderful as breath meditation, is more important than what they want to tell me. But at the second meeting, I teach them this technique and, apart from any strong objection, continue this at all therapy sessions. I often invite them to explore this practice between sessions as well. At various points in the work, when emotions are strong, I remind them to return to their mindful breathing, using the breath not to repress their feeling, but to calm it so they can experience it clearly.

I tell patients that a feeling must be calmed so it can be experienced in a helpful way, so it can be digested and integrated. If we are agitated, if we lose ourselves in the emotion, often nothing much can happen. It can help to learn the art of being fully present to a feeling, of touching it with calm attention, while at the same time not being so distant from it that this constitutes repression.

With many patients, if they have given me an opening on their intake form, I share my belief that true healing involves claiming one's spirituality. I make it clear that I do not intend anything dogmatic by this. I am not proselytizing or trying to make people Buddhists or anything else. In fact, I sometimes explore whether it is possible for them to return to their own tradition, if they have one. For those who can, mindfulness and meditation can be incorporated into this tradition. Many today, however, simply cannot return to the old traditions, and mindfulness may become the cornerstone of their spirituality. While tact is required, one should not be too hesitant to talk about such things. Many people are searching. There is a vast difference between encouraging spirituality, which is inherently human, and encouraging one or another brand of religious dogma.

BETWEEN SESSIONS

There are four general recommendations I make to people, though I do not offer them mechanically to every person. Where appropriate, I advise people to spend a little time each day practicing mindful breathing. This builds on what we are already doing in session. I also discuss how this can be practiced during the day, while waiting in line, in traffic, while on hold on the phone, and so on, so that eventually one learns to be calmer and more present all day long.

My second recommendation is to record dreams. If a patient seems interested in this, but says she does not remember her dreams, I give some basic instructions to facilitate remembering, such as forming an intention to remember while going to bed, setting pad and pen by the bedside, and recording whatever snippets she remembers in the morning, even if they seem nonsensical. I approach dream work as a kind of mindfulness practice as well, extending awareness into the night.

The third thing I sometimes recommend is that patients find some time each day for inspirational reading, whatever that may be for the individual. For some it may be the Bible; for some it may be something quite different. Of course, many therapists will have recommendations to make of their own in this regard, but for additional recommendations, see the references section of this book.

A fourth practice that I sometimes recommend is journaling. Journaling is another way to encourage mindfulness, supporting awareness of what one is really experiencing from day to day. Journaling provides a vessel to contain one's inner processing, much as therapy itself does. But unlike therapy, it is available every day. Of course, many people lack patience for writing anything down these days, and I do not insist on it. Patients who do not seem able to spontaneously discuss their concerns in session may find this especially helpful, using it as a tool to facilitate introspection. They can then bring the journal in and use it to jog their memories, or perhaps even to read a little bit from, though I do not generally have patients read long passages. I prefer the live interaction.

ALLOW SILENCE

One of the most important tools of the mindful therapist is silence. This means, within reason, to let the patient continue to process in silence. It means not jumping in the moment a patient appears to have finished speaking. It means letting the patient own the floor.

Lengthy silence is a violation of the rules of normal social interaction. And as such, silence is one of the things that marks the therapy room as sacred space and differentiates it from other types of interaction. Therapy is not the place for small-talk or chatty conversation. At the same time, some patients will have difficulty tolerating silence. In this case, one can take some responsibility to help the patient feel comfortable by suggesting avenues for exploration, titrating the silence in gradually. In other cases, one might allow an uncomfortable silence to continue, using its gentle pressure to encourage the patient to go deeper and discuss more authentic concerns. Some patients only seem to really get to work with this kind of approach.

Patients' comfort with silence generally increases as therapy proceeds. Even patients who can readily accustom themselves to silence may have less tolerance for it early in therapy. But as they become comfortable with the therapist and with the work, they accommodate longer pauses and silent periods. After a long period of silence, you can also invite the patient to bring mindfulness to what went on in the silence, and how they experienced these moments. Can he share what he was thinking about? Did the silence feel awkward? What were they aware of?

REFLECTIVE LISTENING

Reflective listening is the heart of mindful therapy. In my view, most therapists could benefit from greatly increasing the amount of time they spend listening reflectively. Under pressure to offer something more, one can offer advice and interpretations that are not nearly as helpful as this deceptively simple process. Carl Rogers said reflective listening was his effort to "check his understanding" of what the patient said. That is an excellent way to think of it, since it emphasizes the intention to understand.

Most good reflection is not a verbatim repetition of what the patient said, nor does it always begin with the hackneyed stem, "What I hear you saying is . . ." In most instances, paraphrase is best. Some patients tolerate a very loose retelling of this kind. Others, perhaps more suspicious or more fearful of being misunderstood, reject anything but their own exact words. When comfort is high, reflection can include the unexpressed idea or emotion behind the patient's bald statement. If such deep level reflection is rejected, one can return to a more literal level.

Summary reflections distill a larger chunk of what a patient has been saying. Such reflections can be very useful in helping the patient return to their processing when they seem to have lost the thread. Additionally, they underscore yet again what the patient has been processing. Mindfulness is increased by the patient first saying what he feels, then hearing it reflected back to him, and then hearing it again in a summary reflection. In this way, patients become aware of themselves and what they tell themselves. They can also evaluate whether the view they have of their lives is fully adequate and sense that some aspects of their experience may not fit in.

Often thoughts and feeling circulate and re-circulate through our awareness without sufficient attention to digest them, creating chaotic loops of unfinished thought. Reflection facilitates bringing greater attention to such processes, since the patient formulates a perception, speaks it, then hears it reflected, and then hears it summarized.

Terry was a thirty-five-year-old, twice-divorced woman. Her first marriage lasted one year, her second only eighteen months. It had now been five years since she had dated. Terry worked as a charge nurse and had a lot of responsibility on the job, where she was well-liked and respected. However, Terry considered herself a "loser." She overgeneralized from the unhappiness in her marriages to her whole life.

In the four months that I worked with Terry, I never challenged Terry's story of herself as a loser directly. I simply reflected the other elements of Terry's experience: friends who liked her, her respect and responsibility at work, her many interests and activities, and so on. Hearing this reflected back to her gradually increased her awareness that, while she had trouble in one area of her life, she was far from a loser. From her many strengths, Terry began to work on the patterns that got in her way in relationships. She realized, for example, that the tendency toward perfectionism that made her such a good nurse backfired in the area of love, making her view any difficulty in her relationship as a sign of failure.

A follow-up note from Terry four years later revealed her to be happily married again for two and half years.

METAPHOR AND STORY

If we are to be mindful of our patients and how they perceive the world, we are also aware of the stories, narratives, and metaphors through which they view their lives. By attending to this dimension, more healing and more adequate stories and metaphors may be found. And ultimately, by attending to direct experience, story may even be transcended and, if not left behind, at least employed with greater flexibility.

The logical, reasoning aspects of human beings are a recent development in our evolution. These abilities are not well-established in all people, and even when they are, may be restricted to certain life areas, such as work. The function of logic and reason is to support us in knowing how to go about getting what we want. But these faculties cannot tell us what path to follow. They can't provide in themselves direction or purpose. I find that many people make this mistake, particularly the more intelligent and educated ones, trying to use their intellects to tell them which way to go, when the intellect is actually poorly equipped for this task. The intellect can help us assess the reasonableness of what we want. If we want to become an artist, reason will help us assess whether we have a realistic chance, based on our talent, our drive to make this happen, and knowledge of the odds. It can also help us figure out *how* to get what we want. But is not particularly good at telling us *what* to want.

The language of growth and change is not primarily the language of logic. Logic has its role to play, but the language of growth and change is the language of story, myth, symbol, and metaphor. If we wish to facilitate change rather than hook resistance, we must learn to speak this language. Even more importantly, we must learn to listen for this language from our patients.

The metaphors patients use spontaneously can be important. Since our purpose is not a literary one, these may be very trite, as when a patient says he feels "torn to pieces," or "empty," or many of the other phrases commonly heard in therapists' offices. The mindful therapist contemplates these metaphors, reaching beyond the superficial reaction a trite phrase might normally elicit to the experience lying behind it. The therapist may then invite the patient to explore it further. What is it like to be "torn to pieces?" What else can he say about this? What is the bodily sensation connected with being torn to pieces? Can he engage in a fantasy of the pieces coming back together? What would that be like? How might it happen?, and so on. All of this exploration must be done, of course, in a very gentle way, with an attitude of inviting exploration rather than demanding any particular result. It is important to welcome *whatever* steps a patient can make in this direction as important.

The mindful therapist also listens for a sense of the story of patients' lives and the myth out of which they operate. Piece by piece, the story unfolds, whether it is the story of a Cinderella whose prince never comes, a Herculean tale of overcoming monsters and accomplishing great things, but never finding the way home, or some other such tale. This may also be about more prosaic complexes or schemas, such as "I am always abandoned by the people I love," or the perfectionistic theme of "Whatever I do, it's never good enough."

THERAPIST METAPHORS AND STORIES

Besides listening to the patient with awareness of story and metaphor, the mindful therapist can also provide stories and metaphors that assist in the discovery of more healing and flexible attitudes. When we speak to our patients in the language of story and metaphor, we speak an organic language, a language of growth. If we simply analyze how patients' viewpoints and behavior are incorrect and how they need to change, often we elicit resistance. With such an approach, patients may feel a need to defend themselves against an imperative that comes at them externally, and which may seem threatening.

When instead of analysis or correction we offer a metaphor or a story, we invite change rather than force it, and because change is invited rather than forced, patients can feel free to change, without feeling that they are giving in to another's will and thereby losing something of themselves. Consider, for example, the difference between saying, "You should bring mindful awareness to these difficulties until you know what you need to do, and not do," and "By shining the light of mindfulness gently and repeatedly on your problems, they gradually begin to open, like a flower to the morning sun." Or consider also the difference between saying, "You have to get out and be with people more if you want to stop being depressed. Research shows that people who isolate are more likely to get stuck in their depression," and offering instead, "I knew someone who was depressed like you. He didn't want to go out at all. It took all his energy, but he coaxed himself to do this as much as he could. At times, he lost the battle, and couldn't go out. But at other times, he was able to encourage himself to do this. Each time he went out, though, he noticed he felt a little bit better. It gradually became easier, and eventually his depression began to lift."

Psychologists in particular may be prone to recite research to their patients, hoping thereby to motivate change. And sometimes this may be useful. In my opinion, however, research can some-times become just another external authority that threatens dom-ination and loss of liberty and autonomy. While citing research can be useful, particularly with patients who have some science background, or who think in a more logical way, the mindful ther-apist will consider the *function* of such statements in their inter-personal, therapeutic context. If it is the equivalent of some sort of biblical, "Thus saith the Lord," it may be better left unsaid, or at least accompanied, if not replaced, by story and metaphor.

Like any technique, metaphor and story can be overused. Cer-tainly, you do not want to find yourself preoccupied with inventing metaphors or recalling stories, rather than providing true presence and deep listening. Story and metaphor are crucial ingredients in the therapeutic stew, but like salt, a little goes a long way, and the good cook knows not to overdo it. See appendix II for a recap of metaphors used in this book.

GIVE IT A VOICE

Mindful therapists help patients attend to themselves as embod-ied persons, not just floating intellects. Therapists do well to help patients attend to their bodies, the first of the four founda-tions of mindfulness,[71] and what their bodies are telling them—especially with intellectuals. One of the simplest ways to do this is to ask them to pay attention to the bodily sensation that is connected with a particular issue. After they notice the sensation and describe its quality, I will ask them to "give it a voice," to express what this sensation would say if it could talk. This is a Gestalt technique and a powerful one. The insight expressed may not be novel, but novelty is not the point. What matters is that it connects with the body, with the whole person—that it comes from a deeper level than the cerebral cortex. When an insight is connected in this way, it is more likely to reach the level of effective insight—insight that opens the door to change. The mindful therapist also tracks sighs, posture and changes in posture, facial flushing or paling, hand motions, and so on. I will sometimes ask a patient to express a sigh, a gesture, or a body posture in words.

EMPTY-CHAIR EXERCISE

Another exercise with roots in Gestalt is the empty-chair or two-chair exercise. The point of this exercise is to help the patient give caring attention to both sides of an internal conflict. When patients have such a conflict, the therapist brings over an additional chair, asking them to imagine that the empty chair contains the part of themselves that argues for one side of the dilemma, while the chair they are sitting in contains the other side. Starting with whichever aspect feels closer at the moment, they then tell the other aspect of themselves in the empty chair why this side of the argument is more correct. When they reach a sense of some completion, they switch chairs and take up the other side of the issue, addressing the chair they just abandoned. They then continue this dialogue as though they were writing a two-person play, switching chairs when needed, until the process reaches some natural stopping point.

An example of this is the patient who is ambivalent about a relationship. She may be wondering whether she should continue a relationship, or give up on it. In the exercise, she enacts each argument from its respective chair. In this way, one can facilitate processing without taking a side, which often will only elicit resistance.

Another example is someone contemplating a change in their drinking habits. Most people have some ambivalence about major habit changes. In one chair the patient explores all his worries and concerns about drinking; in the other, he then objects to the change, arguing that he has a lot of fun drinking, and so forth. Once again, this prevents the therapist from being in the role of the nagging parent or spouse and creating resistance to change rather than forward momentum.

Three-Chair Variant

With patients who have a developed sense of the transcendent, and who may have the introspective and verbal skills required, I sometimes add a third chair. I ask them to imagine that their own Wise Inner Self (or Buddha, or Christ, etc.) is sitting in this third chair. As they sit in this chair, I ask them to imagine becoming this wise person, feeling it fully in their body and mind. Then, having already listened with kindness and empathy to both sides of their dilemma in the two-chair exercise, they now express a more transcendent position. This approach should probably be used infrequently, or it may function as an attempt to bypass issues that need more working through.

WORKING WITH DREAMS

As complex mental events, dreams are not always easy to understand. While working with dreams is a subject for many volumes, and not one that I can address fully here, from the perspective of mindful therapy, working with dreams is worthwhile, even when no fully satisfying interpretation is reached. Some patients do not seem to make much progress unless dreams are considered. From a mindfulness perspective, it is the awareness, the process of gentle attending, which heals, in dream work as elsewhere.

The key to working successfully with dreams is to keep the *patient* working and processing, rather than putting yourself in the position of needing to have all the answers. I do not find spot interpretations the most helpful approach. I may begin work on a dream by first asking the patient about particular dream elements, and what comes to mind about them. The simple device of asking them to describe a common object such as a cat, a dog, a chair, a house, and so forth, as though attempting to tell someone from another planet what these things are, can often yield surprising insight. Or I might summarize the content of the dream in a more generic way. For example, if a patient dreams about being back in school, I might translate this as, "I'm currently in some sort of learning situation," and see what this brings to mind.

It is helpful to have familiarity with more than one of the major schools of dream interpretation. Jung offers many helpful insights. While dreams sometimes have a Freudian quality, and seem best understood as a wish fulfillment, particularly those with sexual or aggressive themes, this is too limiting. The Jungian approach, that dreams complement the conscious attitude in some way, is broader, as when a young man who consciously denigrates his father dreams of him as being ten feet tall, implying that there is a lot more to the father than his conscious mind normally understands or accepts. The Gestalt approach to dreams is helpful here, since it emphasizes helping the patient work with a dream rather than interpreting it intellectually.

Familiarity with only one school of interpretation tempts the therapist to impose his concepts on the dream and, more importantly, on the dreamer. Even when the therapist is confident of an interpretation, it should be offered gently, non-dogmatically, and without insisting on its acceptance. For example, one might offer an interpretation with the phrase, "If it were my dream . . . ," which already implies that the dreamer is always the ultimate authority on her own dream. For even an interpretation that is arguably "correct," if rejected by the dreamer, is not helpful, and in this sense, can be called incorrect. In mindful therapy the kind of correctness that matters is correctness that is useful to the patient.

There are many ways to accomplish the therapeutic task of helping the dreamer work actively with a dream. Patients might be coached to imagine the dream story continuing, describing to the therapist how things unfold or writing it down as an exercise between sessions. This is the process Jung referred to as *active imagination*. Or, as a variation of the empty-chair exercise, patients might enact a dialogue between important dream characters. Or they might retell the dream from the perspective of a minor character or object in the dream. Patients may draw something from the dream on a white board or piece of paper. This may be particularly indicated when patients make drawing-like gestures in the air while describing a dream.

From a mindfulness perspective, working with the dream to enlarge awareness is more important than reaching any neat or final interpretation, were that even possible to do. In mindful therapy, we endeavor hold our concepts lightly, because we know our concepts may interfere with a fresh, deep perspective on what we are experiencing.

Sometimes there will be a positive Shadow aspect in a dream. A Shadow element is an element that has been pushed into the unconscious as inferior or otherwise objectionable, but which may contain needed elements. For example, a young man low in self-confidence has a dream in which a character appears who is the opposite of this, very self-assured, perhaps even obnoxiously so. In the enactment, I may ask the dreamer to tell the dream from this character's perspective, becoming him as he narrates the dream from his point of view. Then, I ask him to notice what it feels like to be this character—what his thoughts and emotions are like, what it feels like to be in the character's body. I may suggest that over the next few days, the patient take a few moments now and again to call up this dream character, taking the reality of this aspect of himself into his body, and thereby actively integrating it more fully into his conscious attitude.

VISUALIZATION

I use visualization in two major ways: first, to help a person explore her experience more fully; and second, to imagine positive change, and thereby begin to break the power of old habit and conditioning.

When an emotional complex is triggered, one of the first casualties is mindfulness. For example, in talking with a patient about an argument he had with his wife, I noticed that his memory of the situation was sketchy. He did not remember what his wife said that triggered his anger, or much else about what happened. This is an indication that a schema or complex has been triggered. I then asked him to take a few mindful breaths with me, and put himself back into the situation of his argument with his wife. I asked him to use sensory cues to enter it quite precisely, recalling as best he could what was around them when they were talking, what he was wearing, what she was wearing, what sounds were about them, and any tactile, taste, or olfactory cues. Then I asked him to notice the bodily sensation associated with his anger, and give it a voice, as described above. In this way, he learns to bring mindfulness to such situations, instead of running out old conditioning on automatic. He may not yet be able to bring awareness into the heat of such a discussion, but he has taken a first step by simply imagining doing so.

Regarding the second use of visualization, such a patient can then take yet another step. I may then ask such a patient to visualize himself in a similar situation in the future, this time being able to maintain greater mindfulness, able to notice more clearly what is said, his own reactions to it, including thoughts, emotions, bodily sensations, and how he chooses to respond. He can then also imagine himself responding with greater calmness and skill in this situation.

DWELLING WITH A PHRASE, INSIGHT, OR IMAGE

Some patients say important things and then rush right by them, without appearing to have taken in what they have said. Sometimes this happens with patients who are very intellectual. Or this could happen with patients who are agitated or who have an attention deficit disorder. In these situations, reflective listening already helps to some degree: they at least get to hear the therapist reflect back what they have said. But sometimes the therapist may wish to enhance this still more. One way to do this is ask the patient to breathe in and out, repeating the key phrase or insight, or holding the image or phrase in awareness, just breathing, being present to it, taking it in. This may or may not facilitate more verbal processing, but this is not necessarily the goal. The goal is to slow down the process and bring a deeper level of mindfulness to something that otherwise is too fleeting to be integrated.

DEALING WITH RESISTANCE

Often in therapy, we run up against a patient's resistance to change. The mindful therapist remembers that this is normal and natural. However dysfunctional a patient's way of being in the world may be, no matter how much suffering it may cause, new ways are frightening. The basic tactic in dealing with resistance is to bring mindfulness to the resistance itself, accepting it fully, exploring it calmly. For example, if a patient resists looking at a particular issue, or working actively with a dream, I accept this and do not try to force it, only asking them if they can tell me what they are experiencing that may make this course of action frightening. Then we process that material.

"GOOD NOTICING"

I use this phrase a lot in teaching meditation. For example, someone may report after an initial attempt at meditation that they
were very distracted. I will tell them this is good noticing, which
normalizes the perception and at the same time lets the person
know that they are indeed doing it correctly, since they are being
mindful to the best of their ability.

This phrase also implicitly communicates patience with the
process. After a two-chair exercise, for example, patients may have
the expectation that they should feel immediate resolution of their
dilemma (that expectation of magic, again!). The majority of the
time, of course, this is not the case. Telling them that noticing this
is in itself important strengthens a process orientation rather than
a focus on result. "Good noticing" is an important teaching of
mindful therapy.

NORMALIZING COMMENTS

Often patients are unaware that what they are feeling is experienced by other people, since others may not express it. For example, in our optimistic, extraverted culture, people will not often
express negative sentiments or self-doubt. Because of this, people
get the idea that no one else has such feelings. A bereaved individual may be experiencing anger at the one who died for desert-
ing her. Just saying something like, "Sometimes people feel that
way," without any lengthy elaboration, can already do much to
put someone at ease in such cases. Such normalizing comments
allow patients to be more mindful of what they are feeling by
reducing their level of repression.

PROCESS COMMENTS

The mindful therapist, by being calm and open, can pick up on important aspects of therapeutic process without straining to do so. One such aspect is the quality of the nature of the interaction between therapist and patient. In normal social situations, commenting on this process is taboo. But in therapy, it can be an important source of feedback for the patient, helping increase her mindfulness of how she may affect others.

Process comments facilitate awareness at a different level. In a process comment, the therapist steps outside of the discussion underway, and comments on the nature of the interaction itself. For example, "I'm noticing just now that you seem to be taking a long time answering my question. I wonder what you are aware of about this." (This may also be a form of analysis of the transference, to those who are psychoanalytically trained).

MOST HAPPY/MOST SAD

Where mood is part of the issue bringing a patient to therapy, one way to increase mindfulness from cognitive behavioral therapy is to ask patients to do formal mood-monitoring. With patients who are willing to undertake this, a lot can be learned from such a process about what activities help lessen mood intensity, what triggers mood changes, and what thoughts and feelings come in to play. However, many people experience such a procedure as burdensome and even interpersonally awkward if other people notice them doing it. A simpler alternative is to ask them at the beginning of each session when they felt the most happy and when they felt the least happy between session. This invites the patient to attend to his moods and plants a small seed of mindfulness. It also provides a comforting structure for the therapeutic work, and offers a basis for deeper exploration.

THE PAST IN THE PRESENT

In keeping with a lot of humanistic psychology, mindful therapy focuses on the present. As Thich Nhat Hanh reminds us, life is only available in the present moment. Now is the only time in which we can be alive.

How then do we ever touch the past? Einstein said, "For we convinced physicists, the distinction between past, present, and future is only an illusion, however persistent."[72] We touch the past whenever we touch the present moment deeply. Touching the present moment deeply, we can feel the ghosts of our patient's past in the room with us. When a therapist becomes mindful of this kind of feeling, it is valuable to open the door to exploring it. Sometimes, when a patient acknowledges a certain difficulty, you can ask what her sense is of how it came about. Patients show amazing variability in this regard, some knowing immediately what the origin is. ("Oh, my anger is something I learned from my father. He was always angry.") Others have no idea at all.

Occasionally I will use an affective bridge technique. I ask the patient to be aware of the feelings associated with a present dilemma, and while focusing on these, allow any memories to surface in which they felt a similar feeling, even if the circumstances were quite different. Sometimes after several such iterations, one ends up at an early stage of development. In this way, they learn to deepen their mindfulness of the nutriments that fed their current suffering.

However, in general my approach is to let the past come up insofar as it emerges out of the present moment. In practicing mindful therapy, I do not often find that lengthy histories routinely add a great deal of value (though of course they may reveal important medical details).

IN THE SERVICE OF MINDFULNESS

The techniques offered above are not in any way a complete presentation of what mindful therapy might look like when you practice it. There's no way any list could be. As I've said, it is not my goal here to give a full compendium of technique. The important thing about technique to the mindful therapist is that she remembers that technique is always understood as in the service of greater mindfulness, trusting mindfulness to be the healing ingredient in the therapeutic alchemy.

The purpose of technique in general is not to teach your patients new tricks, but to help them be more deeply, clearly, and acceptingly aware. To achieve this, the mindful therapist relies primarily upon his own mindful presence. He specifically avoids creating "technique fatigue" in patients, forcing them to do his own favorite list of tricks week after week. Ideally, no special tricks of any kind are needed. Rather, one simply allows mindful presence to do the work. Practically however, in some cases the use of some techniques and exercises can facilitate a deeper awareness. They also provide hope.

To be a mindful therapist, one often does not need to learn new techniques so much as reframe and reconceive the techniques already in use as techniques in the service of mindfulness, allowing this reconception to guide the work into a different emphasis.

Above all, the mindful therapist never *overuses* technique, and is always clear about using it to invite greater awareness. When the therapist is mindful, when she is clear and present, technique grows organically out of her presence. In this way it is much less likely to feel forced, artificial, or overdone.

CHAPTER TEN
A Unified Vision of Life

Miraculous power and marvelous activity—
drawing water and hewing wood![73]
—LAYMAN PANG

F OR SPIRITUALLY-INCLINED psychotherapists, it is helpful to find a way to practice a unified vision of life, so that
work is not discrete and separate from who you are in the rest of
your life, but of a piece with it; so that who you are and what you
do are not two. Just as we learn from the Dharma not to identify
with our thoughts, beliefs, emotions, physical form, or life span,
so the mindful therapist also knows that he is not his job. We
may still need protection from unreasonable intrusions into our
non-working life. And in fact, knowing our true career may help
us be even more clear that we need space. For we know that, to
have a chance to be helpful to others, we also need to protect and
nurture ourselves, just as we would have our patients do. But
whether at the office or at home, we see what we are doing as part
of the same path.

A spirituality of mindfulness provides a unifying vision of life.
To adopt this unifying vision gives you a great advantage. In every

situation you know what to do: be as mindful, as in touch as you can be, and let appropriate action or non-action, speech or non-speech, flow from that center of awareness. This is not a burden, not another requirement to meet. To live in forgetfulness is to be at best half alive. Living mindfully is simply being fully alive and aware. Mindfulness is life.

In my training, it was occasionally mentioned that therapists need to take care of themselves and live a balanced life. Coming from a traditional academic psychology program, however, one which seemed more interested in research than in the practice of psychotherapy, such statements were rare. They were also treated as somehow obvious, as though everyone would know how to do this. In truth, many of us did not have a clue about this.

To the mindful therapist, self-care is the *sine qua non* of patient-care. Having a mindful evening is the best thing you can do for your patients the next day. Caring mindfully for your patients also is care of yourself. Your well-being and the well-being of your patients, of your friends and family, are no longer separate, but deeply interpenetrating and interconnected. Ending the split between work and life terminates the cycle of stress at work creating an imbalance that then needs to be compensated for by excess outside of work. Work is no longer a self-depriving experience that you have to make up for. Life is of a piece.

THE LIFE OF A MINDFUL THERAPIST

Mindful therapists do their best to begin their practice of mindfulness the moment they open their eyes. Rather than jumping out of bed immediately, try to spend a few moments breathing and smiling a Buddha-like half-smile. Then take this attitude into each activity as best you can, not trying to impose a rigid perfectionism, but reminding yourself of the advantages of living mindfully, and doing your best to return to mindfulness when you recognize you have lost the thread. Recognizing that mindfulness has slipped is already mindfulness. Remembering this prevents mindfulness practice from degenerating into a superego struggle.

In this way, each thing in daily life becomes the object of contemplation. Each activity becomes sacred. When you sit down with patients, this is just the continuation of the same process you began the moment you woke up. Returning home at the end of the day is just a further continuation of this. Living this way, you cultivate the capacity to be deeply present to your patients. You cultivate the capacity to be deeply present to your family and friends, or even to the person who works at the check out line in the grocery store. Every encounter becomes living and vital.

At times, you may feel that living mindfully is beyond you. But please do not be discouraged. You can do it. "To develop this practice," says Dharma teacher Ajahn Dhammadaro, "the only thing needed is faith and earnestness. Even children, drunkards, madmen, those who are old, or those who are illiterate, can develop mindfulness."[74] When you light up your mindfulness, discouraging thoughts become just more phenomena to encounter mindfully and let be. There are times when you will forget about mindfulness for long stretches at first. This is of no consequence, and is part of the process of learning. But if you see the advantages of mindfulness clearly, if you can find a way to impress this on your mind, and if, as you begin to get more concentrated, you also begin to notice how much lighter and more alive you are, you will find the encouragement you need to continue. Just do your best, and approach the process with joy, not as though doing hard labor.

As your mindfulness deepens, you experience greater depth and ease in your therapeutic work. You will notice things you did not notice before, address things that come up that you might previously have missed. Your work will deepen, which will not only help your patients, but also help you.

241

THE FOUR GIFTS OF THE MINDFUL THERAPIST

The first gift of the mindful therapist is *presence.* This means greater clarity and calm in the therapy room. You are less distracted. Your whole self is present to the person before you. When I look back on my own experiences as a patient, I remember little about the techniques, homework, interpretations, and exercises offered by the therapist. But I remember very clearly the moments when I felt the therapist was truly present.

The second gift of the mindful therapist is *understanding.* You understand because, as your mindfulness deepens, you see the person before you as not other than yourself. Knowing the interconnectedness of all things, knowing that this person's well-being and your well-being are deeply intertwined, you develop an immediacy of understanding without struggle or strain.

From your presence and understanding come the third and fourth gifts: *loving-kindness* and *compassion.* There is an ease and friendliness about you that others begin to respond to more deeply. Other people feel more at home around you. Your desire to ease the suffering of others enables you to be deeply present with people in distress. Your wish to ease their suffering protects you, and guides you in knowing what to do and what not to do in order to help.

These four gifts are very real. You can begin to experience them, perhaps with only a few weeks of effort to live more mindfully.

DAILY PRACTICE SUGGESTIONS

The following are a few general reminders to help you practice mindful therapy.

Give yourself ample time to arrive at the office and be present
    before your first appointment.
Endeavor to walk mindfully, even if it is just from the waiting

room to your office. Feel each step, each contact with the ground or floor.

Stop doing paperwork or making phone calls in every available minute between sessions, so that you can allow yourself a few minutes of mindfulness/breathing before each patient arrives. This will prevent you from having to wrench yourself out of some project to be present with this person.

Deal with scheduling and money issues at the start of the session. That way, you do not have to switch gears back from emotional issues to business ones. You can also end on time, instead of waiting while a patient writes a check and continues to talk. Ending on time in turn helps you be fully present for the next person.

Be mindful of what you feel in the therapy encounter. Consider that it might tell you something about the patient and not just be about you.

Let your patient finish a final thought, but then do your best to start and end on time. Your patients deserve this, and so do you. Again, ending on time helps you be present for the next person.

Breathe for a few moments before making a phone call.

Since you spend your days in the presence of emotions that are often toxic, find ways to breathe, smile, relax, and detoxify in the evening.

Reflect on the following often:

I am here to be deeply present.

I am here to listen.

I cannot change reality for this person.

I cultivate equanimity in myself.

NO INHUMAN SPIRITUALITY

A healthy spirituality is one that works with our human nature and completes it, not one that crushes it or distorts it. We can only be the person that we are. But that is also enough. Indeed, it is more than enough!

If practicing mindfulness starts to feel like a burden, like some sort of rule that you are having to live up to, find a way to ease up on yourself. Whenever we experience spiritual practice in this way, we should stop pushing. Relax. Remember that mindfulness is simply a great way to be fully alive. The exercise below may help you recontact this truth.

For this reason also, when I talk about the gifts of presence, understanding, loving-kindness, and compassion, remember that these are human qualities. This should not be taken in any grandiose sense, as though your patients were coming into the presence of some great guru before whom they should bow. No-self protects from grandiosity because we know that, in a sense, we are not doing anything special. Rather than feeding grandiosity, this book is for reminding therapists who, like myself, need building up from time to time that these simple, human qualities are indeed gifts, and that they can produce a lot of healing without straining and struggling to do more than we can do.

Concluding Exercise

The purpose of this exercise is to help you maintain your motivation to live mindfully. You can use it whenever your enthusiasm wanes.

Sit and breathe mindfully until your mind becomes somewhat calmer—probably at least five minutes.

As always, take your time. Don't rush. If the exercise feels too long, come back to it later rather than rushing through it or pushing yourself.

Now consider what mindfulness is—bringing calm awareness and depth to each moment of your life, being fully alive and aware, not missing any moments as though you had precious moments of life that you could just discard. Remember, it is not about forcing your-self to be peaceful; rather, peace is a byproduct of being willing to acknowledge the truth of your experiencing. Envision yourself going through your daily life with mindfulness. As clearly and concretely as possible, imagine yourself doing all daily activities mindfully:

. . . brushing your teeth

. . . making morning coffee

. . . showering

. . . dressing

. . . meditating

. . . reading

. . . driving to work

. . . preparing to see patients

. . . sitting down with a patient

. . . dealing with difficult feelings in-session

. . . returning home

. . . eating dinner

. . . and other details of your life (be specific!)

Also envision yourself doing your best to bring mindfulness when what you are experiencing is not so pleasant, such as dealing with a difficult patient, struggling with denied insurance claims, encoun-tering personal difficulties of whatever kind may be present in your life right now. Imagine your capacity to handle such things with increasing presence and serenity.

Now recount to yourself the advantages of living mindfully. Feel them in your body and mind as you recount them:

. . . greater serenity

. . . ease in difficult situations

. . . being fully alive

. . . enjoying all your moments of life

. . . greater ease and effectiveness in your work

. . . improved relationships

. . . improved emotional health

. . . improved bodily health

. . . and whatever else occurs to you.

When you are ready, return to mindful breathing for a few moments, just letting yourself rest and be present with the breath, not trying to force anything, in harmony with what is and, above all, not struggling.

APPENDIX I
Case Example

THERAPISTS ARE OFTEN CONFRONTED by cases that seem unsolvable, as is the case, for example, with people who have serious medical problems, where we might seem to lack the capacity to help. But often even in such cases, we can help through mindful therapy, even if we cannot provide a medical cure.

Denise's body had rejected the first liver transplant. And now she faced the prospect of a second. She did not look forward to the long process of waiting. Unfortunately, she would have to get worse before she could get better. Before she would be at the top of the list for a new liver, she would have to be much more sick than she was now. Fiercely independent, she did not relish the prospect of further dependency on her family and on medical personnel. Nor did she relish the dementia that would return as her liver began to shut down.

What could I offer Denise? First, I listened deeply. I came to know her as a particular human being, not "that case of liver disease." I ascertained that Denise did not consider herself a spiritual person, so I could not help to reconnect her with her own tradition, and I had to be careful in what I offered to her. Yet within this context, I gently began to offer spiritual practices that did not involve any dogmatic belief that might present a barrier to her. I taught her breath meditation. I taught her to care for her body with loving attention in body-scan meditation. As fear of mortality sat with us one day in the room, I took the next opportunity to teach her the Five Remembrances meditation—a meditation involving learning to face our impermanent nature with calmness and acceptance.

Months later, after a successful transplant, Denise called to tell me how helpful our work had been to her.

Metaphors Used in This Book

T HE BEST METAPHORS may be ones that you develop on your own, some of them on the spot, others that you employ regularly. Since these grow out of the soil of your own awareness and your own contact with your patients and their issues, you will be able to put more of yourself behind them. But here are some of the metaphors I have used in this book, and a few new ones:

Dumbo's feather; Buddha nature; the jewel in your own pocket; the wisdom of the organism; children of God. These are all ways of saying that each human being already contains the necessary wisdom, which only needs to be unblocked.

Fresh as a flower; Solid as a mountain; Still water; Sky-like awareness. What mindfulness is like.

Two people watching the river. The importance of accepting the true nature of things. Not struggling against what is. Also, the stream of consciousness.

The Pure Land; The Kingdom of Heaven; salvation; nirvana. The state of ultimate realization, always available now.

The stone the builders rejected. The centrality of things we want to avoid, such as our suffering.

Pink elephants; thoughts and feelings as stones or clouds. That thoughts are not controllable. That they are natural facts.

Digesting mental and emotional experience. We need only unblock whatever is hindering the natural processes of digestion, such as forgetfulness instead of mindfulness.

Breath and Spirit. The same word in many ancient languages, indicating the connection between breathing and the ultimate.

The mustard seed; the lump of leavening. Here, the miracle of mindfulness, with a small beginning that in the end becomes powerful and pervasive. Any process that begins small and becomes surprisingly large or pervasive.

Dog chasing its own tail; quenching our thirst by drinking salt water. Activities that don't really satisfy us.

Alchemical transformation; cooking. Human growth and transformation.

Everything is on fire; not leaving a trace. Doing things with a mind that lets go.

Asking the belly. Consulting non-rational bodily wisdom.

Going with the li. Respecting the configurations of nature and working with them.

Pearls before swine. Premature interpretations and suggestions from the therapist. Also, patient behavior that leads to feelings of not being appreciated (countertransference).

Unknown plant. A way for the therapist to contemplate the patient. For the patient, a way to contemplate oneself, one's relationship, one's career path, and so on.

Life as path. We tend to forget that this is a metaphor, and that from another point of view, there is no path. There is only what is.

Mindfulness as sunlight that opens the flower (heals suffering). A primary metaphor for the gentle, transforming power of mindfulness.

Untying a knot. The patient application of mindfulness. Some knots are small and are untangled easily and quickly; big life knots require a lot of time and patience.

Words and actions of people as hurricanes; Chuang-tzu's empty boat. Not taking others' actions personally, but seeing them as the result of impersonal forces.

The world as Rorschach blot. The incredibly all-pervasive tendency for us to experience the world in accord with our desires, fears, aversions, and past experiences.

Smelly old shoe. Our old ways of being, while perhaps unattractive in some ways, can nonetheless feel a lot more comfortable than new, healthier ways.

Therapy room as sacred space (temenos). Evoking a non-trivial attitude, not just making conversation, a place of safety insulated from other concerns. Confidentiality.

Watering positive seeds; transforming negative seeds; changing the peg. Metaphors for taking care of our emotions. Caring for the mind.

You are a flower, a human being—not a puzzle or a problem to be solved. The purpose of life is to be fully alive.

Other trees in the garden. When there has been one kind of loss, it is like a tree dying. We need to be in touch with the loss, but not forget the other trees.

Crying baby. The gentleness required to calm inflamed emotions.

Skier adjusting to the contours of the hill. Close attention teaches us what to do.

Not touching a hot stove. Effective insight.

Sickness, pathology; id, ego, superego; conscious/unconscious; individuation, self-actualization, wholeness; self. Let's not forget that a lot of the words we use regularly in psychology have a metaphorical quality. From a Buddhist point of view, this is especially so with the word "self."

Metaphors and story may also be used from a patient's religious heritage, insofar as the therapist is aware of these. A Jewish patient may relate to the idea of freeing herself from bondage, in this case emotional bondage, as her personal continuation of the story of the exodus from Egypt. A Christian patient may see his movement toward greater self-acceptance as claiming the freely-given grace of God through Christ.[75]

Endnotes

1. *The Path of Emancipation*, p. 152.
2. *Zen Buddhism and Psychoanalysis*, p. 28.
3. *Transformation at the Base*, p. 115.
4. "The Importance of Modern Physics for Modern Medicine," in *Healing East and West*, p. 410.
5. [There is evidence . . . advancement.] See e.g. Seligman, *Authentic Happiness*, pp. 168–169.
6. "The Importance of Modern Physics for Modern Medicine," in *Healing East and West*, p. 413.
7. *The Heart of the Buddha's Teaching*, p. 130.
8. *Anguttara Nikaya*, 8:83.
9. *Gestalt Therapy Verbatim*, p. 17.
10. [Ajahn Chah . . . water buffalo.] Kornfield, *Living Dharma*, p. 41.
11. ["Buddhism" . . . a western invention.] See e.g. Bowker (ed.), *The Oxford Dictionary of World Religions*, entry on Buddhism, p. 171.
12. *Touching Peace*, pp. 11–12. Used with permission.
13. Quoted in Watts, *The Way of Zen*, p. 89. Seng-tsan was the third patriarch in the Ch'an Buddhist lineage.
14. *Creating True Peace*, p. 36.

253

15. "Chinese Medicine: The Law of Five Elements," in *Healing East and West*, p. 84.
16. *Vajracchedika*, cited in Watts, *The Way of Zen*, p. 45.
17. The Sutra of Forty-two Chapters, quoted in *The Heart of the Buddha's Teaching*, p. 131.
18. See *Family Therapy in Clinical Practice*.
19. *The Spiritual Teaching of Ramana Maharshi*, p. 68.
20. *Breathe! You are Alive*, a translation and commentary on the Anapanasatti Sutra, p. 74.
21. The Dalai Lama, for one, accepts the value of teaching people compassion through self-interest. See e.g. *The Art of Happiness*, esp. pp. 113–130.
22. *Zen Buddhism and Psychoanalysis*, p. 128.
23. This follows the translation and commentary on this sutra by Thich Nhat Hanh titled *Transformation and Healing*, see esp. pp. 3–4.
24. *Dhamma Cakka Pavattana Sutta*.
25. See *The Heart of the Buddha's Teaching*, pp. 18–22.
26. Adapted from Thich Nhat Hanh, *The Heart of the Buddha's Teaching*, p. 116.
27. From the cassette series, *The Science of Enlightenment*.
28. Quoted in Watts, *Tao: The Watercourse Way*, p. 97.
29. Paraphrasing Watts, *Tao: The Watercourse Way*, p. 31.
30. *The Human Adventure*, p. 12.
31. Quoted in Huxley, *The Perennial Philosophy*, p. 106.
32. *Zen Buddhism and Psychoanalysis*, p. 53.
33. For details and relevant research see Miller and Rollnick, *Motivational Interviewing*.
34. This is one of Thich Nhat Hanh's favorite metaphors for the need to protect ourselves from toxins. See for example *The Heart of the Buddha's Teaching*, p. 32.
35. Not all teachers emphasize going slowly as important in living mindfully. For Thich Nhat Hanh, however, the two seem more

or less inseparable. For example, in *Peace is Every Step* (p. 26), he writes about washing dishes, "I enjoy taking my time with each dish . . . I know that if I hurry . . . the time of washing dishes will be unpleasant and not worth living."

36. *The Heart of the Buddha's Teaching,* p. 233.

37. *Toward a Psychology of Being,* p. 184.

38. The Dalai Lama, for instance, questions the primacy of matter over thought assumed by western science. See *The Art of Happiness,* pp. 5–6.

39. The discussion in this section largely follows Brazier, *Zen Therapy,* pp. 87–94.

40. For an example of this kind of analysis of language, see *The Way of Zen,* p. 5 ff.

41. Hostility triggers the release of the hormones epinephrine, norepinephrine, cortisol, and for men, testosterone. Testosterone and cortisol in turn trigger the creation of cholesterol. Anger also triggers high blood pressure and poor digestion. For a summary of the relevant research see McKay, Rogers, and McKay, *When Anger Hurts,* pp. 23–32.

42. Compare Tanahashi and Levitt, *A Flock of Fools,* p. 134.

43. The idea that deep understanding creates love is a basic teaching of Thich Nhat Hanh. For example, he writes: "When we are mindful, touching deeply the present moment, we can see and listen deeply, and the fruits are always understanding, acceptance, and love." [*The Heart of the Buddha's Teaching,* p. 61] And later in the book he writes: "If we can offer understanding to someone, that is true love." [p. 197] In *Being Peace,* the connection is even more explicit: "Understanding and love are not two things, but just one." [p. 14]

44. [to know you don't know . . . is the beginning of knowing] Cited in Thich Nhat Hanh, *Teachings on Love,* p. 84.

45. [benefits from love and compassion . . . continue the practice]

Anguttara Nikaya, following Thich Nhat Hanh in *Teachings on Love,* p. 17.

46. [no one more worthy of love . . . than oneself.] *Samyutta Nikaya,* cited in Kornfield, *After the Ecstasy the Laundry,* p. 169.

47. Quoted in Huxley, *The Perennial Philosophy,* p. 27.

48. The story of the Buddha's life largely follows Armstrong, *Buddha.*

49. The simile is from the Sutra on the Better Way to Catch a Snake, which reads:

    "There are always some people who do not understand the letter or the spirit of a teaching, and, in fact, take it the opposite way of what was intended . . . There are always some people who study only to satisfy their curiosity or win arguments, and not for the sake of liberation . . .

    "Bhiksus, a person who studies that way can be compared to a man trying to catch a poisonous snake in the wild. If he reaches out his hand, the snake may bite his hand, leg, or some part of his body. Trying to catch a snake that way has no advantages and can only create suffering."

    [Translation from Thich Nhat Hanh, *Thundering Silence,* p. 6]

50. *The Heart of the Buddha's Teaching,* pp. 122–132.

51. Quoted in Goleman, *The Meditative Mind,* p. 132.

52. *Transformation at the Base,* p. 69.

53. Quoted in Mitchell, *The Gospel According to Jesus,* p. 48.

54. *Two Essays on Analytical Psychology,* p. 226.

55. Quoted from the *Vinaya* in Boorstein, *It's Easier Than You Think,* pp. 81–82.

56. *The Farthest Reaches of Human Nature,* pp. 115–116.

57. *A Still Forest Pool,* p. 168.

58. [As the Buddha . . . produce the pleasing sound.] *Vinaya Mahavagga Khuddaka Nikaya 5.* For commentary see Thich Nhat Hanh, *The Heart of the Buddha's Teaching,* p. 93.

59. The full quotation reads: "Among all my patients in the

second half of life—that is to say, over thirty-five—there has not been one whose problem in the last resort was not that of finding a religious outlook on life. It is safe to say that every one of them fell ill because he had lost what the living religions of every age have given to their followers, and none of them has been really healed who did not regain his religious outlook." "Psychotherapists or the Clergy," *Collected Works,* vol. 8, 2nd ed. (Princeton: Bollingen, 1969) pp. 327–347. First published in German, 1932.

60. "The Over-Soul," *Selected Writings of Ralph Waldo Emerson,* p. 282.

61. Freud is one who espoused this model, basing his views partly on the available technology of his day, the steam engine. In such a model, it makes perfect sense that energy builds up and must be released or there will be an explosion. More recent models frequently draw on the technology of the computer, where there is no clear necessity that anger must build up in such a way.

62. Research showing that anger ventilation can be harmful has been around awhile, as can be seen in Tavris's discussion in *Anger,* esp. pp. 120–150. From a Buddhist perspective see Thich Nhat Hanh, also titled *Anger,* esp. pp. 115–117, a passage entitled "Dangers of Venting."

63. This principle is from Hayes, Strosahl, and Wilson, *Acceptance and Commitment Therapy,* a mindfulness-based approach.

64. The source of this story is no longer traceable.

65. This does not meaning *saying* that you empathize or feel sorry, but empathy in the Rogerian sense of using reflective listening to demonstrate your understanding.

66. [. . . changes a wooden peg . . .] Discussed in *The Heart of the Buddha's Teaching,* p. 195.

67. See e.g. *Touching Peace,* p. 39.

68. *The Way of Zen,* p. 176.

69. [joy] I follow Thich Nhat Hanh in translating *mudita* as joy rather than sympathetic joy. He comments that sympathetic joy "is too limited. It discriminates between self and others." [*The Heart of the Buddha's Teaching*, p. 161]
70. *The Practice of Psychotherapy*, p. 3.
71. The others are *feelings, mind,* and *objects of mind.* See Thich Nhat Hanh, *Transformation and Healing.*
72. Quoted in Greene, *The Fabric of the Cosmos*, p. 139.
73. Quoted in Watts, *The Way of Zen*, p. 133.
74. Quoted in Jack Kornfield, *Living Dharma*, p. 267.
75. For a fuller explication of the value of story in a Judeo-Christian context, see my "Story and Narrative" in Miller and Delaney (eds.), *Judeo-Christian Perspectives on Psychology.*

Bibliography

Armstrong, Karen. *Buddha*. New York: Penguin Putnam, 2001.

Bien, Thomas. "Story and Narrative," in *Judeo-Christian Perspectives on Psychology: Human Nature, Motivation, and Change*. W.R. Miller and H.D. Delaney (eds.). Washington, D.C.: American Psychological Assoc., 2005.

Bien, Thomas, and Beverly Bien. *Mindful Recovery: A Spiritual Path to Healing from Addiction*. New York: Wiley, 2002.

————. *Finding the Center Within: The Healing Way of Mindfulness Meditation*. Hoboken, N.J.: Wiley, 2003.

Bowen, Murray, M.D. *Family Therapy in Clinical Practice*. New York: Jason Aronson, 1978.

Bowker, John (ed.). *The Oxford Dictionary of World Religions*. Oxford: Oxford University Press, 1997.

Boorstein, Sylvia. *It's Easier Than You Think: The Buddhist Way to Happiness*. New York: HarperSanFrancisco, 1995.

Brazier, David. *Zen Therapy: Transcending the Sorrows of the Human Mind*. New York: Wiley, 1995.

Chah, Ajahn. *A Still Forest Pool: The Insight Meditation of Ajahn*

Chah. Compiled by Jack Kornfield and Paul Breiter. Wheaton, Ill.: Quest Books, 1985.

Cortright, Brant. *Psychotherapy and Spirit: Theory and Practice in Transpersonal Psychotherapy.* Albany: State University of New York Press, 1997.

Dalai Lama and Howard C. Cutler, M.D. *The Art of Happiness: A Handbook for Living.* New York: Riverhead Books, 1998.

Diagnostic and Statistical Manual of Mental Disorders (DSM-IV), 4th ed. Washington D.C.: American Psychiatric Press. {intro p. xxii}

de Silva, Padmasiri. *An Introduction to Buddhist Psychology,* 3rd edition. New York: Rowman and Littlefield, 2000.

Emerson, Ralph Waldo. *Selected Writings of Ralph Waldo Emerson.* William H. Gliman, ed. New York: New American Library, 1965.

Gendlin, Eugene T. *Let Your Body Interpret Your Dreams.* Wilmette, Ill.: Chiron Publications, 1986.

Goleman, Daniel. *The Meditative Mind: The Varieties of Meditative Experience.* New York: Tarcher/Putnam, 1988.

Greene, Brian. *The Fabric of the Cosmos: Space, Time, and the Texture of Reality.* New York: Alfred A. Knopf, 2004.

Hayes, Stephen C., Kirk D. Strosahl, and Kelly G. Wilson. *Acceptance and Commitment Therapy: An Experiential Approach to Behavior Change.* New York: Guilford, 1999.

Herrigel, Eugen. *Zen in the Art of Archery.* New York: Random House, 1953.

Huxley, Aldous. *The Perennial Philosophy.* New York: Harper & Row, 1945.

Jung, Carl Gustav. *Two Essays on Analytical Psychology.* Princeton: Bollingen, 1953.

———. *The Practice of Psychotherapy.* Princeton: Bollingen, 1954.

———. *Dreams.* Princeton: Bollingen, 1974.

Kirschenbaum, Howard, and Valerie Land Henderson (eds.). *The Carl Rogers Reader.* Boston: Houghton Mifflin, 1989.

Kornfield, Jack. *Living Dharma: Teachings of Twelve Buddhist Masters.* Boston: Shambhala, 1996.

———. *After the Ecstasy, the Laundry: How the Heart Grows Wise on the Spiritual Path.* New York: Bantam, 2000.

Kornfield, Jack, and Paul Breiter (eds.). *A Still Forest Pool: The Insight Meditation of Achaan Chah.* Wheaton, Ill.: Quest Books, 1985.

Maharshi, Ramana. *The Spiritual Teaching of Ramana Maharshi.* Boston: Shambhala, 1988.

Maslow, Abraham. *Toward a Psychology of Being.* 2nd edition. New York: D. Van Nostrand, 1962.

———. *The Farthest Reaches of Human Nature.* New York: Compass, 1971.

Mattoon, Mary Ann. *Understanding Dreams.* Woodstock, Conn.: Spring Publications, 1978.

McKay, Matthew, Peter D. Rogers, and Judith McKay. *When Anger Hurts: Quieting the Storm Within,* Oakland: New Harbinger, 1989.

McNamara, William, O.C.D. *The Human Adventure: Contemplation for Everyman.* New York: Doubleday, 1974.

Miller, William R., and Stephen Rollnick. *Motivational Interviewing: Preparing People for Change.* 2nd edition. New York: Guilford, 2002.

Miller, William R., and Harold D. Delaney (eds.). *Judeo-Christian Perspectives on Psychology: Human Nature, Motivation, and Change.* Washington, D.C.: American Psychological Assoc., 2005.

Mitchell, Stephen. *The Gospel According to Jesus: A New Translation and Guide to His Essential Teachings for Believers and Unbelievers.* New York: HarperCollins, 1991.

Nhat Hanh, Thich. *Being Peace.* Berkeley: Parallax, 1987.

————. *Transformation and Healing: Sutra on the Four Establishments of Mindfulness*. Berkeley: Parallax, 1990.

————. *Touching Peace: Practicing the Art of Mindful Living*. Berkeley: Parallax Press, 1992.

————. *Thundering Silence*. Berkeley: Parallax, 1993.

————. *Breathe! You are Alive: Sutra on the Full Awareness of Breathing*. Berkeley: Parallax, 1996.

————. *Teachings on Love*. Berkeley: Parallax, 1997.

————. *The Heart of the Buddha's Teaching: Transforming Suffering Into Peace, Joy, and Liberation*. Berkeley: Parallax, 1998.

————. *The Path of Emancipation*. Berkeley: Parallax, 2000.

————. *Anger: Wisdom for Cooling the Flames*. New York: Riverhead, 2001.

————. *Transformation at the Base: Fifty Verses on the Nature of Consciousness*. Berkeley: Parallax, 2001.

————. *Creating True Peace: Ending Violence in Yourself, Your Family, Your Community, and the World*. New York: Free Press, 2003.

Perls, Frederick S. *Gestalt Therapy Verbatim*. New York: Bantam, 1976.

Rogers, Carl R. *On Becoming a Person*. Boston: Houghton Mifflin, 1961.

————. *A Way of Being*. Boston: Houghton Mifflin, 1980.

Segal, Zindel V., J. Mark G. Williams, and John D. Teasdale. *Mindfulness-Based Cognitive Therapy for Depression: A New Approach to Preventing Relapse*. New York: Guilford, 2002.

Seligman, Martin E.P. *Authentic Happiness: Using the New Positive Psychology to Realize Your Potential for Lasting Fulfillment*. New York: Free Press, 2002.

Sheikh, Annees A., and Katharina S. Sheikh. *Healing East and West: Ancient Wisdom and Modern Psychology*. New York: Wiley, 1989.

Siegelman, Ellen Y. *Metaphor and Meaning in Psychotherapy*. New York: Guilford, 1990.

Suzuki, D.T., Erich Fromm, and Richard De Martino. *Zen Buddhism and Psychoanalysis*. New York: Grove Press, 1960.

Tanahashi, Kazuaki, and Peter Levitt. *A Flock of Fools: Ancient Buddhist Tales of Wisdom and Laughter from the One Hundred Parable Sutra*. New York: Grove Press, 2004.

Tavris, Carol. *Anger: The Misunderstood Emotion*. New York: Simon & Schuster, 1982.

Watts, Alan. *The Way of Zen*. New York: Vintage Books, 1957.

———. *Tao: The Watercourse Way*. New York: Pantheon, 1975.

Yalom, Irvin D., M.D. *Existential Psychotherapy*. New York: Basic Books, 1980.

———. *The Gift of Therapy: An Open Letter to a New Generation of Therapists and Their Patients*. New York: HarperCollins, 2002.

Young, Shinzen. *The Science of Enlightenment*. (Audio cassettes.) Boulder, Colo.: Sounds True, 1997.

Index

About the Author

THOMAS BEN, PH.D., is a psychologist in private practice in Albuquerque, New Mexico, and a meditation and mindfulness teacher. He is author of number of book chapters and articles, as well as the books *Mindful Recovery: A Spiritual Path to Healing from Addiction* (Wiley, 2002) and *Finding the Center Within: The Healing Way of Mindfulness Meditation* (Wiley, 2003). Further information can be found at his website, mindfulpsychology.com.

About Wisdom

WISDOM PUBLICATIONS, a nonprofit publisher, is dedicated to making available authentic Buddhist works for the benefit of all. We publish translations of the sutras and tantras, commentaries and teachings of past and contemporary Buddhist masters, and original works by the world's leading Buddhist scholars. We publish our titles with the appreciation of Buddhism as a living philosophy and with the special commitment to preserve and transmit important works from all the major Buddhist traditions.

To learn more about Wisdom, or to browse books online, visit our website at wisdompubs.org. You may request a copy of our mail-order catalog online or by writing to this address:

Wisdom Publications
199 Elm Street
Somerville, Massachusetts 02144 USA
Telephone: (617) 776-7416
Fax: (617) 776-7841
Email: info@wisdompubs.org
www.wisdompubs.org

THE WISDOM TRUST

As a nonprofit publisher, Wisdom is dedicated to the publication of fine Dharma books for the benefit of all sentient beings and dependent upon the kindness and generosity of sponsors in order to do so. If you would like to make a donation to Wisdom, please do so through our Somerville office. If you would like to sponsor the publication of a book, please write or email us at the address above.

Thank you.

Wisdom is a nonprofit, charitable 501(c)(3) organization affiliated with the Foundation for the Preservation of the Mahayana Tradition (FPMT).

Psychoanalysis and Buddhism
An Unfolding Dialogue
Edited by Jeremy D. Safran
456 pages, ISBN 0-86171-342-7, $19.95

"An extraordinary book. While Jack Engler's brilliant opening essay sets the bar high for the other contributors, the entire volume is full of wonderful surprises. This is a beautifully conceived work: innovative, provocative, fascinating and useful. Jeremy Safran deserves much praise."—Mark Epstein, M.D., author of *Thoughts without a Thinker*

Ordinary Mind
Exploring the Common Ground of Zen and Psychoanalysis
Barry Magid
Foreword by Charlotte Joko Beck
224 pages, ISBN 0-86171-495-4, $15.95

"Magid's book has a broad appeal; many people will find something useful here. [. . .] A valuable step forward in making two radically different healing techniques available to each other in both thought and practice. With the help of this book, teachers and students in both camps reflect fruitfully on the benefits of the other."—*Psychologist-Psychoanalyst*

Mindfulness in Plain English
Revised, Expanded Edition
Bhante Henepola Gunaratana
224 pages, ISBN 0-86171-321-4, $14.95

"An extremely up-to-date book written in an approachable, engaging style. The instructions are pithy and practical, and often by the numbers. The book also serves as a very thorough FAQ for new (and not-so-new) meditators."—*Shambhala Sun*

"Of great value to newcomers...especially people without access to a teacher."—Larry Rosenberg, Director, Cambridge Insight Meditation Center

The Essence of Jung's Psychology and Tibetan Buddhism:
Western & Eastern Paths to the Heart
Radmila Moacanin
144 pages, ISBN 0-86171-340-0, $12.95

Moacanin cuts to the heart of two very different yet remarkably similar traditions, touching on their major ideas: the collective unconscious and karma, archetypes and deities, the analyst and the spiritual friend, and mandalas. Within Tibetan Buddhism she focuses on tantra and relates its emphasis on spiritual transformation, also a major concern of Jung's. This expanded edition includes new material on the integration of the two traditions, and their importance in today's unsteady world.

The Wisdom of Listening
Edited by Mark Brady
320 pages, ISBN 0-86171-355-9 $16.95

"A very helpful anthology of 19 essays on the promise, practice, and power of listening. Among the contributors are spiritual teacher Ram Dass; Marshall Rosenberg, founder of the Center for Nonviolent Communication; Anne Simpkinson, an editor for *Prevention* magazine; Kathleen Dowling Singh, a therapist and workshop leader; and Rodney Smith, director of the Hospice of Seattle. They offer suggestions, perspectives, and practices that will reinforce your intentions to be a good listener."—*Spirituality and Health*

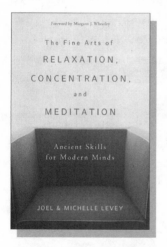

The Fine Arts of Relaxation, Concentration, and Meditation
Ancient Skills for Modern Minds
Joel and Michelle Levey
Foreword by Margaret J. Wheatley
304 pages, ISBN 0-86171-349-4, $14.95

"A skillful blend of time-proven antidotes to the stress of modern life."—Daniel Goleman, author of *Emotional Intelligence*

"What a beautiful book!"—Larry Dossey, M.D., author of *Healing Wounds*

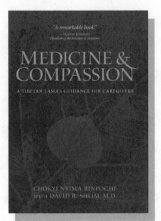

Medicine and Compassion
A Tibetan Lama's Guidance for
Caregivers
Chokyi Nyima Rinpoche with David
R. Shlim, M.D.
Foreword by Harvey and Donald
Fineberg
224 pages, ISBN 0-86171- 512-8, $14.95

"I was dumbfounded by how much Chokyi Nyima Rinpoche comprehends the emotional challenges facing doctors in relationship to their patients. He nails it time and time again. Magnificent!"—Jon Kabat-Zinn, M.D., author of *Full Catastrophe Living*

"A delightful book."—*New England Journal of Medicine*

Meditation and Relaxation in Plain
English
Bob Sharples
208 pp, ISBN 0-86171-286-2, $14.95

"This book speaks to the reader in a warm voice and simple language for understanding the often confusing topics of meditation and relaxation practices. It is a good and friendly introduction for exploring the landscape of the inner life."—Dr. Jeff Brantley, author of *Calming Your Anxious Mind: How Mindfulness and Compassion Can Free You from Anxiety, Fear, and Panic*